September 27, 1993
For the Staff and Patrons
of the Robinson Township
Public Library, with
the author's very
best wishes,

Wiert Hays, Jr.

Come Home With Me Now. . .

The Untold Story of Movie Czar Will Hays
By His Son

Will H. Hays, Jr.

Come Home With Me Now. . .

The Untold Story of Movie Czar Will Hays
By His Son

Guild Press of Indiana, Inc.
Indianapolis, Indiana

Guild Press of Indiana, Inc.
6000 Sunset Lane
Indianapolis, IN 46208

Printed in the United States of America

Library of Congress
Catalogue Card Number
93-78168

ISBN 1-878208-21-7

FOR

Ray Russell and Miss Fischer

Preface

Politician, statesman, "Movie Czar"—Will Hays had a remarkable talent for friendship as well as leadership.

From Theodore Roosevelt to Franklin Roosevelt, from Theda Bara to Calvin Coolidge, from Thomas Edison to Loretta Young, from Charles Lindberg to Mary Pickford to Herbert Hoover to Irene Dunne to Will Rogers to Gloria Swanson to Henry Ford to Joseph Kennedy to Walt Disney to Marion Davies to Louis Mayer to Buster Keaton to Pope Pius XII, to W.C. Fields, to cowboys to coal miners to farmers, on and on. The variety of his friendships was spectacular and unique. The reader is going to meet a lot of these friends.

Will Hays' entire career was a panorama of varied successes: admission to the Sullivan, Indiana, bar association at age twenty-one, chairmanships of the Indiana and national Republican parties, Postmaster Generalship of the United States, and quarter-century presidency of the Motion Picture Producers and Distributors of America—the "Hays Office"—among others. He was offered the powerful movie job because the filmmakers feared industry-devastating censorship, threatened in the early twenties by state legislatures and Congress. A great many Americans were voicing their anger at the movies' sexual and nude displays and at some of the stars' shenanigans.

Believing profoundly that statutory censorship was wrong, and self-regulation by the industry the better course, Will Hays took the job and set about convincing those government agencies to withhold action until the movies had a chance to clean up their own act. He did convince them, and the studios did clean up their acts, by contract with him and among themselves. His office steadily grew larger to encompass numerous all-industry matters beyond self-regulation.

My dad's and my relationship varied from the norm and in many respects I think was unique. My purpose with this book is not only to record his doings and, because of the nature of our relationship, my own doings over a dozen or so years, but also to reveal him as a man and a father. This isn't a biography of either of us; it's the story of the two of us, of an apart–close father and an occasional–always son, one famous and the other far from it. Such space as there often was between us was never empty of feeling. This book is more a mirror than a story; it reflects images of love, guilt, generosity, reserve, anger, sexual fire and ashes, but never indifference.

Putting the thing together has caused me some painful times, as well as pleasant ones. But as a rodeo cowboy once said to me, "When the chute opens, you better damn well go with the bronc."

WWH, Jr.
19 February 1993

Father, dear father, come home with me now,
The clock in the steeple strikes one;
You said you were coming right home from the shop
As soon as your day's work was done.

Henry Clay Work
"Come Home, Father"

Chapter One

ONE summer Saturday morning in 1935, on vacation from Indiana's Wabash College, I was saddling Will Hays'—my dad's—and my cow ponies in the corral of his one hundred-acre "ranch" in Hidden Valley, forty miles northwest of Hollywood. He was in the house studying some files he'd brought out from his Hollywood office where he spent about a third of his working year. The rest of the time while he was president of Motion Picture Producers and Distributors of America, the movies' self-regulating conglomerate, he spent in New York City. That morning, he had said he'd take an hour for a ride with me if I'd bring his saddled horse up to him, giving him an extra half-hour for paper work.

As I tightened the cinch of his pony, a dusty coupe pulled into the barn lot, and Will Rogers swung out from under its steering wheel. I recognized the world-famous humorist, raconteur, newspaper columnist, and actor immediately, of course; in fact, I'd had lunch with Dad and him a couple of times at the Rogers ranch (today a state park near Santa Monica). We shook hands, he smiling, I being awed. He said he'd come out to ask Dad to go driving with him, so they could talk "a spell."

Taking Dad's horse by its reins, I loped our two animals up the hill to the house and told him that Mr. Rogers was down at the corral; and we rode back down together. After their affectionate greeting, the two Wills exchanged a few quiet words as I made myself scarce; and then Dad called to me, referring to my stepmother, "Tell Jessie Will and I are going for a drive," and they took off in the coupe. I got a kick out of Dad's almost reckless tone.

Mr. Rogers' "spell" turned out to be until late afternoon; and after declining dinner because he still had to drive forty miles or so, he went home. At dinner Dad told us that they'd driven almost to Santa Barbara, talking about national affairs and some personal matters and stopping for hamburgers at a roadside stand (where the proprietor had recognized them and refused payment in return for autographs). Mr. Rogers had said he was to fly within the next few days with pilot Wiley Post to Russia by way of Alaska. On their return Mr. Rogers was going

1

to send out to the ranch, as a present for Dad, a fine cow pony named "Chevito."

Mr. Rogers also had told Dad he'd never spoken the words so often ascribed to him, "I never met a man I didn't like," but actually had said, "I never kidded a man I didn't like."

Within the week, the whole world learned that Will Rogers and Wiley Post were killed when their plane crashed at Point Barrow, Alaska. Within the following week the Rogers' foreman, Buddy Sterling, hauled a horse trailer into our barn lot with Chevito on board, saying that before starting for Russia Will Rogers had told his wife he wanted Will Hays to have the horse, and Mrs. Rogers was making good the gift. Dad said that if he were a drinking man, it was a time when he'd have got drunk for a week.

Fifty-six years before that summer my father Will Hays had been born in a small Indiana coal-mining town named Sullivan. Twenty years before that summer, I'd been born in the same town. Our lives' paths were to diverge many times in many ways, but never our heritage. Or our father–son love.

My own consecutive memories began when I was about five. The summer early-morning sounds I remember hearing in Sullivan in the 1920s undoubtedly were like those in every American small town; and I'm sure their lifelong nostalgic echoes have remained alike for everyone across the land who has lain in bed listening to them. Screen doors slammed, dogs barked, milk bottles clinked as milkmen carried them up walks in wire baskets, broom straws whisked concrete, lawn mowers fluttered metallically, cardinals whistled, turtle doves cooed, rubber tires whispered or squeaked, an occasional horse's hoofs clopped, maybe a train whistle wailed—that more often was a night sound—a newsboy dragging a wagon caroled the Sunday papers as church bells tolled, sometimes rain spattered window panes and sills, the courthouse or the bank clock chimed, breezes rustled thick leaves, babies cried next door, my friend Ray Russell sang a hymn softly as he washed our family car.

It was an adventure on a summer morning to ride on the rear step of the ice wagon from one house to the next, sucking ice chips, the horse moving and stopping without command. It was fascinating to watch the iceman pick away an exact weight of his stock in trade from a yard-long, rectangular block as ordered by a numbered cardboard sign hung next to a house's front door and to follow him as he carried the ice over his shoulder with tongs around to a back porch icebox, and to imagine what it should be like to be as strong as he.

It wasn't much fun to go to church on Sunday with my real mother, Helen Thomas Hays, and my surrogate mother, Helen Valentine Fischer (she'd been a schoolteacher hired to "look after" me because of Mother's lifelong frailty) and my Uncle Hinkle and Aunt Lucile and cousins, Chuck and John T., and to sit in our (no other!) uncushioned pew in an unaccustomed suit, squirming surreptitiously through an earnest sermon by sweet, tired old Reverend Gray. But it wasn't painful either, because there was Jesus to stare at in the stained-glass window which sometimes glowed with the outdoor sunlight and sometimes was dimmed by a rainy day's gloom, and there were heroic, ecstatic, bloody, peaceful happenings to imagine. There also were things to ponder: why were "quick" people (fast runners, I supposed) judged along with the dead? In all fairness, why oughtn't people who owed us money pay their debts?

One of my earliest Sullivan memories is of the time Dad came home from Washington after Warren Harding had been elected President, which must have been in the fall of 1920. Dad had been the Republican National Chairman in charge of Harding's campaign and soon was to be appointed by the President as Postmaster General of the United States.

Previously, Will Hays had been his party's Indiana chairman and an attorney in his father's small, respected Sullivan firm and Sullivan's city attorney (his only elective office ever) and a 1900 graduate of Crawfordsville's (Indiana) Wabash College. Throughout his life's seventy-four years of varied, famous, hyperactive accomplishments and vast acquaintance he began, continued, and ended as a Hoosier. His values were rooted permanently in Indiana's solid earth. Incidentally, he once told me that his father, John T. Hays, had middle-named him "Harrison" in honor of my grandfather's Indiana friend and occasional lawyering colleague, Benjamin Harrison, later to become the United States' twenty-third President. In fact, Dad said that one evening in Sullivan when he'd been about nine years old, his father's and Harrison's card game had been interrupted by a messenger at the Hays' front door to say that a request had come over the town's only phone at the railroad station for Harrison to get right up to Chicago, because the Republican National Convention wanted to nominate him for the presidency.

Speaking of presidential nominations and particularly of Warren Harding's, I recall a contemporary of Dad's telling me years later that at the deadlocked 1920 Republican convention the party's leaders met for four successive days in what the press dubbed the "smoke-filled room" (404) of Chicago's Blackstone Hotel before agreeing on a nominee: Will H. Hays. When they gave Dad the news in an anteroom where he'd been sitting out their deliberations, he declined their offer, telling them that his job was to "elect, not select," and that "In Indiana we have a saying: 'A man doesn't bid at his own auction.'" As things turned out, of course, he'd have been the next president, even though, as the same contemporary said, "He wouldn't have had Will Hays running his campaign."

Anyhow, on that fall day after Harding's election, when I was going on five years old, the Sullivan townspeople gathered on the lawn in front of our home on West Washington Street to call for Dad to come out onto our front porch and make a speech to them, as befitted a hometown boy who'd made good. Our house was two-story, yellow-painted, board-sided, with pillars in front rising from the porch past the second-story smaller porch to the eaves. I later learned Dad had built it in 1910 at a cost of ten thousand dollars. I don't know whether Dad had any warning that the crowd was going to gather, but I recall that the first I became aware of it was hearing clapping and whistling from outside. I guess I was playing in the living room and hadn't looked out of the window as the people had congregated quietly before starting to call for him. Mother and Dad and I went onto the front porch and found the crowd extending across the lawn and the street beyond to its farther curb and overflowing into our neighbors' yards. Dad began to talk to the people, and I think I sat down on the steps at his feet. Later in my life I heard records of some of his political speeches, and on that day I suppose he addressed the crowd in the same oratorical style those records revealed—not at all pompously, but theatrically and with warmth and humor. I think he was introduced by our neighbor and his boyhood friend, a hunchbacked man called "Cuppy" Stratton. I have the impression his speech was interrupted several times by cheers and laughter.

As I remember it, this occasion was the first on which I had seen Dad function in the context of his public life. It was like a big birthday party—noisy and friendly and laudatory—and it made a happy impression on me even though I didn't know what it was all about. It was exciting, and I realize now that it probably was characteristic of the sense of excitement which being around him generated in me throughout the rest of his life, as he rushed on into his Washington and New York and Hollywood careers.

I gathered Dad was something special to other people as well as to me. I can think of hundreds of instances when we were together, as walking on the streets of New York some years later, when I saw people recognize him and nudge one another and smile at him. And after we'd passed I was aware they were turning to look after him, whispering to one another, "That was Will Hays!" When we walked into restaurants or theaters or other such places, the people in charge greeted him cordially and escorted us to the best tables or seats, and often he and they had friendly chats. I always was perfectly aware that I was just a body next to him and that none of this attention remotely was directed to me or even included me. I got a kick out of it, nevertheless, a feeling of pride and empathetic stimulation.

In Sullivan during the fall when I was approaching seven years old, nineteen-year-old Ray Russell took me on the handlebars of his bicycle to the first day of my second grade in the public schools. Ray just had been hired long-distance by Dad (who already was away most of the time) to take care of the house and yard and to help Helen Fischer keep an eye on me. A couple of years later Ray was to marry Bonnie and within the next several years to have three sons in addition to his "adopted" one—me. He was to become my surrogate father. He lived on North Court Street and rode his bike daily to and from our house on West Washington. I heard him every morning in the wintertime shaking down the night's embers in the basement furnace before shoveling the new day's coal into it. The reverberation of that shaking-down was carried up to my second-floor room through the radiator pipes. A few minutes after the shaking-down, noise the radiator in my room started pounding as it heated up. I slept in what once had been a so-called "sleeping porch," as houses used to have for summertime, which had been walled in to make a room. This room was separated from the one in which Miss Fischer slept by a wall which apparently had been the back wall of the house because there were windows in it. Usually those windows were kept open between Miss Fischer's room and mine, I suppose so she could hear me if I should call during the night.

Back to Ray's taking me to the second grade on the handlebars of his bike: I don't remember that my southern Indiana classmates even noticed my somewhat exotic chauffeuring by one of Sullivan's very few black residents. I do remember, however, that both Ray and I got along fine with everybody—pupils, teachers, townspeople—during my six more years of schooling there. He and I shared with each other and them a kaleidoscope of experiences.

One early such experience, for instance, happened on a day, probably in the second grade, when I was sitting near the classroom's front row, not paying close attention to what the teacher (Miss Maple? Miss Neal? Miss Lyons?) was saying, day-dreaming a bit with my eyes almost closed—not dozing but sort of seeing how things looked through that narrowed, dimming perspective. Suddenly, much to my embarrassment I realized that the teacher was speaking to me. I heard my name mentioned for what may have been the second or third time, and I think I realized that the girl, Catherine Furgeson, sitting at the desk in front of me was giggling. Instead of opening my eyes then and responding to the teacher's words, inexplicably I kept my eyes almost closed as they had been and looked toward her and said, probably, "Yes, Miss Maple?" She said something like, "Billy, why are you squinting?" At this point I felt it necessary to keep squinting. I think I said, "I don't know, Miss Maple," and probably added, "Something wrong with my eyes, I guess." She now became somewhat concerned and walked over to me, leaned down and peered into my eyes; and I peered back, squinting, smelling her perfume. Her concern seemed to turn to alarm and she asked me to walk with her to the principal's office, which I did, she leading me by the hand. The principal's name was Mr. Sinclair; we called him "Hadie." He used to whip boys with a length of enema tubing he carried in his hip pocket. At his office he peered into my eyes too and I squinted back at him, and after asking whether my eyes hurt, to which I said "No," he phoned my home and told Miss Fischer there was some sort of problem with my eyes and she or someone had better come and get me right away and take me to a doctor.

There was nothing for me to do but sit in the principal's office, squinting and waiting. In about twenty minutes Ray arrived on his bicycle and after one look at me and a few brief words with the principal and the teacher, he took me on his bike's handlebars to Dr. Crowder's office, which had a gas-log fireplace in the waiting room and always smelled of iodine. We waited in the tile-floored outer room for a few minutes and then Ray took me to the next room to see the doctor. (For years several of the tiles in the waiting room floor were loose; evidently they were accepted by the doctor and everyone else as naturally, inevitably loose.) It's a pretty good bet Ray had a twinkle in his eye when he told Dr. Crowder there seemed to be something the matter with my vision; but I was in a state of almost fainting mortification. Now it was the old doc's turn to peer closely into my eyes. He lifted each of my lids with a gentle thumb and said "Hmmmmm" and leaned back and said to Ray "Well, Ray, I think it probably would be best for you to take Billy home and tell his mother or Miss Fischer maybe he'd better stay there the rest of the day. I think that ought to take care of the eye problem pretty well."

I had got very tired of holding my eyes in a squint, and was glad when we went back outside and headed home on Ray's bicycle. I spent the rest of the day in my room there with the blinds drawn as though I had the measles. Not long after we reached home I opened my eyes wide and my tunnel vision was replaced by normal sight, presumably to everybody else's relief and certainly mine. Nobody at home, as I recall, ever mentioned the incident again. I know I didn't. The next day I was back in school and nobody there mentioned the matter either.

Ray Russell was—and is—a wonderful human being. So was Miss Fischer. It seems as though I've known them both all my life. The Russells weren't called "black" then; their race was "Negro" and they were generally referred to by sensitive people as "colored" and by the insensitive or ignorant as "niggers," a word I still hate worse that any other in our language. About the time Ray came to work at our house Dad persuaded Mother, again long-distance, to hire a girl also to help her look after the house and me. Mother was more or less an invalid, certainly in delicate health. She'd had two stillborn children before me, which was why she'd been taken to Robert Long Hospital in Indianapolis for my birth. Years later I was to learn that her ill health, both physical and emotional, accounted in part for her refusal to accompany Dad to places his expanding career took him. The other part was her disdain for such flamboyances as politics and public office and association with motion pictures. Mother found Miss Fischer, a young white school-teacher, in Crawfordsville, Mother's home town; and Miss Fischer came to Sullivan when I was about seven years old to serve as a sort of governess-without-uniform.

Ray and Miss Fischer "raised" me.

Miss Fischer's and my relationship, and Ray's and mine, were distinct in some ways and melded in others, in the same way a mother's and father's relationships are with a son. Miss Fischer bought my clothes and saw that I had breakfast and started me off to school and read to me at night before bedtime and helped me with my homework. I remember lying on the floor in the living room at her feet as she sat in a wicker rocking chair next to a fringed lamp reading aloud such books as *Uncle Wiggly* and *Tom Swift's Electric Rifle* and *Roy Blakely's B-Line Hike* and *The Boy's King Arthur and His Round Table* and *Tarzan of the Apes*. Later I remember her helping me with the multiplication tables and geography in the little den under the stairs. We loved each other very much; our letters when we were apart always ended with "xxx."

Ray on the other hand played football with me and my "gang" of friends after school. That group of about a dozen kids later took the name "Mix-Mixers." The name was inspired by Western movie star Tom Mix's gift to me, after he and Dad became friends in Hollywood, of a pinto pony named Tony, Jr., which was shipped to Sullivan from California by train. The first time I got on him Tony reared and fell over backwards on me, giving me a bad back for life. Ray taught me to shoot guns—first a Daisy B-B air rifle, then a .22 rifle and after that a 20-gauge shotgun—and took me on many squirrel, rabbit and quail hunts in the woods and fields around Sullivan. I remember his impressing on me that when we were hunting squirrels in the fall, it was very important to tread very softly so we wouldn't crackle the dry leaves and twigs and scare the squirrels away or at least to the backsides of trees, putting the tree trunks between us and them. I never enjoyed shooting anything, but I loved the Indian-like stalking of game in the countryside in the company of my beloved friend and mentor.

We also had a series of cooks in Sullivan, one named Ella Shaw and another Mrs. Adams. Ray ate his breakfast and dinner at his own home on North Court Street but his lunch with the cook in our kitchen. Miss Fischer ate with Mother and me in the dining room. Miss Fischer lived with us, and Ray lived at his home, leaving our house every evening between five and six o'clock. In the wintertime he came back about nine o'clock every night to "bank" the furnace, to keep its coals hot throughout the night. For a few years, I think probably when I was from about seven to nine, we had a succession of chauffeurs of our Cole and then Hudson and then Essex automobiles: two nice young white guys from Indianapolis named Herman Lord and Paul Kester and finally Ray, in addition to his other chores. Miss Fischer developed a crush on Paul, Ray told me much later.

It seemed even in those days that most of the time Mother was not only indoors but upstairs, although she took her meals with Miss Fischer and me, and once in a while she went to bridge club and, surprisingly and much more rarely, to a movie with us at the Sherman Theater on the Square. Aside from my name and Miss Fischer's and Ray's and Mother's in-laws across the street and more remotely Dad's, the important names in Mother's life seemed to be limited pretty much to her father's, Judge Albert D. Thomas of Crawfordsville, and our good neighbors', Mrs. William Jamison and Mrs. Paul Poynter. Sometimes it seemed that the most important tangible object to her (if the most embarrassing to me) was the police whistle with which she called me from my backyard play at suppertime.

After Herman Lord left, Paul Kester drove me the twenty-seven miles to the Terre Haute YMCA for my first swimming lessons. Earlier,

Ray and I had played in Buck Creek at the edge of town before I actually learned to swim. The gang played football in a lot behind our backyard which Dad bought after Tom Mix gave me the pony; it was to be the latter's pasture. Dad had carpenters build a one-stall shed for Tony, Jr., and on one of Dad's periodic trips home he had a local sawmill haul in enough sawdust to cover the entire acre to a depth of about six inches so we wouldn't get hurt falling on hard ground. Hence the lot's name, "Sawdust Park," not only in the neighborhood but throughout town. This sawdust business was slightly embarrassing to me for a few days; then my friends and I forgot about it.

The early and middle 1920s were for me mostly Sullivan-related, although there were vacations in Michigan and Colorado. I was either sitting in a varnish-disinfectant-sweat-smelling grade school, or skating the town's sidewalks, or sledding Stratton's hill, or playing under our backyard maples and hickories with boys and dogs and Ray and Miss Fischer, or stalking squirrels with Ray, or being read to or drilled in the multiplication table by Miss Fischer, or splashing in Buck Creek beside Center Ridge Cemetery, or flying kites, or spinning tops. The names I knew next-best to Ray's and Miss Fischer's and my natural father's and mother's were those of my pals Brandy and Murph and Dave and Hindu and Maurice Lee and Wayne and Waldo and Ruth and Mary and Catherine and my across-the-street cousins, John T. and Chuck, and Uncle Hinkle and Aunt Lucile.

Dad, of course, was far removed from my very much less hectic doings. The first couple of years of the 1920s for him must have been a dizzying montage: sitting impatiently in the United States Cabinet after running the cross-country, successful Harding–Coolidge campaign against Ohio Governor James Cox and future President Franklin Roosevelt (then and thereafter his friend); mending political fences, mediating factional disputes, appeasing administration critics; among other postal reforms, creating a carrier-clerk welfare system, putting postmasters under Civil Service rather that political patronage, revitalizing the sickly airmail service, motorizing rural delivery, and improving foreign mailing; resigning from the Cabinet to accept the lucrative offer of a new consortium of major movie companies to lead their fight against economically ruinous censorship, and as the group's president setting out to persuade—successfully, it turned out—American churches, fraternal orders, women's clubs, city and state and the Federal governments, and United States citizens generally that self-regulation, not legislation, was the American way to corral Hollywood's widely perceived licentious stampede.

There were some names beyond Sullivan that were important to him in those days, with whose owners he associated and which were probably also important in one way or another to most Americans. They included those of President Harding, Vice-President Coolidge, Secretary of Commerce and future President Herbert Hoover, Secretary of State and later Supreme Court Chief Justice Charles Evans Hughes, Secretary of the Treasury and aluminum multimillionaire philanthropist Andrew Mellon, Secretary of the Interior and subsequently "Teapot Dome" rascal Albert Fall, Attorney General and also alleged miscreant Harry Daugherty, oil tycoon and alleged "Teapot Dome" briber Harry Sinclair. Also there were former President Theodore Roosevelt and William Boyce Thompson (multimillionaire copper baron, dedicated in his retirement to unofficial public service). Included were the ruler of his namesake, industrial dynasty and United States Senator from Delaware Coleman DuPont; brilliant lawyer and international statesman and New York Senator Elihu Root; newspaper chain titan William Randolph Hearst; and wealthy banker and wise counselor to United States Presidents then and thereafter Bernard Baruch. He also knew anti-labor steel mogul Henry Clay Frick, Senator (and to become Coolidge's Vice-President) Charles G. Dawes, pioneer airmail pilot and later first Atlantic solo flier Charles A. Lindberg, anti-League-of-Nations Senators Henry Cabot Lodge and William Borah, and former Wilson Democrat George Harvey, whom Harding appointed Ambassador to Great Britain and whose Blackstone Hotel suite during Chicago's 1920 Republican National Convention the press dubbed the delegates' "smoke-filled room." Also there was respected lawyer-banker Dwight Morrow who later became Coolidge's Ambassador to Mexico and father-in-law of Charles Lindberg, General William ("Billy") Mitchell who initially was derided for his belief in the future wartime importance of airplanes and who sank an obsolete battleship with air bombs in a test exonerating this theory, syndicated (over 1,000 newspapers) national affairs columnist Arthur Brisbane, commanding general of World War I's American Expeditionary Forces John J. Pershing, New York Symphony conductor and nationally influential music educator Walter Damrosch, motion picture bosses Adolph Zukor and William Fox and Carl Leammle and Samuel Goldwyn and Robert Cochrane and David Selznick.

Chapter Two

THE PEOPLES STATE BANK

George R. Dutton   J.T. Akin   R.W. Akin
Chairman   President   Cashier

SULLIVAN, INDIANA
May 25, 1920

Will H. Hays,
New York

Dear Will:

    I enclose check of W.H.H., Jr., and wish to inform you, as his father, that the young man is putting quite a number across the counter.

    I wish to assure you it is quite a pleasure to me to honor his checks, but at the same time felt it my duty to inform you of his activity in that direction. Some Boy!

Very Truly, Joe. T. Akin

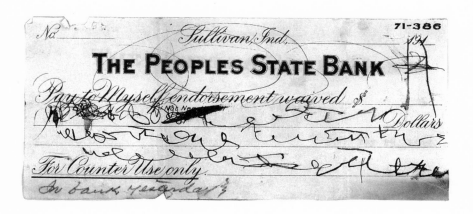

REPUBLICAN NATIONAL COMMITTEE

Will H. Hays, Chairman
19 West 44th Street
New York City

May 29, 1920

Mr. J.T. Akin,
Sullivan, Indiana.

My dear Mr. Akin:
Thanks very much for your letter and the enclosure. I am crazy about the enclosure . . .

Sincerely yours, Will H. Hays

* * *

Tuesday, March 29 [1]

. . . *Cabinet meeting at eleven mostly on Railroad Labor situation. See first evidence of Hoover's alleged solo playing . . .*

Tuesday, April 5

. . . *Cabinet meeting mostly on policy of Dep't. of Justice in re big business. Lunch with President and Mrs. Harding at White House and Harry Daugherty. <u>Harding O.K.</u> Evening . . . dinner with Geo. Harvey, now settled for English Ambassador . . . These things are brought about . . .*

Friday, April 29

. . . *Breakfast at Dwight W. Morrow's. Lunch at Mrs. E. H. Harriman's with Averill, her son and two others. Then call on Payne Whitney & then Morrow & Cochran at Morgan's . . . Payne Whitney very good—also Morrow and Cochran.*

---

1. *Personal diary entries by W.H.H., from March 29, 1921, through December 31, 1921, are italicized.*

Sunday, May 8

. . . *To White House and go to Church (Calvary Baptist) with President & Mrs. Harding & Mr. and Mrs. J. T. Pratt. Beautiful Mother's Day serive. Lunch at White House. Walk in garden. Very good day . . .* <u>Remember Mother's Day</u>. *Dine alone in room.*

Tuesday, May 17

. . . *Am much worried about Harding's lack of decision . . . Long talk with Harry Sinclair who is very friendly in re future . . .*

Saturday, May 21

. . . *H. Hoover comes by at 10 and we go to funeral Chief Justice White . . . 1 o'clock motor to Boling Field and start with General Wm. Mitchell in airplane to New York . . . Great business & good way to die . . .*

Wednesday, May 25

. . . *Office all morning except hurried trip to Post Office Committee of Congress . . . Afternoon give out statement that I had granted second class privilege to "Liberator."* [2] *This will make a noise . . .*

Friday, May 27

. . . *Unable to sleep. Am still not well and hate this job and Washington . . . After Cabinet meeting, Weeks, Daughtery, Fall & I get the President in room and ride him about hurrying patronage. He agrees to appoint Scott Bone Governor of Alaska . . . Could chuck this job with glee.*

Tuesday, May 31

. . . *Sen. Wm. E. Borah writes a very complimentary letter. Fainting: He approves "Liberator" decision. Makes me doubt it some. Do not really mean that . . .*

---

2. *"Liberator" was considered a "radical" paper by many who sought to penalize it by making it pay more costly first–class rate.*

Wednesday, June 8

. . . I resign as Chairman of Republican National Comm. . . . Feel relieved with end of Chairmanship. It has been a very active and interesting experience and I liked it. Of the future I'm in doubt . . .

Tuesday, June 28

. . . Cabinet—where Chas G. Dawes makes a speech and a good deal of fool of himself. Believe he and I will fuss a good deal. I know we will if he undertakes any funny business. Lunch with Mr. and Mrs. Howard Chandler Christy of Shoreham. Afternoon see 15 people . . .

* * *

Saturday, July 2

. . . On train to Indiana, work until noon on Postal Savings . . . Reach Terre Haute at 12:46. Hinkle at train . . . Drive home . . . Billie continues to grow and is fine boy . . .

Sunday, July 3

. . . Church. Communion Sunday. Conscience hurts very much. My dear father & mother . . . On to Terre Haute and take four o'clock Penn. for N.Y.

Tuesday, July 12

. . . Stay after Cabinet to see W. G. H. about request of W. R. Hearst for a revenue collector in Calif. . . .

Tuesday, July 19

. . . No cabinet meeting on account bombing tests at Hampton Rhoades. Lunch at White House . . . All afternoon see people . . . Evening see Dempsey–Carpentier fight pictures.

* * *

Sunday, August 14

... Am determined to find out where I am with things generally ... Really do not believe I'll be content at all until I am out at work for money again—and yet I feel that won't do it.

Monday, August 15

... Down at 9 AM to meet Adolf Zukor & J.E. Watson. A. H. Smith, Pres. of N.Y. Central, calls. He has patent mail car he wants to sell government. Lunch in office in re Peace Conference ...

Tuesday, August 16

... Delegation from Indiana says Ed Wasmuth will run for Governor there if I do not. I will not of course ... Staff meeting & Cabinet. Hughes still a little stiff. Harding looks worn. I do not care for this life ...

* * *

Monday, August 22

... Leave at 7:15 for motor trip to N.Y. .. have accident in N.Y. .... Too bad ... Evening till one o'clock with H. F. Sinclair. He is a brick ... Return to Washington at one a.m.

Tuesday, August 23

Arrive Washington at 7 ... Sorry about the Collision. Have some difficulty ahead about failure to change license that someone is to blame for. You can't delegate anything much. N.Y. Times have scurrilous (accident) article absolutely without any foundation in fact. Must find out who responsible for that and get ahold of them ...

Monday, August 29

... I am all shot inside, in spirit certainly ... Letter from Coleman DuPont suggesting I go into Empire Trust Co. Don't think I'm interested but

appreciate his thoughfulness . . . Dinner <u>alone</u> as usual. Movie nearby, "Four Horsemen."

* * *

Friday, September 2

Staff meeting and cabinet. West Va. strike and riot about only thing. Harding keeps head. Hoover not too sound . . .

Monday, September 5

. . . Arrive St. Louis at 6 o'clock . . . 3000 at station—Glee Club and bands . . . Convention of Letter Carriers. Never had a better meeting <u>anywhere</u>. Start back East at 10 o'clock . . .

Wednesday, September 21

. . . Take J. C. Shaffer to call on Henry Wallace . . . Give out story about killing the mail bandits at Ft. Worth, Texas. Osteopath. Dinner at Hoovers . .

Sunday, September 25

. . . Spend day again on Coleman DuPont's yacht. This is real vacation and he is splendid . . .

Thursday, September 29

. . . We are starting a good many things in this job. I believe the service will be improved permanently . . . Worried about conditions at home. Whole situation very wrong . . . Pack to leave for Sullivan tomorrow . . .

Friday, September 30

Failure of Senate and House to keep platform pledge in re taxes is serious. Am shaken in faith in popular government. All right so long as men keep unselfish just a little and they have leaders . . . Merchant Marine matter precipitated into discussion by President. He has his hands full . . . Leave for Sullivan—much worried.

* * *

Saturday, October 1

Chas. Edward and W. H., Jr. all at station in football suits . . . Helen[3] not well . . . Dr. Crowder agrees to take up immediately. Billie seems all right and a great boy. Am deeply upset about it all.

Sunday, October 2

. . . Hinkle & Lucile to take care of Billie when Helen away. Am seriously worried about her condition. Developments might be an explanation for un-understandable things of the past. Will cure her if it is humanly possible and feel sure it is . . .

* * *

JOSEPH A CAPPS, M.D.
Peoples Gas Building
Suite 1401
Chicago

Referred by Dr. J. H. Crowder [4]

Hays, Mrs. Will H.   October 10, 1921
250 Washington St.,
Sullivan, Indiana

. . . Complaint — Last March attack of dizziness— "black out momentarily" —extraction of all teeth . . . Recently double vision . . . Loss of memory.

Prev. Ill. — Malaria or typhoid at 12.

---

3. *Helen Hays, his wife.*
4. *Handwritten notes by Dr. Capps*

F. H. — Father 1v. Mother d. of T. B. 2 children died in few hours. 1 lv. and well, 6 yrs. old.

Supplementary — Thinks hearing is growing less acute. Ringing of ears, esp. left. 2 yrs ago attack of dizziness (from food?). No reoccurrence. Tremor of hands of late & trembling of voice but no palpitation.

* * *

Monday, October 10

... *Telephone from A. Brisbane about purchase of Detroit Times. Evening all in* ...

Thursday, October 20

... *At 4:50 left for Sullivan on Pennsylvania R. R.* ... *Strike on railroads may be imminent, but I doubt it. Greatly worried about Helen's condition. Had no idea it was so bad. Dictated Boy-Scout speech between Washington & Baltimore* ...

Friday, October 21

... *Helen & Billie meet me at Terre Haute station, they from Crawfordsville en route to Sullivan. Condition of Helen very serious. Lucile also meets us. I ride home in her car* ... *Play with Billie all afternoon and evening. Helen partially realizes her situation, only. Billie <u>seems</u> entirely well. Get him gun. Mattie[5] great help* ... <u>*Very sad*</u> *situation. I am <u>completely undone</u>.*

Saturday, October 22

... *Dr. Crowder* ... *will go with us to Chicago tomorrow. Everything seems so minor in this real crisis. Take Billie long walk.* ... *Helen condition very*

---

5. *W.H.H.'s half–sister*

18

serious it seems to me. I am <u>very very</u> deeply moved. I seem so helpless and I am so utterly unworthy . . .

Sunday, October 23

Up early. Helen packs. Mattie helps. Billie goes to Sunday school. He seems OK. Great comfort that Lucile can care for him . . . Very sad—but <u>everything</u> will be done . . . Dr. Crowder, Helen & I go to St. Luke's Hospital immediately on arrival in Chicago. See Dr. Capps who will care for her.

Thursday, October 27

. . . Start early in N. Y. this A.M. by visit to main P. O. and interview chauffeur Frank Haverack who was driving the truck which was robbed . . . Go with H. F. Sinclair to Roosevelt Memorial meeting . . . says he will want me to be President of Consolidated Company. Have some doubts . . . Take train for Washington and get <u>wrecked</u>. Shaken a little. Back to N. Y. . . . Walter Damroch & porter and conductor kind. Waldorf, where Dr. <u>Geo. Riley</u>[6] comes . . . <u>He also real friend</u>. Might have been serious.

* * *

Tuesday, November 1

. . . Awaken very early, very nervous. Staff and Cabinet meetings. Then with President 12 to 1. Propose Hoover for Advisory Council of Disarmament Conference . . . Lunch in office and all afternoon in office on new Envelope Contract. Dinner alone, then theatre with Booth Tarkington, et ux. Osteopath afterward. Am not well yet.

* * *

---

6. *Osteopath*

JOSEPH A. CAPPS, M.D.
Peoples Gas Building
(Suite 1401)
Chicago

Dr. Joseph R. Crowder,   November 2, 1921
Sullivan, Indiana.

Dear Dr. Crowder:

You will be interested to know about Mrs. Hays . . . There has been no definite change as yet in her condition . . . Her mental confusion was certainly a great deal more than on her previous visit . . . At times she has an obsession that someone was spying on her from a room across the court, but this seems to have been a passing notion . . .

With kindest regards, I am

Yours sincerely, Joseph A. Capps

Saturday, November 5

<u>42 years old today</u>. Work in office all day . . . <u>Forty two years</u>. Would they were finishing differently in many respects.

Tuesday, November 8

Staff and Cabinet meetings. Much talk about mail robbers —nothing else. Lunch with Hoover. He is OK, I guess. Afternoon with Gen. LaJune in re 1000 marines for mail protection . . .

Wednesday, November 9

Tired all the time. Office all morning. Lunch at White House . . . Afternoon office until late . . . H. G. Wells, English author . . . very interesting.

Friday, November 11

<u>Father's birthday</u>. Armistice Day . . . Procession from Capitol to Executive Ave. March with Cabinet . . . Harding makes <u>great speech</u> . . .

JOHN T. HAYS
WILL H. HAYS
HINKLE C. HAYS
ALONZO C. OWENS

HAYS & HAYS
ATTORNEYS-AT-LAW
SULLIVAN, IND.

Dear Father

letter I am writing you a
for your birthday
and when are you going
to send the Ingersoll
And kiss us for
all

Will H. Hays Jr.

I love you

Received by W. H. H., November 5, 1921.
The first letter written by W. H. H. Jr.

The correspondence that kept father and son close over the miles and the years began with letters like this one, written when Will Hays, Jr., was five years old and in the first grade.

Wednesday, November 16

Up at 7:30 . . . *Call on Bernard Baruch . . . Call on R. J. Cuddahy, Literary Digest, who is friendly . . .*

Thursday, November 24

<u>Thanksgiving</u> . . . *Calvary Baptist Church. Harding and many foreigners. <u>Very</u> fine ceremony. Lunch with Col. & Mrs. William Boyce Thompson at Shoreham . . .*

Friday, November 25

See the result of test of pistol shots on glass in mail truck. Cabinet. Coolidge asks me up to Boston for Bankers meeting on Jan 6. Get new suit from a Washington tailor and can't wear it . . .

* * *

Saturday, December 3

Arrive Chicago eleven. Go to hospital. Helen some better . . . Afternoon with Joseph Medill Patteson and Robert McCormick in re the giving away money by Tribune and Chicago Examiner. On phone to N.Y. with Hearst. We work it all out . . .

Monday, December 5

To hospital and begin thorough physical examination of <u>myself</u> . . .

Wednesday, December 7

. . . Leave Hospital at noon . . . Ordered to take 3 weeks rest . . . Bad headache. Old friend Connery has a spine doctor over from Battle Creek. He jerks me badly, I think.

Thursday, December 8

. . . Helen better. Leave for Washington at 12:40 . . . Headache bad. Porter a gentleman, a characteristic not determined by color or station.

Friday, December 9

 Arrive Washington 9:15. All in. Bad headache . . . Have Dr. Swope & Dr. Work. Begin the rest by necessity! . . . Lewis Selznick and Saul Rogers (att'y for Wm Fox) call and leave written offer for $100,000 from Movie Producers.

Sunday, December 11

 <u>*Billie Hays, jr. six years old today*</u>. *I stay in bed all day with head and neck & back . . .*

*   *   *

Monday, December 12

 . . . Will either go to White Sulphur or to Col. Thompson's house at Yonkers tomorrow for bed rest. Telephone Hinkle to come East. Want to talk movie matter with him . . .

Friday, December 16

 . . . <u>Times publishes where I am</u>. Must remember their unfriendliness. Must see who is their city editor . . . Head worse. Very nervous. Worried about what is matter with me . . .

Sunday, December 18

 . . . Hinkle comes out [7] from N.Y. He reports his week's work, which is marvelous. There and in W.H., Jr.—and indeed in all of them—is my future devotion . . .

Tuesday, December 20

 . . . H. C. H. goes to Chicago to arrange matters re Helen there . . . Reports <u>Billie</u> all right. God grant that is so . . .

---

7. *To Col. Thompson's home in Yonkers.*

Saturday, December 24

... Take walk of 12 minutes ... Evening go down for dinner in dining room. Very weak. An odd Christmas Eve—in bed. Col and Mrs. Thompson very kind, however.

Sunday, December 25

Christmas Day, 1921 ... I eat dinner with family at 1 o'clock ... Odd Xmas. Wonder what then? But must not worry ...

* * *

Monday, December 26

In bed all morning ... H. F. Sinclair comes at 1 and stays till five. Very anxious that I do not take movie job but stay where I am and later go with him . ..

Tuesday, December 27

... Spend hour with Col. in his room at house in bathrobes. He tells me Texas Gulf Sulphur has gone up enough to pay off my losses on Sinclair Oil. Lunch with family ... dictated letters for hour to Col's stenographer and find myself mentally very disinterested. Bad sign must wait ...

* * *

HAYS & HAYS
Attorneys-at-Law
Sullivan, Ind.

Dear Father,[8]
 I love you very much. I had my hair cut yesterday. I look very nice. Aunt Bertie was down here and wanted me to go home with her.

---

8. *Written on December 28, 1921. (Hereafter, dates of letters by W.H.H. Jr. not dated by him, will be noted numerically in parenthesis, as indicated by Helen Fischer, or by recipient, or as post marked.)*

Aunt Cile though it was too cold. Please thank Santa Clause for me.

your loving Son, Will H. Hays Jr.

P. S. Uncle Hinkle has been sick but is better. W.H.H.Jr.

* * *

(1-1-22)

Wednesday, December 28

. . . Simply have to come back slowly mentally as well as physically, that's all . . . Up at noon, lunch in room and to N.Y. See Henry Rosen at Harriman Bank—good friend—then to meet movie men Fox, Zukor, Selznick, Abrams, Atkinson, Glums, Cole, Laemmle, Cochran, Goldwin, etc. . . . Will consider till Jan. 15 . . .

Saturday, December 31

. . . I am very, very grateful Col. Thompson . . . Feel <u>very weak today</u> . . . In bed in room 754 Waldorf about asleep when year out. Has been odd year. Hope 1922 is different in some ways. But anyway God is good.

* * *

(1-1-22)
Dearest Father

I love you and Charles thanks you for his oranges and his pictures. I thank you too.

I went to the dentist and had my tooth filled. I went to Sunday school and Church today. I am learning to skate.

Your loving son, Will H. Hays Jr.

Chapter Three

AMONG my childhood pals in Sullivan were some pretty tough kids from coal mining families and others with fathers who worked around town or even owned a store like Bradbury's Grocery. One of my best friends was Junior Henderson—we called him "Hindu"—who lived with his younger brother and older sister over the fire station, their parents being dead. Today he's a retired DuPont chemist and executive.

In the other end of town by the railroad station another gang had formed called the "Depot Towners" and we played football against them on many Friday afternoons and Saturday mornings in Sawdust Park for an audience of townspeople standing around the sides of the pasture. The audience knew about the games because we advertised them by tacking crayoned posters on telephone poles around the courthouse square. Once we even were invited by the high school to play between halves of one of its games and another time Ray drove us to Palestine, Illinois, to play a pick-up team there. I remember Tony getting out of his shed several times in the middle of games and Ray, who was the referee, having to call time out while he caught Tony and put him back in his stall.

Dad gave us sweat shirts with "MM" on their fronts, except for the "manager's," which had just one "M"; they arrived one day from New York in a big box, as a surprise. I also got for my birthday a football helmet and padded pants. Our team was "coached" by a high school halfback named Waldo Wheeler, with the occasional assistance of high school center Stewart Hartfelter. Waldo's dad worked in the mines; Stewart's "kept up" the cemetery, and his sister was an acrobatic dancer.

Several years before the Mix-Mixers days—I was age four or five—I came down with pneumonia. I remember being in bed for a time, not in my room which used to be the sleeping porch but in the large bedroom upstairs where usually my mother slept. On my dad's trips home I never knew for sure where he slept; maybe in her room or maybe in the guest room. I never remember seeing them kiss each other, which didn't occur to me until much later. Anyhow, I suppose I was moved into

Mother's room so she could keep an eye on me during the nighttime. Miss Fischer hadn't arrived on the scene yet and Ray had been there only a short time, it seems to me. I remember there being a nurse around during my illness. She was a rather young person, I think, and one day she didn't appear but a different one did, this one somewhat older than she. Some years later I realized the reason for this switch of nurses but at the time I was aware simply of the fact that the first nurse, the day before her disappearance, told me she'd had an operation and asked if I would like to see the scar. I must have said I would because she stepped close to the bed and raised her skirt above her hips and pulled down her undergarments and took my hand and pulled it out to touch her "scar." I had an unidentifiable feeling about this and was pulling my hand back when Ray appeared in the doorway of the bedroom and the nurse quickly jerked down her dress and hurried out of the room past Ray. I have the impression she was laughing. I never saw her again. Ray never mentioned that episode, and the next day the different nurse arrived. That was my first exposure to what later in my growing up I became aware was the vast and complicated and wonderful area of "sex"; and in long retrospect I've sometimes mused that it was too bad I hadn't been, say, eighteen at the time.

Another incident involving Ray, also before the Mix-Mixers days, probably when I was just about starting to grade school, had to do with his old Model T Ford which sometimes he drove to work instead of biking and parked at the rear of our yard where an alley ran between the backyard and the lot that later became Sawdust Park. I remember I crawled under the automobile, as though it were a cave and I were an Indian after a day's hunt, and took some twigs I'd gathered and a couple of matches I'd got from the kitchen and built a little fire under there and lay on my stomach with my chin propped on my fists staring at the blaze from a foot away, feeling the warmth on my eyeballs. Suddenly Ray's feet appeared beside the car and then his head upside down looking at me under it and then I felt my ankles in his grip and my body hauled out from under the car. Ray threw some handfuls of dust onto the fire which was burning under the Ford's gas tank. He suggested I give up for all time the building of fires underneath automobiles.

One sad time I remember with Ray—there's still pain in the memory—I got mad at him about something I don't recall now and threw a handful of sand out of the sand pile in our backyard into his face; and he picked up a handful and threw it into my face. I can remember my surprise and the gritty feeling of the sand in my mouth; and I cried and he did too; and we hugged each other tighter that usual before he left for his house.

This doesn't involve Ray or Miss Fischer, but Uncle Hurley Drake, who lived with Dad's half-sister Aunt Bertie in Farmersburg, about ten miles north of Sullivan. Ray used to drive Mother and me, without Helen, on an occasional Sunday afternoon up to Farmersburg to visit Uncle Hurley and Aunt Bertie; and while the older people talked I played out in a soft, garden-like spot between the Drake's house and their driveway, building little roads for the toy automobiles and trucks they kept at their house for me. They didn't have children of their own. Sometimes Uncle Hurley and Aunt Bertie would come down on Sundays to visit us in Sullivan. One day after Sunday dinner at out house, Uncle Hurley and I walked out into the backyard, talking and strolling around, and he found a bird—probably a sparrow—which was flopping around on the ground with a broken wing. Sort of casually he picked up the wounded bird and held it by its head and whirled its body around a couple of times, wringing its head off, and tossed its head and body into some bushes. I never felt quite the same about Uncle Hurley again.

Ray used to wring chickens' necks that way in the backyard whenever we were having chicken for Sunday dinner, but somehow—although I don't think I could have brought myself to do that and Ray never asked me to—I didn't hold Ray's doing it against him; it was something necessary, if unpleasant, which was part of his job. I used to watch him in the dimly lighted basement in front of the furnace skin rabbits or squirrels he had shot in the fields or woods; and because they were dead and he was skillful and quick at the job the anatomical aspects of it fascinated me, rather than repulsed me. He threw the skins and entrails into the furnace fire and took the cleaned carcasses home for Bonnie to cook for his family. Once he dried a squirrel or rabbit skin, I forget which, and nailed it on a board for me to hang of the wall of my bedroom upstairs, like a picture. Helen accepted this trophy display. Mother, if she noticed it, probably didn't know what it was.

After school and on Saturdays in my earliest grade-school years, several of my classmates and I often gravitated to our backyard, before Sawdust Park was attached to the rear of the yard across the cindered alley, and we played cowboys and Indians or pirates of the Spanish Main or Robin Hood or whatever kind of movie had inspired us the previous Friday night at the Sherman Theatre. (The three-story theater building's third floor was occupied by the Hays & Hays law firm which had been founded by my grandfather, John T. Hays, and was where my father had begun his practice of law after graduating from Wabash College.)

Ray taught all of us to play "shinny," a sort of iceless hockey, and in the wintertime he often played this with us (or with me alone when the other kids weren't around) in the driveway that ran from the street beside out house back to a circle around the sand pile. The puck was a tin can which quickly became battered into a more or less compact object about the size of a tennis ball, and the sticks were branches cut from saplings in a way which gave them shafts and curved heads like golf clubs.

In the spring Ray and the gang and I played baseball, first in the backyard between the back porch and the sand pile, later in Sawdust Park. The grounders didn't roll in the sawdust, but it made sliding into home plate easier on runners' hips if not catchers' eyes. In the late spring after it got warm enough and in the summer weeks when I wasn't away somewhere, we all often went out into the woods and fields, led by Ray like the Pied Piper; and as often as not these meanderings involved skinny-dipping in Buck Creek, which flowed through Powell's pasture between the west edge of town and Center Ridge Cemetery. Incidentally, upstream about a half-mile from our swimming hole was the community slaughter house. I don't remember our realizing the juxtaposition at the time; it wasn't until quite a while later that we became aware of the slaughter house operator's practice of throwing offal into the creek. I don't recall our getting ear infections or pinkeye after those swims, but of course we didn't open our eyes under the water because it was so muddy a boy couldn't see anything.

Chapter Four

January 28, 1922

Dr. J. R. Crowder,
Sullivan, Indiana.

Dear Dr. Crowder:
    ... The tremor of the hands is much less marked, but she still has the attacks of petit mal, although they are not as frequent as they used to be ... A few weeks ago, as you know, she had very definite delusions and hallucinations, and now she seems to have imperative ideas and often is rather suspicious of the actions and motives of others. There is also a definite impairment of memory. On the whole, I would say her mental condition has improved appreciably in the last month. At the present time, however, I think it would be impossible, or at least extremely difficult, to take the responsibility of her care at home unless she had her two nurses and was seen very frequently ...

    I am sorry I cannot give a more glowing outlook about her mental condition, but there are certain deep-seated changes in the brain that may prove permanent, or at least not amenable to treatment.

    With best regards, I am

Yours sincerely, Joseph A. Capps

* * *

March 4, 1922

Mr. H. Will Hays, Jr.,
250 West Washington Street
Sullivan, Indiana.

My dear Billy:
    I have just heard from your Uncle Hinkle about your report. I am delighted to know that the G which you got in spelling and arithmetic

last month have gone to E this month. That is fine. I note that the conduct grade slipped a little and I know you will bring it back to E next month.

Your Uncle Hinkle is here in New York and Aunt Lucille and we are having a nice visit. I will be out in a couple of weeks and we will have a great play . . .

Affectionately yours, Will H. Hays

* * *

March 10, 1922

Dr. Joseph L. Crowder,
Sullivan, Indiana.

Dear Dr. Crowder:
. . . Mrs. Will Hays has been steadily improving . . . Her mental symptoms, such as delusions, suspicions, hallucinations, etc., have been conspicuous by their absence for many weeks . . .The only fly in the ointment is that she does persist in having these attacks of petit mal, two or three, or more, times a day.

. . . She certainly would not go to an institution voluntarily, and it would be very difficult at the present time to commit her, as she is not at the present a source of danger to herself or to others, and moreover, she is not suffering from any serious mental confusion or derangement . . . It would seem best to have her under competent supervision at home with a reliable trained nurse and companion . . .

With regards, I am

Yours sincerely, Joseph A. Capps

* * *

FUTURE BOSS OF THE MOVIES

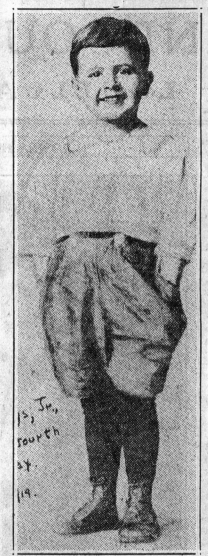

WILL H. HAYS, JR.

His dad, Will H. Hays, Sr., gives the motion picture industry orders, but Bill tells his dad what to do. A command to spend Sunday at Bay View, Michigan, and bring along a new canoe was obeyed to the letter by the dictator of motion pictures, who knows it's wise to always give heed to the power behind the throne.

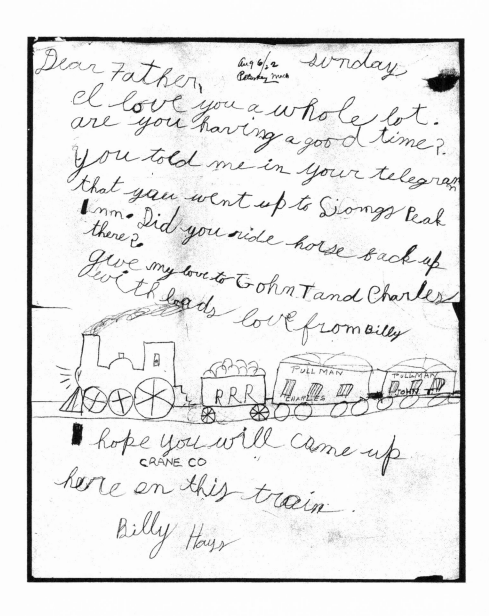

Aug 6/'2
Peterkey mich

Dear Father, Sunday
I love you a whole lot.
Are you having a good time?
You told me in your telegram
that you went up to Siongs Peak
mm. Did you ride horse back up
there?
Give my love to John T and Charles
with loads love from Billy

PULLMAN
RRR CHARLES
PULLMAN JOHN T
CRANE CO

I hope you will come up
here on this train.

Billy Hays

33

MOTION PICTURE PRODUCERS & DISTRIBUTORS OF
AMERICA, INC.
522 FIFTH AVENUE
NEW YORK CITY

Will H. Hays   Telephone
President[1]   Vanderbilt 2110

September 1, 1922.

Master Billie Hays,
West Washington St.
Sullivan, Ind.

Dear Billie:

     I sent you by express from here yesterday a very fine horsehair bridle which William S. Hart sent to me for you with his compliments, and said that when you are a little older he hopes you will have a regular cowboy horse and ride it hard. This is the finest bridle you ever saw, or anybody ever saw, and you ought to take good care of it, of course.

     I think you should write Mr. Hart.

     Love to all.

Affectionately, Father

* * *

THE WILLIAM S. HART. COMPANY
5544 1/2 Hollywood Boulevard
Hollywood, California
September 11, 1922.

Dear Bill:

     I sure was glad to get your fine letter and to know that you liked the bridle.

     Don't be in any hurry to get a horse. Wait until you are bigger and stronger then you can handle a better horse. One that has some get up and get to him . . .

---

1. *W.H.H. had accepted this position in March, 1922, resigning as Postmaster General*

... I know you are a big boy now but you'll be a whole lot bigger after awhile and stronger. Play outdoors all you can in the fresh air and you'll get bigger—quicker . . .

My Pinto Pony has written a new book and when it is published I'll send you one. You know he didn't really write it, Bill, but I knew what he wanted to say and I wrote it for him. And when I sent it to the people that print books they sent back word they'd make the book if the English was a little better. And I wrote back to them and told them, "that was the best English my horse could talk" . . . Mr. James Montgomery Flagg, a great artist, is painting a whole lot of pictures for it and I hope you like it when I send it to you.

Well—so long, Bill. Be a good boy and always do what your Daddy and your Mama wants you to do, because they love you and will always tell you what is right and what is wrong. And when a boy does what is right, he never needs to be afraid of anybody.

Always your friend, Bill Hart

* * *

HAYS & HAYS
Attorneys-at-Law
Sullivan, Ind.

Nov. 24, 1922.

Mr. Will H. Hays, Jr.,
Sullivan, Ind.

Dear Billy:
Your birthday is December 11th, and at that time you are seven years old . . . At this time I want to wish you the best birthday you ever had, and that each year may always be as happy, and remember, old kid, that your hard-boiled Uncle Hinkle loves you more that all the rest of them put together . . .

Affectionately, Hinkle C. Hays

* * *

WESTERN UNION TELEGRAM

. . . WA NEW YORK NY DEC 10 1922
WILL HAYS JR

CARE HAYS & HAYS SULLIVAN IND
TODAY IS GREAT DAY BILL EVERY BIRTHDAY MEANS
A LOT TO A BOY THAT IS GROWING UP INTO A BIG MAN
BECAUSE EVERY YEAR THAT GOES PAST MEANS THAT
SOMETHING FINE HAS BEEN ACCOMPLISHED AND WE
ALL KNOW YOU ARE MAKING GOOD EVERY YEAR YOUR
FRIEND
BILL HART

* * *

(1/11/23)

Dear Father,
I have been very busy in school or I would have written you
sooner. We are now reading the story of Robinson Crusoe.
I had such a nice Christmas and I want to thank you for the nice
toys you gave me. I have had on my cowboy suit all after noon. I am well
and am being a very good boy . . . Do you love me as much as I love you.
I love you a whole world full.
Good bye
Billie Hays

* * *

THE WHITE HOUSE
WASHINGTON

8:30 p.m. Thursday, 1/18/23

Dear Billie:[2]
I am down in Washington today and have been visiting with Col.
George Hárvey who is the American Ambassador to England. An
Ambassador from one Country to another Country is the man who is sent

---

2. *Originally handwritten*

to represent the Country he comes from and see that his country's interests are looked after. Col. Harvey is a good friend and is back here on a short visit. He is going back to New York tonight and on to England on Saturday to help work out a settlement of the 5,000,000,000 dollar debt which England owes this Country. This mission is confidential, so you must not tell . . .

I got your letter and am always very happy to get them. . . . I am very anxious to see you all and will be home at the first possible minute. I hear from others that you are doing fine at school and I am glad. I know you will. Love to all.

Affectionately, Your Father

* * *

522 FIFTH AVENUE
Sunday,
January 21, 1923

Dear Billie:

. . . Of course, I knew your would get promoted because you have been getting fine grades every day and when a boy or girl does good work in the little things every day, then when the end of the month comes they always know that the big job has been well done . . .

When I get home next, which will be soon, I want you to tell me all about Robinson Crusoe.

Give my love to all and write often.

Affectionately yours, Father

Here are some reloads for your revolvers. Give John T. and Charles some of them, too.

* * *

(1-28-23)

Dear Father

I love you and how are you getting along.

Ray is now putting up my punching bag in the basement. I am having a good time with Charles. We played with my electric train. We will now say Good-Bye.

Billie Hays

(1-29-23)

Dear Miss Ficher [sic],

how are you geting along on your visit to Crawfordvil. I am well and I hop you are to. I am sending you this letter to ask you if you love me. I love you.

good-by   Billie Hays

* * *

February 12, 1923.

Dear Dr. Crowder:

... The most remarkable phase of Mrs. Hays' improvement is the practical cessation of the attacks of petit mal ...

With regards, I am

Yours sincerely, Joseph A. Capps

* * *

HOWARD CHANDLER CHRISTY
1 WEST 67th STREET
Feb. 23rd, 1923.

Dear Billie

I'm glad you like the knife—I thought you would like it because of the patent spring making it easy to open—and of course every real boy likes a jack knife anyway! When you come to New York to see your

Father you must come up to see us and I'll show you some fine old swords and guns of all kinds . . .

Your Father was here yesterday. I am painting his portrait. He is very well indeed but has a little stye on his eyelid. I'm not putting that in his picture! Your Father is a very wonderful man and we are very fond of him and he talks so much about you we feel we know you quite well.

With all good wishes to you always from,

Howard Chandler Christy

* * *

April 4, 1923.

Dear Billie:

I am just back and want to send this word of appreciation and congratulation about Sunday. I am mighty happy that you joined church. I want to congratulate you, too, on the fine speech you made at the Sunday School service in the morning. The day was one of the happiest in my life.

Affectionately, Father

* * *

HAYS & HAYS
Attorneys-at-Law
Sullivan, Ind.

April 6, 1923.

Dear Bill:

. . . I told Billie I was going to send his Easter story to you and asked him if he had made a 100 today in school number work and that I wanted to send it to you, too, he was so pleased . . . It is very great pleasure to teach him because it gets so quick and it sticks.

Love, Martha[3]

---

3. *Martha "Mattie" Hays, W.H.H.'s half-sister.*

(6-15-23)

My Dear Father.

I have just written a letter to President Harding and attorney General Daugherty thanking them for my baseball . . . [4] We boys enjoyed our hunt with you when you were home.

I love you.

Good Bye, Billie Hays 2d

* * *

4. *Thrown by the President into a D.C. big league game, autographed by the President, Babe Ruth, Connie Mack, John McGraw, and Gabby Street.*

Chapter Five

IN the summers before I started to school and before each of the first few grades, Mother and Helen Fischer and I went to resorts for perhaps a month—I remember places like Estes Park, Colorado, Bay View, Michigan, Big Moose Lake in New York—and when I became Cub Scout age I was sent to the summer school of Culver Military Academy on Indiana's Lake Maxinkuckee.

I think we were at Estes Park for two summers, staying the first one in a cottage across Big Thompson River from Elkhorn Lodge and the second in the Lodge itself. Paul Kester was with us the first summer. Behind the hotel a couple of hundred yards was the stable where riding horses were kept for the guests. At least the second summer, a little bay Shetland pony named "Brownie" was reserved at the stable for me to ride. He was just the right size for my years, well-broken, neck-reined, a bit strong-willed but altogether a sweetheart and I loved him. This was before the "Mix-Mixer" days of Tony in Sullivan; I learned to ride well on Brownie, taught by the cowboys around the stable including a red-headed hand named Tex who wore a white Stetson like Tom Mix's. At first I was allowed to ride only with a group led by a wrangler; but after a while I was allowed to go out alone.

It was beautiful country, surrounded by mountains with Long's Peak predominant in the background. Immediately behind the Lodge was a small mountain called "Old Man Mountain" because the rocky top of it was shaped like an old man's profile. I climbed it a number of times with Miss Fischer and once alone, secretly. Its peak probably was less than a thousand feet above the Lodge. Miss Fischer climbed Long's Peak, a vastly more difficult undertaking at more than fourteen thousand feet.

The cottage we lived in, which probably was owned by the Lodge, was made of logs and stood at the foot of the ridge forming one side of Estes Park valley. The first summer Paul and I used to play a game with a huge ball three feet in diameter which I was told President Harding and Attorney General Daugherty sent to me. That summer must have been boring for Paul; mostly he drove Mother the mile from the cottage to the Lodge and to a few other hotels in the vicinity for lunch and maybe some bridge games with ladies while Miss Fischer and I rode horses and climbed hills and big rocks. I think Paul almost always had the evening off because I remember his driving down the road toward the Lodge and beyond it to the village of Estes Park after he brought us back from dinner at the Lodge in the evening. Often, as he got ready to leave, I went down the road a hundred yards or so and hid behind a sagebrush and waited for him to come along in the Model A Ford we acquired that summer from somewhere; and when he came along I jumped out from behind the bush and pretended to shoot him and waved good-bye to him. Sometimes he took a nap in the afternoon in his cabin beside our cottage and I lay under his bed chewing Blackjack gum and reading western magazines. He didn't seem to mind as long as I was quiet. He needed his rest for the evenings. I don't recall Miss Fischer going with him on these occasions but maybe sometimes she did, now that I think about it. It was while playing around our cottage I first discovered the foot-high anthills scattered among the sagebrush. I sometimes poked them with a stick and watched the hundreds of ants come pouring out over the pile. The principal flower in that country was "Indian Paint Brush," which Miss Fischer loved.

While I was at Estes Park the second summer, an issue of *Cosmopolitan* magazine came out in which an editorial by Editor Ray Long reprinted in facsimile a letter I had written the previous school year to one of our gang, Jimmie Collins, whose father had been killed in a mine explosion close to Sullivan, one of fifty-one miners who lost their lives in that disaster. Mr. Long had some nice words to say in his editorial about the importance of taking time in periods of friends' grief to console them in a personal way. I learned later that Jimmie Collins' mother had showed my letter to Miss Fischer, who had borrowed it and sent it to Dad in New York, who in turn had showed it to his friend, Ray Long, at a dinner party. Evidently Mr. Long got Dad's and Mrs. Collins' permissions to use the letter in his magazine. Anyhow Dad wrote us in Estes Park to watch for that issue and Miss Fischer one day came back with it from the village and showed it to Mother and me. I went for a ride on Brownie; and after a couple of hours I came riding back past the Lodge veranda toward the stable, feeling an acute urge to go to the bathroom. I saw Miss Fischer and Mother and a cluster of other ladies in rockers on the veranda and I rode toward them thinking to tie Brownie there for a few minutes while I went to the men's room in the Lodge. As I approached the group I realized they were handing around the *Cosmopolitan*, and as I arrived in front of them I suddenly was very uncomfortable at their exclaiming over me about the editorial with my picture and letter. In a sort of hot-cheeked spasm of rashness, not really conscious of my words until I'd said them, I swung off the horse, handed its reins to Miss Fischer and said, "Here, hold the son-of-a-bitch a minute," and clumped across the veranda into the lobby. After going to the bathroom I stumbled back out through the group and took Brownie's reins, swung into the saddle and trotted off toward the barn, the back of my neck feeling roasted. Miss Fischer told me later with a grin that the ladies had been shocked speechless at the contrast between the little boy of the magazine and the cussing one in high-heeled boots and Stetson. She also said she seemed to hear Tex in there somewhere. Mother simply said something like, "Mercy, Billy, you must watch your language." Throughout her life "Mercy" was Mother's favorite exclamation.

At Estes Park also, probably on my second summer there, I felt the first conscious stirrings of sexuality when I encountered in the Lodge on our first day a ravishing eleven-year-old blonde. When our gazes locked for a long instant across some wicker lobby furniture, my chest tightened and my throat dried up and my bowels felt loose and my ears hummed and I had to look away for fear of—I don't know what. It took a week of hanging around the Lodge until I learned her daily routine so I could pass her several times a day while pretending not to see her before I got up the nerve to say "Hello." When I did greet her she responded immediately with a friendly smile and cheerful words— I think we were walking in opposite directions on the little road between the hotel and the stable—and after that I took every possible occasion, contriving most of them, to speak to her and gradually to stretch our greetings into conversations and then into a horseback ride with Miss Fischer along. I think I asked the latter to go along on that first ride with the breathtaking creature because I still wasn't up to being alone with her; that would have been too terrifyingly wonderful. Somewhere about this time my awe of her was invaded suddenly and wildly by a carnal urge; I wanted to kiss her. I think I happened to be staring at her parted pink lips and beautiful teeth when it happened. I think Miss Fischer probably had tumbled already to my crush; no doubt it was obvious. Also, in retrospect, I imagine Miss Fischer was sensitive to the general realm, given Paul's proximity that summer. Certainly she was sympathetic one evening when one of us brought up the subject of the girl while she and I were taking a walk before bedtime. Indeed my pal not only was sympathetic, she was encouraging. And the next day when she and the beauty and I were out for a horseback ride and the girl dropped the bombshell that her parents were taking her away from Estes Park the

A Lesson I've Learned from a Boy of Nine

By Ray Long

JIMMIE COLLINS   BILLIE HAYS

WE reproduce here a letter which is one of the finest expressions of sympathy I have ever read.

It was written, as you will have guessed, by a youngster, by a boy of nine, Billie Hays, son of Will Hays, head of the motion picture industry. It was to Billie's chum, Jimmie Collins, whose father had been killed in a mine disaster in their home town of Sullivan, Indiana.

You will have guessed it came from the pen of a youngster, because you know, as I know, that no grown-up expresses sympathy with such direct, spontaneous, heartfelt simplicity.

As I read Billie Hays' letter I contrasted it with the wire I sent recently to a friend who had lost one dear to him. I *felt* sympathy, but instead of taking the time to think out and write a letter, I called my stenographer and dictated a telegram. And the result was a stilted, conventional expression which read like a form letter. And that, I'll venture to say, is just what Billie's father and every other busy man does under similar circumstances.

"Busy men." That's the trouble. We're busy, we're hurried, we're worried. But a boy of nine has inspired me to a decision never again to be so busy that I can't take the time and the thought to write a real letter to a friend in distress.

I shan't be able to write with the feeling that Billie showed (nor will Billie when he's as old as I am); but at least my friend shall know that I have written from the heart.

(Editorial reproduced by courtesy Cosmopolitan*)*

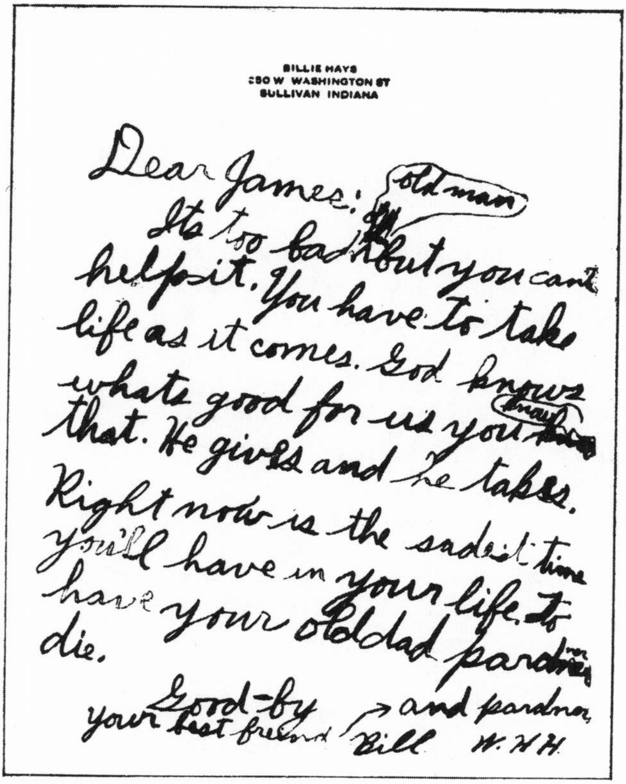

BILLIE HAYS
250 W WASHINGTON ST
SULLIVAN INDIANA

Dear James: old man
Its too bad but you cant help it. You have to take life as it comes. God knows whats good for us you know that. He gives and he takes. Right now is the sadest time you'll have in your life. to have your old dad pardner die.

Good-by
your best friend → and pardner,
Bill W.H.H.

next day forever, my pal suggested that the girl—I ought at least to remember her name, given her impact on me—and I ride ahead and explore an old barn at the far end of the meadow. When Miss Fischer winked at me, I had two sensations simultaneously: the thrill of anticipation and the fear of rejection. (I've had those same mixed feelings a thousand times since.) Astonishingly, the girl laughed and said something like, "Great, come on!" and spurred her horse into a lope toward the barn; and it didn't take me more that a couple of deep breaths to lope after her on Brownie. As clearly as though it happened yesterday I remember our dismounting outside the barn, tying our ponies to a hitchrail, entering the cool shade, and climbing up a rough ladder to explore the hayloft as though we really cared what was up there. Suddenly we were standing close to each other, knee-deep in hay, not looking at each other but at least I'm damn sure excruciatingly conscious of our nearness. We probably stood like that for only a few seconds, surely not more that half a minute; but it seemed to me an age while I tried desperately to turn toward her and lift my arms to touch her and press my lips against hers. And I just didn't have the courage. It was hard for me later to admit it to Miss Fischer, but I was just plain cowardly. I don't remember today whether or not I saw the girl off the next morning; probably too embarrassing; even now.

I don't know whether I remember another Estes Park incident or simply remember hearing Mother tell about it. Probably the latter. As I think of it now it does make me realize that Mother and I were at Estes Park once before Miss Fischer was with us, because I think this happened there when I was only about three or four years old. We stayed in a second-floor room of the Elkhorn Lodge with a railed balcony overlooking the Lodge's entrance driveway and its decorative pile of antlers. The way I remember Mother telling it, she had invited some rather "staid" (her word) ladies to drop by one Sunday afternoon for tea. They didn't play bridge because these particular ladies belonged to a church which frowned rigidly even on dominos on Monday, let alone cards on Sunday. Since Miss Fischer wasn't there I don't know who was sitting with me while I played on the balcony upstairs with an extra deck of cards. As the ladies were saying good-bye to Mother and climbing into their automobile, I grabbed up two fistfuls of the Devil's ducats, ambled to the railing and threw them down onto the suddenly up-staring, clucking assemblage like manna from Hell. I'm sure when Mother got upstairs she said something on the order of "Mercy, Billy!" But I'm also sure she said it with a twinkle in her eye.

My mother's sense of humor was one of the three characteristics I remember most as being hers. A second was her impressive attunement to the arts, an almost aristocratic sense of elegance, evidenced, particularly in her early years, by such things as the really beautiful watercolors I salvaged from her few possessions after her death and which she once told me she had painted as a twenty-year-old on a "Grand Tour" of Europe after graduating from Miss Somebody's finishing school in the East. A third characteristic, increasingly apparent as the years went by, might in all gentleness be termed eccentricity. There isn't any doubt about it, Mother was a character—stubborn, haughty, frequently nagging, but patient in her sad infirmities, very funny both intentionally and unintentionally, and surely gallant. She called tradespeople and other social non-acquaintances "creatures," referred to going upstairs as "ascending to the upper regions," said things like "The preacher regaled us with the horrors of Hell," and never referred to my dad's second wife as anything but "that woman" (emphasizing "that"). All her life she considered all politicians and show-business people—including her famous husband's political and motion-picture colleagues—to be "common," and never failed to return a word of greeting from anyone, whether or not she knew the greeter, or in her increasing deafness heard the nature of the greeting. Especially in her later years, after her divorce from Dad had formalized their long separation and she'd returned from Sullivan to her girlhood home in Crawfordsville, she walked across neighborhood and downtown street intersections without pausing or looking in either direction, as though no automobile should have the effrontery to bring her low. It was pure luck, relatively speaking, that she died in bed of hardening of the arteries and a broken hip and at least her sixth stroke instead of in the middle of a street. I thought sometimes her deafness, which increased with middle age, was intermittent, either physically or psychologically or both. Often it seemed to be selective. She tuned out most of the world and missed a good deal doing it, both good and bad; but she heard the summer rain begin in the night so she could get up and close the window and lean over my bed to listen to my breathing when she thought I was asleep and hear the postman's morning step on the front porch the few times she wasn't watching for him to come up the walk.

One of Mother's and my first summer sojourns—if not the first—was in Bay View, Michigan, or maybe Petoskey, or maybe in each place on successive summers. This must have been after my earliest

Estes Park trip, the pre-Miss Fischer card-throwing one, but before the other two Estes Park summers. The main things I remember about Bay View—really the only things—were the sweet, reedy smell of the toy birch-bark canoe somebody bought me; racing down a long boardwalk from one beach where I could see a distant freighter enter some sort of channel to another beach where I could see it emerge; riding in a car with Mother and Uncle Hinkle and Aunt Lucille and my cousins, John T. and Charles ("Chuck"), to visit a Hays family friend who had a summer cottage in the middle of a glowering woods on a glassy, gloomy lake called Loon Lake, I think; fishing with Dad off a dock in Lake Michigan during a visit there by him, my excitement alloyed by my mortification at his tying us together with a twenty-foot length of clothesline to keep me from drowning. My mortification arose not so much from the prospect of rescue as from what I felt (although, I realized Dad's concern) was the rope's implication of my clumsiness.

Another resort which Mother and this time Miss Fischer and I visited in our pre-Estes Park summers was a large, wide-porched hotel on an Adirondack Mountains lake called Big Moose. A shifting montage of that stay's images, like a mobile of memories in a lake breeze, brings around a toy square-rigger bobbing on the tiny waves of its harbor Miss Fischer and I scooped out of the sandy beach; the first professional "deep-sea" divers I'd seen—other-worldly, round-helmeted, rubber-suited, lead-shod—descending to the lake's bottom from an off-shore scow in search of a diamond ring dropped from the hotel's launch by the world-famous opera singer, Madam Schumman-Hienk; Miss Fischer showing up one day after a beauty shop visit with a new-style hair "bob," concerning which Mother probably said, "Mercy"; the fabulous, sur-prise arrival—I don't remember by what means—of a Scotch collie puppy as a gift from Dad; immediately naming my first beloved dog Glenn, after Hotel Glennmore where we stayed, not imagining that distemper was to take him from me the next spring in Sullivan; with friends in a combination boathouse and dancehall next to the hotel lighting the ends of drinking straws and taking puffs of hot smoke before the flames got to our lips (this experiment preceding cornsilk in Sullivan); out of Mother's and even Miss Fischer's sight several times racing alone ahead of snorting hogs across the hotel's pig lot from its fence to its center shed and, after resting, back again; watching a man at the table next to ours in the hotel dining room, oblivious of my interest, eating bread with a kind of reserved but exquisite enjoyment that was strangely fascinating and somehow momentarily unreal, like a common word a person stares at sometimes and thinks he hasn't seen before; on Miss

Fischer's day off, counting on Mother's vagueness and perhaps earliest hearing difficulty for unawareness of where I was for an hour, renting a tall, English-bridled, fortunately very gentle mare from the hotel stable's groom whom I assured this was old stuff for me—although in fact only from seeing movies to that point—and going for my first horseback ride.

Chapter Six

July 7, 1923.

Master Will H. Hays, Jr.
Elkhorn Lodge,
Estes Park, Colorado.

Dear Billy:
      Enclosed is a picture of yourself and an envelope to mail it in. I want you to write across the bottom of this, on straight lines which Miss Fischer will help you with:

> "Dear Mr. Daugherty; This is the ball which you and the President sent me. Thank you very much.
>
>   Billy Hays."

Love to all.

                Affectionately, Father

(Estes Park, 7-17-23)

Dear Father,
      I got the big camp ball last night. Paul knocked me over with the ball. we have lots of fun with it. Miss Helen takes golf lessons with me. I sent Mr. Daugherty the picture this afternoon. I forgot to thank you for the ball.
           good by,
                Hotdog. I love you
                    Billy Hays.

* * *

August 13, 1923.

Dear Billie:

I got back[1] yesterday from Marion, Ohio, where I went to attend President Harding's funeral. President Harding was a great and good man. You must save the ball always which he sent you.

I am glad to know from your letters that you and Charles are having a good time. Be outdoors all the time, climb the mountains, eat dirt, throw snowballs, kick the camp ball around, turn somersaults and everything . . .

Love to all.

Affectionately, Father

* * *

August 25, 1923.

Dear Billie:

I'm sorry you may have to have teeth braces when you get home. But when I was a boy you should have seen my teeth. My, they were as crooked as a trail up Old Baldy . . . I believe if I were you I would get me a lawyer to manage the case and beat the teeth. The best lawyer I know of anyplace is your Uncle Hinkle and I believe if I were you I would go to him, show him this letter, and tell him you want him to take charge of the case.

I wonder how you are getting along learning how to play ball. In addition to learning how to play golf, you want to learn how to be a big baseball pitcher.

Love to all.

Affectionately, Father

(8/27/23)
Monday

Dear Father

How are you I am having fun out here playing with charles and John T. I ate dinner at the Elkhorn yesterday. I went to the cowboy stampede. I will see you in Chicago and want you to go home with us.

good by

Billie Hays

1. *To New York City*

S. S. LEVIATHAN
UNITED STATES LINES

Thursday evening 6:10
Sept. 13

Dear Billie:

We have just seen land, off to the left. It's a light house and a lot of island, called Scilly Islands—we have had a fine trip. I've slept most of the time. Have not been sea sick at all. This is the biggest boat in the world . . . Will cable from London.

Love to all

Affectionately, Dad

* * *

Dictated enroute
Chicago to Sullivan
Sept. 13, 1923

Dear Will:

Concerning purchase of dogs, if you want any dogs bought, you buy them. In addition, confine your purchases to your own family. I am not situated so as to take on the additional burden at home, and, therefore, do not want John T. and Charles to have one, and do not want to be a party to buying Bill a dog or any other presents, until he comes clean with my request that he must stand up straight, which he certainly is not doing . . . even then I would get out of buying the dog, if I were you, because they are a bug-carrier and a nuisance . . . Although I do not want to become involved in this dog maelstrom at all, I know your intention is good and I love your for the kindness.

Affectionately, H.C.H.[2]

* * *

Was talking to HCH on telephone and tried to coax him into different opinion on this matter, but he said that he had the situation in

---

2. *Hinkle C. Hays*

splendid shape and that even Little Billie was not disappointed and had quit talking about the dog.[3]

* * *

Dear Father

I hope you are having a good time back in New York. I saw Harold Lloyd in Why worry and I liked it to, hotdog. I can't hardly wait until my book and sweater comes. Mother and aunt Sallie went to church to-night. charles and I have races with our pushmobiles. mine is a Dusenburg Special.

Billie Hays

Be sure and come home this week

* * *

C. H. STRATTON INVESTMENTS
SULLIVAN, INDIANA

Monday, November 5, 1923

Mr. Will H. Hays
522 Fifth Avenue
New York City

My dear Bill:

Yesterday morning about nine o'clock the telephone rang. Mrs. Stratton answered, and a gentleman asked for Mr. Stratton . . . I asked him what he wanted to communicate with me about and he informed me there was something for me fastened to my mail box on the front veranda. Am herewith inclosing the "for sale" sign for my house which I found here. Later I called him up and while I could not get much satisfaction out of him about it, he seemed to be inclined to sell the property very cheaply. If I remember correctly his price was $150.00 and I told him I would take it . . .

Yours truly, C. H. Stratton

---

3. *From secretary Julia Kelly to W.H.H.*

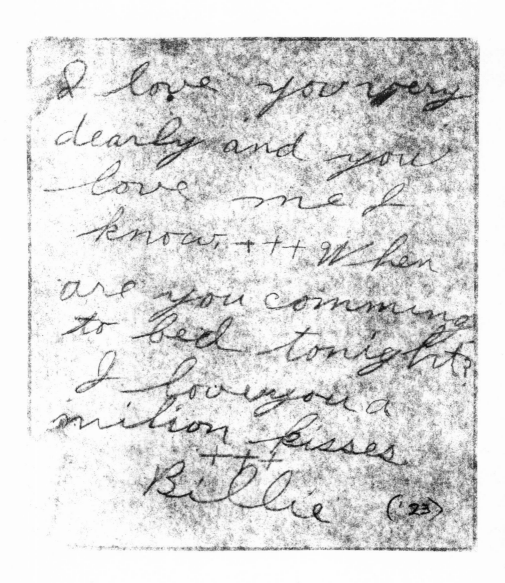

Note to Helen Fischer

Sullivan, Ind.
Nov. 25, 1923
Sunday

Dear Father,

I was sorry that I was not here when you called up yesterday. I wood have liked to have talked to you very much. Mother and I are planning to go to Crawfordville for Thanksgiving I am sorry too that you can't come to see Grandfather. Oh boy it's not very long till Christmas then I can see you hotdog we will have a hunt won't we? I had a letter from Bill Hart the other day in answer to my letter. He said for me to never mind about the lasso part for it will always be the hardest part

I love you
Good-by
Sir Bill

* * *

Dec. 5 - 23

Dear Santa Claus

I would like a "Uncle Wigley" game and a little play telephone and a book about boy-scouts and one of those things you make bridges with, you now. I live in Sullivan Ind. I just told you because I thought you might have forgotten.

good-by
Billie Hays

* * *

December 7, 1923.

Dear Billie:

I have ordered some scales sent to you and they ought to reach you any day. They will be your birthday present. You can put them in the bathroom and weigh yourself every day. I am going to give you a dollar every time you gain a pound. You can keep them until you are an old man, take them to college with you and use them there.

I am glad to have your letter this morning enclosing your report. I think it is fine. I am delighted with the "G plus" and "Ex" marks. Next month we want to whip up a little on spelling and music . . . Fine business, kid.

Love to all.

Affectionately, Father

* * *

THE PEOPLES STATE BANK
SULLIVAN, IND.
Dec. 11th, 1923.

Hon. Will H. Hays,
New York City

Dear Will:
. . . The Sullivan Advertising Club had its drawing yesterday, and gave away an Overland sedan and one hundred fowls. Bill Jr. drew a goose, and he was right on the job when the time came to get it. He swung onto its neck and started home with it. I walked up the street with him this morning and he told me that he was going to have it for dinner today. He sure is <u>some</u> boy.

Yours, R. W. Akin

* * *

Sullivan, Ind.
Dec. 16, 1923.

Dear Father
I received the scales that you sent me but they did not come on my birthday they came the day after but I am counting it as a birthday present. Last Thursday I weighed 51 pounds with my clothes off . . .
The goose that I got was a big one . . . We had the goose for dinner and it was very good. Uncle Hinkle, Aunt Lucile, John T and Charles were here. Only 9 more days till Christmas hotdog then we can play. good-by
I love you
Billie Hays

BILLIE HAYS
250 W. WASHINGTON ST.
SULLIVAN, INDIANA

Sunday, Jan. 6, 1924.

Dear Father,

I hope you and Uncle Hinkle are haveing a good time in California. I am haveing a good time here at home. It snowed here Thursday and I played on Strattons hill with my sled. Today was Communion Sunday. Mother and I went to church. I made a radio yesterday. I've listened to New York and Denver Its a pretty good one too. I hope I can hear from Hollywood.

I love you

good-by, Sir Bill

to a Good Hunter

* * *

THE BLACKSTONE
CHICAGO

Sunday

Dear Aunt:[4]

Just a word of appreciation for what you are doing for Billie . . . Don't you think also you could teach him some physical exercises like they do the children in school and it will make his muscles grow.

I'm going to give you a check the next time I'm home.

Love

from Bill[5]

February 2, 1924.

Master Will H. Hays, Jr.,
Sullivan, Indiana.

Dear Billie:

I just have your card showing your promotion to 3A and am returning the card herewith. You are a fine boy. I'll tell you what I want

---

4. *Miss Sarah M. Cain (Sally)*
5. *W.H.H.*

you to do next month: I want you to try to bring Self Control back to G-plus or better; also I want you to try to bring your writing up to Ex, and your language-grammar and arithmetic . . .

> Affectionately yours, W.H.H.

(2/3/24)

Dear Father,
    . . . The Bill Hart pictures came here safely and I like to look at them. You dont need to worry about me. I understand why you couldn't come home. I wish I could have seen you but I was so happy that I got to talk with you over the telephone from Chicago.

> Good-by
>   I love you.
> > Sir Bill.

* * *

New York City
February 9, 1924

Dear Bill:
    Under separate cover I am sending the desk set which I promised to send you . . . From this you will note that my promise has been kept. I want you to register the fact because I propose never to be in position of breaking a promise made to you . . .
> With love to all,

> Affectionately, Hinkle C. Hays

* * *

(3/2/24)

Dear Father
    I am so anxious for that old cold to leave you so you can come home.
    Charles is down stairs waiting for me to finish my letter and play with him. I have gained almost two pounds since you were here last and

that time seems a long time to me. I don't want any money til you can pay me personally. I hope you and Uncle Hinkle are having a good time now I am. I love you

Good by

Billie Hays

* * *

April 9, 1924 [6]

Dear Billie:

. . . I am going to look into the dog matter the next time I am home which will be in a very short time. I think a Collie is allright, but I believe you will want to think about whether or not a Collie will be too big after it is full grown . . . Maybe you will decide that you want to get a little kind of a dog when it gets grown.

Love to all.

Affectionately, Father

* * *

(4/13/24)

Dear Father

. . . I'll bet him a new bridle that I <u>am</u> standing up straight, I mean Bill Hart. O Boy I'll get the bridle and you'll get the saddle because I am going to stand up straight.

I saw "The Covered Wagon" and boy It was good Charles got scared and went home I didn't tho. The other night at the show charles got so excited that he yelled out loud "Hot Dog" and every body laughed.

Good-by I love you,

Bill

---

6. *From Hollywood*

(5/4/24)

Dear Father

It is a pretty day here in Sullivan and the flowers and leavs are all out on the trees. I wish you were here to go out in the car with me.

Uncle Hinkle got me a new mit to play ball with. Ray and I have been playing ball in the back yard. The children at school had a race and I did to and I won It was over the tables of 6es, 7s, and 4es. The other day a dog was under the window and I barked and he barked back. Just now there was another dog under the window and I barked at it he looked at me and then ran.

I love you

Bill

*   *   *

May 8, 1924 [7]

Dear Billie:

. . . I wish I had been there to go with you in the car.

I am glad Uncle Hinkle got you the "big mitt." The more you play ball the better. I want you to learn to be a good pitcher. I note about the race and am glad you won it. You ought to practice running to get so you can run a hundred yards real fast. Remember you are going to get that dog and you can get it whenever you want to and any kind you want.

With love to all,

Affectionately, Father

*   *   *

(5/11/24)

Dear Father

. . . I ment an arithmetic race In stead of foot-race. I know you would like that better. I saw Jackie Coogan in the boy of Flanders and I liked It so much, Charles and John are here to play. I ordered a baceball facegard.

I love you

Bill

---

7. *From New York City*

89

The William S. Hart Company

5544½ HOLLYWOOD BOULEVARD
HOLLYWOOD, CALIFORNIA April 20, 1924

Master Will Hays,
Sullivan, Indiana

Hello Pardner!

It is a long time since I have written you but then
Bill I have been mighty busy and have only just returned home from a
several weeks' trip East.

I saw your Dad in New York and we had a couple of pow-wows
and parted still being friends. My principal kick against your Dad
is that he doesn't bring you out to California when he makes a trip
out here. (May be I am getting him in wrong in saying this but I do
not care a doggone bit.) I told him that the next time he came out
here if he did not bring you the Pinto Pony, 'Lizabeth, Cactus Kate,
Yucca Sal and King Valentine would sure set up an awful howl. And
then besides, Bill, I want you to see our country out here.

I know you have been in Colorado but Colorado aint California no matter what Colorado folks may say and don't you believe it
is either. The farther you get West the better they git. Now I
will tell you by example just what I mean. I noticed in Chicago that
all the boys stooped over a whole lot, and as a matter of fact in the
middle west they are all doubled up like jack knives, but the farther
you travel toward the setting sun the straighter they seem to become
and when you get out in this country they all stand straight up on
both feet so straight that you could use their spine for a ridge pole
of a house . And I tell you it looks a whole lot better, Bill. I
like to see boys stand straight up as it makes them grow up straight
and when a fellow has grown up straight it sort of follows that he
will go straight in life, which means a whole lot.

I am sorry I haven't had the time to write you for so long
but I promise you not to be guilty of the same offense again - so any
time you feel like it you just drop a line to your

Old Friend and Pardner,

61

May 17, 1924.

Will H. Hays, Jr.,
250 West Washington St.,
Sullivan, Indiana.

Dear Billie:

On next Saturday I have to be in Grand Rapids attending the General Assembly of the Presbyterian Church. I am Chairman of a committee of Laymen with the job of raising a large sum of pension money[8] to help aged and infirm ministers. I think I can get away from there at seven o'clock Saturday night and get to Indianapolis Sunday morning . . . It would be a lot of fun if you could be in Indianapolis and you and I could start out together that morning in an automobile and go wherever you wanted to go, getting home that afternoon . . .

Love to all.

Affectionately,

Father

* * *

June 23, 1924

Master Will H. Hays
Sullivan, Indiana.

Dear Billie:

. . . I have been hoping to get up to Utica, New York, to be there when you all get there and go up to Big Moose Lake with you, but it is not going to be possible to do this . . .

With love to all,

Affectionately,

Father.

---

8. *$15,000,000*

July 8, 1924

Will H. Hays, Jr.,
Glennmore Hotel,
Big Moose, N.Y.

Dear Billie:

We have got the dog! Mr. Maurice McKenzie of my office has been hunting all over New York and all the country around it to find just the Collie pup we wanted. It is going forward by express this afternoon . . . It is two and one-half months old—just exactly what you want, I think—and you can name him whatever you want to. He may have fleas as all dogs do. Every once in a while you ought to throw him in the lake.

Love to all.

Affectionately, Father

* * *

WESTERN UNION TELEGRAM

1924 JUL 9
BIGMOOSE LAKE NY 9

WILL H HAYS
300 PARK AVE NEWYORK NY

DOG IS SAFE. IT HAS FLEAS BUT DOCTOR CROSS AND I ARE TAKING CARE OF HIM. I HAVE NAMED HIM GLENN WHICH IS SHORT FOR GLENNMORE. GLENN IS BARKING. EVERYBODY LIKES HIM AND SO DO I. HE BROKE HIS COLLAR AND I HAD A SWIM TODAY. THANKS AND LOVE

BILLY.

* * *

July 10, 1924

Dear Billie:

I just have your telegram . . . Fleas won't hurt a boy much. I am glad you went swimming. You want to learn to play tennis, to row, to swim, eat lots, etc. I know you will carry out the rules and that Mother and Miss Fischer will do likewise.

I am leaving tomorrow for California, but will be back soon and then be right up to see you. Write me a lot of letters.

Love to all.

Affectionately, Father

July 11, 1924.

Dear Billie:

Enclosed are two copies of your food schedule from the Doctor which I sent your mother. I want you to have one and Miss Fischer to have one, because you and Miss Fischer are also parties to the contract.

Love to all.

Affectionately, Father

* * *

HOTEL GLENNMORE
Adirondacks   Big Moose, N.Y.

(7/20/24)

Dear Father

I have been having a good play with my friend Jack. There is another dog here that will sneeze for the ball. I am going to teach Glenn tricks like that. I am so glad you came here. Miss Fischer and I are minding the rules and so is Mother. I hope you have a good time at California and if you see Mr. Hart tell him I am still a cattle ranger.

Good by

I love you

Bill.

July 24, 1924.

Dear Billie:

...Your father told me before he left for California that you were taking care of Mother and Miss Fischer. When a man has two ladies to look after he certainly needs some one to call him up once in a while and ask him how he is getting along, which is why I did last evening.

Sincerely yours, Julia Kelly[9]

* * *

(Aug. 11, 1924)

Dear Mr. Hart:

I am writing this letter to thank you for the quirt you sent to me. Oh boy it is a good one. If I ever got behind a mule and hit him with it I would land on the other side of the lake. Some boys and I played lion trainer and it works as good with lions as it does with ponies.

Good-By

Billie Hays

* * *

Aug. 13

Dear Mr. McKenzie

I thank you for getting the dog for me. You picked out a very nice one. I named him glenn. He knows me and wags him tail and liks his chops when he sees me bring his food to him. Boy he's a frisky little fellow. He will play tag with me. Oh boy he is the best little pup in the world. Come and see Glenn and his Master some time

Good-by

Billie Hays

August 18, 1924 [10]

Dear Billie:

. . . I had a fine time yesterday on my stop-over there from

9. *Principal secretary to W.H.H., New York City Office.*
10. *From New York City*

California and enjoyed it thoroughly. Give the whole gang my love—
Jack, Tom and Arthur.

With much love for yourself, I am

Affectionately, Father

P.S. Remember the three things we talked about last night
before I left: Standing up straight, minding Miss Fisher and eating more
bread and butter.

W.H.H.

* * *

August 27, 1924.

Dear Billie:

This is an important business letter. You must show it to Mother
and Miss Fischer. You will be the only man in the party when you leave
Big Moose so you have got to take some responsibility about getting
them safely home . . .

It seems to be a problem to get pullman reservations on the New
York Central for you from Big Moose to Utica, so yesterday I telephoned
Mr. W. J. Jackson, President of the C. & E. I., of which I'm a board
member, and he's wiring Mr. Crawley, President of the New York
Central . . . I rather think they will have the reservations all right from
Big Moose to Utica. If they don't you will have to get on a day coach. I
guess you can control the two young ladies on the day coach for three
hours. Anyway, you will want, of course, to check all the baggage you can
direct from Big Moose to Terre Haute. When you get to Terre Haute
you can check it through to Sullivan. I have written to Paul[11] telling him
when you will arrive in Terre Haute and asking him to meet you at the
station there with the automobile and take you home.

You have your own job of getting Glenn home. To do this maybe
you ought to build a little crate. I don't know how to do it, but you can
get him home all right. They will take him in the baggage car at Utica

---

11. *Kester, chauffeur in Sullivan*

and feed and water him. The station agent there at Big Moose will tell you how to do it.

I would come up myself but it is mighty hard to get there and back from New York right now, and one man is enough to get everybody home all right. You are some man.

Love to all.

Affectionately, W.H.H.

(9/1/24)

Dear Father

I asked Mr. Calahan to build a crate and he did it. It is a good one with air holes.

Yesterday I was in a shoe race and a sack race and potato race and I won a prize my prize was box of candy and a base ball. it is very hot today and I am going in swining.

Glenn is fine.

I love you

billie Hays

* * *

HOTEL UTICA
Utica, N.Y.

(9/2/24)

Dear Father

I am at hotel utica waiting for the train to Indiana so I thought I would rite to you to let you now we are safe and this far on our trip. Glenn is fine but he is a mighty frightened little pup.

I love you

Billie Hays

* * *

September 10, 1924

Dear Billie:

Now you are in the fourth grade—my. In your next letter let me know what you are studying in school this year and which subjects you like best.

I got your Sunday letter and am sorry I forgot it was John T.'s birthday. The fact is I was so busy working Sunday that did not get a chance to think of anything, although I don't think anybody ought to work on Sunday. Everybody ought to go to Church and Sunday School on Sunday and you don't want to let anybody or anything keep you away from them and don't let anybody around the house miss a Sunday. I will write to John T. today.

Love to all.

Affectionately, Father

* * *

(Sept. 15, 1924)

Dear Father—

I have arithmetic, Spelling, Language, Geography, Reading, physiology, and Health, Music and art. I like Geography the best. Aunt Cile,[12] Aunt Sallie and John T. and Charles[13] were here for dinner today we had a good time. I just fed glenn and he is barking for me to play.

Good-by
I love you
Billie Hays

* * *

12. *Mrs. Hinkle Hays (Lucile)*
13. *Cousins of W.H.H., Jr.*

September 20, 1924.

Dear Billie:

. . . Keep me posted every week just how you are getting along in school. Also tell me what you are doing with Paul about playing football, learning to box, learning to hit the baseball with the bat, learning to wrestle, etc. . . . I am going to make a real athlete out of you . . .

Love to all.

Affectionately, Father

*   *   *

September 22, 1924.

Dear Billie:

Enclosed is a pistol which is also a knife. I am sending this to you at the request of Mr. Howard Chandler Christy, who is giving it to you . . . Be sure to keep it away from your eyes when you pull the trigger . . You want to write a letter to Mr. Christy.

Love to all.

Affectionately, Father

*   *   *

November 14, 1924.

Dear Billie:

Two or three things I want you to do. You are already doing them but I want you to keep on doing them. (1.) Put on a clean waist every morning. (2.) Don't forget to eat the green vegetables. (3.) Don't forget to wash your teeth real often. (4.) Be sure and send me the size of your shoes. (I want to get you a pair of high shoes like we talked about.)

Love to all.

Affectionately, Father

*   *   *

November 14, 1924.

Dear Billie:

Don't forget to take exercise. You must play hard and learn to play football, box, pound that punching bag, etc. And don't forget to teach the dog tricks. I am going to send you a book on dogs. Also, when you boys[14] come to New York next week, I am going to give you a book on gymnastics and boy's food.

Did you get the check from Paul for the two and a half pounds? Love to all.

Affectionately, Father

* * *

THE WALDORF ASTORIA
NEW YORK

(11-23-24)

Dear Miss Fischer

I am having a good time in New York. I am just fine and I hope you are too

I love you
Bill

* * *

WARDMAN PARK HOTEL
WASHINGTON, D.C.

11-27-24

Dear Miss Helen [15]

I just got at Washington and I just finished my meal. I have just written to Paul, Ray, and mother so I thought I would write to you.

I love you
Your old pal
Bill

---

14. *Cousins John T. and Charles and I, with Hinkle and Lucile, for Thanksgiving with W.H.H.*
15. *Fischer*

John T. Hays, W.H.H., Jr., President Calvin Coolidge, and Charles Hays (left to right) in the Rose Garden of the White House, Thanksgiving Day, 1924.

Chapter Seven

MY first trip to New York City was when I was almost nine years old. Uncle Hinkle and Aunt Lucille took John T., Chuck and me to visit Dad over Thanksgiving. Evidently Mother was either ill or didn't want to go. Dad lived at the "old" Waldorf Astoria, before the present one up Park Avenue was built in the 1930s, and it was beautiful. And although eating and sleeping on the train had been fun, and looking out of the hotel's high windows at the City's bustle was exciting, my most memorable New York experience then was my visit with Dad to the Central Park West studio of his friend, the famous and kindly artist, Howard Chandler Christy. I was standing beside Dad when Mr. Christy opened his studio's door to the hall (thinking, it turned out, that Mrs. Christy had forgotten her key and knocked); and on a pedestal not twenty feet from me stood the most beautiful woman I'd ever seen—stark naked.

The model snatched up a blue kimono, threw it on and stepped down. After the artist's warm greeting of his guests, he motioned her forward and introduced her to us. My initial, gulping embarrassment was quickly dispelled by his unperturbed joviality and her utter poise, not to mention her lovely smile. We all sat down and pretty soon Mrs. Christy arrived and the five of us chatted for half an hour before Dad and I took our leave. At least, the four of them chatted. I mostly alternated mutely between staring at the blue vision and at my lap.

From New York, we all went down with Dad to Washington, where we'd been invited by President and Mrs. Coolidge to share a turkey given to them by Billy Sunday (that day's Billy Graham). We stayed at the Wardman Park Hotel, where many years later my wife, Ginny, and I were to spend our wedding night on the eve also of my Army service in World War II. While the Hayses waited in the lobby for the limousine that was to take us to the White House, I remember nervously tilting forward a wing-back chair and pressing my hips against its rear and feeling—absurdly, given the circumstances—a warm sensation in my groin and mentally glimpsing the New York model.

I imagine that my nervousness then was caused, at least partly, by my having been cautioned several times not to spill my milk at the

White House, as I had done for the past two Sundays in Sullivan at Uncle Hinkle's dinner table, and my thinking how horrible I and everybody else should feel if I did. And also I'd been tipped off by Dad that I might be called on to say grace; I suppose President Coolidge had hinted as much to him, although the reportedly humorless Chief Executive was known by Dad, through their association in Harding's administration and otherwise, to be gently mischievous at times. Anyhow, about an hour later the phrase "self-fulfilling prophecy" was validated on this planet once again: after getting through grace and the soup and part of a turkey slice, I reached too stiffly for my milk glass and knocked it over. The instant's howling silence was broken by the President, gazing expressionlessly at me: "Don't worry, Billy; did the same thing myself last week." If he had chosen to run again—twenty times—he'd have had my vote. A couple of years later, at lunch with Dad and President Hoover, I managed not to replay the scene, and was rewarded by having my picture taken in the Rose Garden with the latter President and his English setter. In some ways that was a better day, in others not.

Chapter Eight

December 6, 1924.

Dr. J. R. Crowder,
Sullivan, Indiana.

Dear Joe:

When Billie was here for Thanksgiving, he complained of a pain in his leg. One night it bothered him a great deal and kept him awake. Several times he talked about it. Probably, it was some muscular matter or it may only be a cold. I will be grateful if you will look into it . . . I will be home for the holidays if not before.

With best wishes always, I am

Sincerely yours,

W.H.H.

* * *

December 12, 1924.

Dear Billie:

. . . I hope you had a good time yesterday. I would like to have been with you. I got the report card and have made four little crosses on the four things that you ought to work a little harder on. I am glad to note that Geography went up from G to G-plus . . .

Love to all.

Affectionately,

Father

(12/14/24)

Dear Father

... We went to Dr. Crowder and he could not find the pain altho he twisted my leg all up he said he would answer your letter.

I got the telegram that you sent me on my birthday. I had Uncle Hinkle and Aunt Cile, Mrs. Marlowe,[1] and the boys I wish you could have been there. I am in another Sunday School class now I was poot there this morning the teacher is Mr. Russell Thompson and he said you taught him when he was a little boy.

Good-by

I love you, Billie Hays.

* * *

December 16, 1924

Will H. Hays, Jr.,
West Washington St.,
Sullivan, Indiana.

Dear Billie:

Your Uncle Hinkle has written me about the fact that he has been giving Charles and John T. about three months a year Scotts Emulsion of Cod Liver Oil ... I think it would be a good thing for you. You can, therefore prepare to take some of this delightful stuff beginning when I get home.

Love to all.

Affectionately, Father

* * *

You are always wellcome where ever I am. You know that picture with Jeases and he has his arms out? Well if that was me the arms would be out streched to you. [2]

Bill

---

1. *Mrs. Eugene Marlowe, sister of Lucile.*
2. *Handwritten note to Helen Fischer, circa Christmas, 1924. The picture of Jesus referred to was probably a stained glass window in Sullivan's First Presbyterian Church.*

(1/11/25)

Dear Father

I got the clock you sent me and it is <u>very</u> nice. It's ticking away on my dresser now. I have gained 1 1/2 pounds since you left. I am reading *With the Indians in the Rockies* it is good too. Miss Fischer is reading to me *Heidi* it is a story of a little girl in the Alps.

I love you

Your son.   Billie Hays.

* * *

(2/8/25)

Dear Father:

... Ray has taught glenn to go in his house when you knock on the door. When we put him in his house we used to have to push him in but now all you do is to knock on the door and he goes in. I have had lots of fun with the little locomotive you sent me.

I love you

Your son, Will H. Hays Jr

* * *

February 28, 1925.

Dear Will:

Concerning two things:

First, I thought you worked it out for little Bill to come over to our house to eat when we asked him and when he wanted to. Last Friday night, we asked him and met his mother's response, "Oh, it's so cold I hate to have him go out again," or something equally foolish.

Second, I want to report that little Bill put Navajo blankets up that you gave him, and when he came home they had been taken down and put on the floor. He then hid them, and was all disturbed because his property, which his Dad gave him, had been gotten out, without his consent, and against his wishes, and when he came home that afternoon, after school, they were out again, having been taken from the place where they were hidden, and are now being so used.

I report these two things for what they may be worth. If the kid was my kid, I would have the blankets put wherever the kid wanted them, and if the kid was my kid I would let him go across the street to his uncle's to eat, irrespective of whether it was 0 or 92 in the shade.

Affectionately, H.C.H.

* * *

(3/1/25)

Dear Father:

Today is a snowy blowy day. March came in like a lion in our part of the country.

This is a lonesome week for me without Glenn. I miss him a lot. He was awful sick at the end.

Good-by

I love you, Bill

* * *

March 6, 1925[3]

Master Billie Hays,
Sullivan, Indiana.

Dear Billie:

. . . I am wondering what you have done with the Navajo blankets. They will stand a lot of wear, but are very fine and you will want to keep them a long time, and you will probably want to put them up on the wall in the "camp." However, I do not want to tell you what to do with any of these things, because they are yours absolutely and you can do with them just want you want to do. Don't forget that.

With love to all, I am

Affectionately, Your father

* * *

---

3. *From Hollywood.*

March 6, 1925

Master Bill Hays,
Sullivan,
Indiana

Dear Billie:
Well, Pardner, how are you and Charles and John T. getting along? Remember, they are to come over to your house a lot and you are to go over there a lot. You know the agreement when I was home was that you could go back and forth there the same as in your own yard, but before you cross the street you must stop and look up and down, just like the automobiles do before they cross Section Street up at Dr. Thompson's corner . . .
with love to all,

Affectionately, W.H.H., your father

* * *

(3/14/25)
Dear Billie:
. . . Some of these days you and I are going to ride a lot on ponies just like this one Bill Hart sent us a picture of. For hours and days we are going to ride together!
Love to all.

Affectionately, W.H.H.

* * *

March 17, 1925

Mrs. Lucile B. Hays,
West Washington Street,
Sullivan, Indiana.

Dear Lucile:
I wish you would have Charles write me a letter telling me how much he wanted Billie to eat supper with him the other night and how sorry he was he could not. I want to use such a letter from Charles as the basis of a new appeal in the situation.
Love to all.

Affectionately, W.H.H.

(3/22/25)

Dear Father:

Saturday Paul and I went to Terre Haute about taking swiming lessons. The man was not there that we were to ask so we will go again . . .

Mr. Fred Schader sent me some copies of *Variety* with my picture in them and it said when Billie Hays got his cowboy suit he said he wanted to be Tom Mix and I said I wanted to be Bill Hart I hope he don't take the *Variety* magazine. I mean Bill Hart because I don't want him to think I have gone back on him.

I love you

Will H Hays Jr

* * *

March 23, 1925.

Dear Will:

Little Bill got to come over Saturday night. We sat down to eat at a quarter to seven, and his mother made him go home and go to bed at seven-thirty. This morning she received your letter, and she came over to the house and climbed over Lucile about "being tired of being bossed and other people butting into her business", etc. . . . One suggestive thing she said was that she "did not want little Bill to leave the house in the evening because it left nobody to talk to her" . . .

Affectionately, H.C.H.

* * *

(4/5/25)

Dear Father:

I have just been drawing a map of North AMERICA and South AMERICA . . . I got a telegram from Tom Mix saying he was leaving for Europe.

I have missed my dog awfully much since he died. When I come home from school in the evening and he is not there I feel so bad I could cry which I have done often. I can hardly wait till my other dog comes.

This was communion sundy at church.

Your Loving Son

I love you

Will H Hays Jr.

(4/19/25)

Dear Father

I just ate dinner Miss Fischer read to me before dinner. I have been practising on the punching bag I can do it fast. I have been playing base ball at school . . . I made some home runs too. I made three strate. Ray has also been teaching me to box which we have done eveings when I come home from school . . . My blank cartridge pistol came. Paul ordered some cartradge. You listen and if you hear a bang you'l know what it is.

I picked these violets for you in the back yard.

I love you
Will H Hays Jr.

* * *

(4/26/25)

Dear Father:

. . . I am going to begin to take the cod liveroil as you want me to do.

I received a letter from Mr. Joseph Kennedy saying he was going to send me a football used by the Harvard team and it came. Mr. Kennedy said Please remember me to your Father . . .

I love you.
Will H. Hays. Jr.

* * *

Dear Miss Fischer[4]

I love you very much and I always will and I know you feel the same way about me, don't you?

Bill

* * *

4. *Note possibly handed to her, or left for her to find.*

May 1, 1925 [5]

Dear Billie:

You are a fine boy.

... Cod Liver Oil may not taste so very good, but it will make you fat and every pound is one dollar. I have been glad to learn that your swimming lessons have started. You know, if you are a real good swimmer before you go to Culver next year, it will be a great advantage to you your first summer there. Let me know what you need, if anything, for scouting, horseback riding and other fun in the mountains at Estes Park this summer.

I wish you would have Paul take a real good Kodak picture of you and Jimmie Collins together.

... Don't forget to see that Ray teaches you to box and knock that punching bag.

With love to all.

Affectionately.

*   *   *

(5-31, 1925)

Dear Father:

School was out last week and I was promoted to the fifth grade ... Yesterday at the Terre Haute "Y" I dived off the diving board at the deep end where it is over Mr. Huffman's head standing on his tip toes and swam to the other end.

I am going to Crawfordsville with Mother and Miss Fischer and I am going to have fun with Eugene Fischer. Hes her brother. I fixed up a tennis court in the back yard and miss Fischer and I are practicing in it. I have gotten a few places on the radio.

Your Son

I love you, Will H. Hays Jr

---

5. *From New York City.*

June 10, 1925

Mr. Will H. Hays, Jr.,
c/o Hon. A. D. Thomas,
Crawfordsville, Indiana.

Dear Billie:

I am sending you today at Sullivan a regular Boy Scout axe. It doesn't look to me like a Boy Scout axe, it looks like a man axe. However, you are a careful boy and won't hurt yourself.

Love to all.

Affectionately, Father

* * *

June 20, 1925.

Mr. Will H. Hays, Jr.,
West Washington Street,
Sullivan, Indiana.

Dear Billie:

About Colorado:

You should take your golf sticks. There is undoubtedly a golf course out there . . . Also, I think you should take your tennis racket . . You and Miss Fischer ought to have some pretty good games . . .

As the only man in the party, I think you should begin to see that the arrangements are getting properly made . . . I will call up in a day or two and see whether you want me to wire to Denver and arrange for an automobile to go from Denver right up to Estes that same day. I probably will not get out to Sullivan before you start, but I hope to stop in Estes Park on my way back from California.

Love to all.

Affectionately, Father

* * *

CONGRESS HOTEL & ANNEX
CHICAGO

(6-30-25)

Dear Father:

I got the telegram you sent me and I'll do my best in taking care of the three young ladies thats a pretty big job for one man to do.

I love you

Your Son

Will H Hays

* * *

WESTERN UNION TELEGRAM

July 4, 1925

BILLIE HAYS
ELKHORN LODGE
ESTES PARKCOLORADO

HOPE YOU RIDE HORSEBACK A LOT BUT THOSE MOUNTAIN HORSES ARE SOMETIMES FRISKY . . . SEE IF YOU CANNOT GET A WELL BROKE SHETLAND PONY AND LET MISS FISCHER OR AUNT MARTHA RIDE THE BUCKING BRONCHOES . . . AM LEAVING TODAY FOR CALIFORNIA AS PLANNED LOVE TO ALL

FATHER.

* * *

ELKHORN LODGE
Estes Park, Colo.

(7/5/25)

Dear Father:

I got your letter about riding. I went to Harry the stable man and he said he had a very gentle Shetland pony the gentlest one in the farm named Brownie. Miss Fischer and I are saving the brono for you to ride . . . We have been climbing small mountains around here soon we will start on the bigger ones . . . One of the boys had a partie and I sat at his table.

> Your loving Son
>> I love you
>>> Will H. Hays Jr.

* * *

Privat
(7-5-25)

Dear Father:

When are you going to send my dog I want to know because I can tell the carpenter about fixing his house.

> Our Privat Code
> 1. If your bringing him when you come say "Attaboy"
> 2. If he will come before you come say "Hot dog"
> 3. If you don't know say "ride him cowboy"

> Will H Hays Jr

* * *

WESTERN UNION TELEGRAM

July 14, 1925 [6]
WILL H. HAYS JR.
ELKHORN LODGE
ESTES PARK COLORADO

I HAVE TALKED OVER THE DOG BUSINESS WITH MISTER CHARLES CHRISTIE WHO OWNS A PICTURE STUDIO AND A KENNEL AND IS A FRIEND STOP HE WILL PICK YOU OUT A FINE SCOTCH TERRIER IN A FEW DAYS WHICH WILL BE OLD ENOUGH TO BE TRAINED AND OVER THE DISTEMPER AND FINE IN EVERY RESPECT STOP WILL LET YOU KNOW THE DETAILS IN A FEW DAYS. LOVE TO ALL.

> WILL H. HAYS

---

6. *From Hollywood*

(July 18, 1925)

Dear Father:

I know all the men down at the stable. I know Tex, Archie, Harry, Lee, Archie is the one who goes with me on my rides. I just got out of church they have it in the Ballroom. I do a lot of hiking up on the rocks.

A boy friend of mine and I go out to the wood pile and take pieces of wood and hold them at our arms length to make our arms strong.

I saw Jackie Coogan in *Long Live The King.*

I love you

Will H. Hays Jr.

* * *

(7-26-25)

Dear Father:

... I got my boots, thanks very much. I am riding in them and it is much more better than puttees I think. Harry thinks they are dandy. Tex wanted to buy them I am going to wright to Mr. Long and tell him I appreciated his article very much.

I love you

Will H Hays Jr.

* * *

Aug. 8, 1925

Dear Father:

... Brownie and I are having such a good time together Brownie still follows me around like a big dog. I am very careful when I climb the mountains ... The sun has been shining most of the time since you left. I hope you feel better now.

I love you. Your Son.

Will H Hays Jr.

* * *

Y. AUGUST 2, 1925

SON OF CZAR HAYS OF MOVIES PAL OF COWBOYS IN ESTES PARK

Billy Hays, son of Will Hays, director of the motion picture industry, who is spending the summer at Estes Park.

Boy Recently Wrote Letter of Sympathy That Attracted National Attention.

Son of Czar Hays, Pal of Cowboys, in Estes Park.

August 10, 1925

Dear Billie:

Herewith is a telegram I got from Charles Christie just before I left Chicago on the way back to New York. You will see he is perfectly pleased to send the Scottie direct to Sullivan soon after you arrive home in September. You will notice the pup's name is Don. Of course, if there is some other name you would like better, you can change it.

Love to all.

Affectionately, W.H.H.

* * *

BILLIE HAYS
250 WEST WASHINGTON ST.
SULLIVAN, INDIANA

(9-6-25)

Dear Father:

I am having lots of fun with Don. I think he is the cutest little fellow. He follows me around and knows I'm his master I'm going to try to be the best master I can to him. I am going to try to make very good grades in school . . .

I love you

Good-by

Will H Hays Jr

(9-13-25)

Dear Father:

I have just written to grandfather Thomas in Crawfordsville telling him about Don. I told him If he wanted to know what color Don was to go down in the coal bin and look at a pice of coal . . . I will go back to school in the morning again . . .

Good-by

I love you (and Don)

Billie

* * *

(10-4-25)

Dear Father:

     . . . I am so glad you are comming home, I have some business to talk over with you when you get here.

     Don is just fine he is barking at something now, some imaginary thing I suppose. Some times he sees a caterpillar or something on the ground and he picks it up with his mouth and it stings him. He is so funny. . .

                I love you

                    Will H Hays

* * *

WESTERN UNION TELEGRAM
(NEW YORK)

OCTOBER 9, 1925.
BILLIE HAYS
250 WEST WASHINGTON STREET,
SULLIVAN, INDIANA

     IMPOSSIBLE FOR ME TO LEAVE HERE BEFORE SOME-TIME NEXT WEEK STOP VERY SORRY ABOUT THIS BE-CAUSE VERY ANXIOUS TO SEE YOU STOP BE HOME VERY SOON AND WE WILL HAVE LONG TALK ABOUT THE BUSI-NESS MATTER YOU MENTIONED . . . PLAY HARD STUDY HARD AND FEED DON BEEFSTEAK NOT CATERPILLARS STOP LOVE TO ALL

                  WILL H. HAYS

* * *

*O*ut in the forest the
   things are growing,
And all the while the
thunder is roaring.
Rabbits and squirrels
are snug in their houses,
While in the pond the
duck carouses.

                  By W.H.H., Jr.

"Dear Miss Fischer . . . "

Chapter Nine

IT took a long time for Mother to admit she was hard of hearing. Years after my early Sullivan days, when I was attending Wabash College in Crawfordsville, Indiana, I stopped at what then had become her home to see how she was, as I often did, and I noticed she was sporting a hearing aid. Carefully not making a big thing of it I asked her where she had got it. She said she'd ordered it from a salesman who had called on her a month before. I silently credited him with enormous tact, but of course he was a pro at it. Anyhow I was pleased to think I wouldn't have to speak to her so loudly and precisely from then on, as I had done for years. My pleasure in this lasted for only two or three weeks, however, because one day when I visited her she wasn't wearing the gadget, and when I asked her where it was she said she had thrown it away because its amplification had got fainter and fainter and finally it had quit working altogether. I asked her if she had tried new batteries and she said she didn't know what I was talking about, the salesman hadn't said anything about batteries, and if that meant she had to keep spending money to keep the gadget working on which she'd already spent $90.00, she was glad she'd thrown it in the trash. I wondered if the trashman had a hearing problem; maybe somebody had got some good out of it.

While I'm talking about Mother in her later years—giving an idea of where maybe her earlier ones had headed her—I'm reminded of some other scenes. One was while I was visiting her in Crawfordsville from Riverdale prep school in New York, another while I was in Wabash College, and a third after I'd got out of the World War II army and was living with my wife and children in Beverly Hills and had stopped by Crawfordsville on my way to deliver the manuscript of my novel *Dragonwatch* to its New York publisher, Doubleday and Company.

According to the terms of Dad and Mother's divorce, I was to spend my Christmas and spring and half my summer vacations from Riverdale with her in Crawfordsville. I went to Riverdale in September of 1928, when I had three months to go before I'd be thirteen. I think my folks got their divorce when I was about a third of the way through my five years at that prep school. I entered the eighth grade, which Riverdale called the "second form," and I graduated from the sixth form (senior in high school at home) in the spring of 1933.

One spring vacation at Mother's house I was cleaning a .44-calibre, single-action Frontier model Colt revolver which I'd bought at a pawnshop in Hollywood, California, and had been out shooting for practice that afternoon in some woods near Crawfordsville. Ray had taught me always to be careful in handling guns and I simply don't know how it could have happened that there was a bullet left in the revolver or why I pulled its trigger as I started to clean it; but there was and I did. Mother had gone to bed upstairs when the damn thing went off with an ear-splitting roar, its bullet crashing through the door at the back end of the hall and, as I learned a few minutes later, on through the side of the refrigerator in the pantry beyond the door. As the reverberations echoed into awful silence Mother called from upstairs, "Mercy, Billy, what on earth was that?" In my numbness I managed to yell back the first thing that came to my head: "I dropped a book." She replied that it certainly must have been a big one and went back to bed. When Nellie Akins, a warm-hearted black lady who was Mother's Crawfordsville cook and housekeeper for many years, arrived for work early the next morning I told her what had happened and showed her the refrigerator, which wasn't refrigerating things well at that point, and she agreed there was no reason to bother Mother with the details. Nellie was an understanding friend. Since Mother went into the kitchen and pantry only on Nellie's days off, my friend and I had the rest of the week to convince Mother that her household needed a new refrigerator in place of the worn-out one. Nellie told me later that the appliance dealer hadn't asked how a bullet hole had got in the refrigerator—either through tact or indifference—but had said he couldn't give Mother any trade-in value on the old item in view of what he called its advanced wear and tear. I've always been intrigued by his savoir-faire.

A few years later after the revolver episode, when I was a Wabash College student, Nellie and I were involved in another nighttime misadventure. Again Mother played a part in it without knowing the whole story. Incidentally I footed the bill this time, although it took me several months to do that. I suggested a deal with Mother which she bought: I would take her for afternoon drives two or three days a week if she would supply a small car, which turned out to be a Ford. I didn't own a car until Dad gave me a Buick coupe in 1937 as a Wabash graduation present. The Ford was to be kept in the one-car garage behind Mother's house and (by implication, at least) to be used for no other purpose. As far as I was concerned—and I think Mother, too—everything went well with this arrangement until very early one moonless fall morning. On that nightmarish occasion, after a lovely date, I drove slowly and quietly into her driveway with the headlights out so she wouldn't see me if she had happened to be up for some reason at the still-dark hour. I barely could make out the driveway in the dim glow of a streetlamp and there was no way I could see into the black interior of the garage as I eased the car through its open doorway. That was the end of the quiet and most of the darkness. The grinding clatter of the car's wheels crushing the wicker front-porch furniture—without warning me, she had ordered that moved in the afternoon around to the garage for the winter—awakened a good part of the neighborhood, including Mother, and caused a number of upstairs lights to come on in all directions. A couple of minutes later the beam of a neighbor's flashlight preceded him cautiously across the driveway to the garage, where I let him know in a stage whisper that all was well—not exactly the case—and urged him to turn off the flashlight. He didn't help matters by booming, "Oh, it's you!" and then laughing loudly, "What you trying to do, Bill, tear the place down?" At my hoarse urging he went back to bed. I didn't get to bed for the additional hour it took me to clean up the worst of the mess and walk back through the darkness to the Phi Delt house. The next morning I returned to the scene of the debacle, told my buddy Nellie about it and went into the living room to see how Mother was. She said she'd slept well except for a brief time during the night when she'd been awakened by "a great tumult of some kind in the neighbor's backyard," adding, "I can't imagine what they were up to at that unearthly hour." This time, instead of the rest of the week to get a new refrigerator, I had the rest of the winter to find and pay a carpenter to repair the porch furniture.

About twenty years later, on the occasion when I stopped in Crawfordsville en route to New York with the manuscript of my novel, a college-days friend named Charlie Groves was driving me back to Mother's after dinner at his house when a car going pretty fast crashed into the rear of his, knocking it, with him hanging onto its steering wheel, off the side of the street. With nothing to hold onto when the door on my side flew open, I was thrown out and narrowly missed being run over by the car which had rammed us. At the hospital my abrasions and contusions were cleaned up and I was discharged, but not before I was given a shot of horse serum to prevent tetanus. The doctor offered Charlie and me rides home and I had him let me off for a drink at another friend's house about a block from Mother's, and by the time I walked on to her place and let myself in quietly it was pretty late. She had fallen asleep in her hospital-style bed in the living room off the downstairs hall. I tiptoed past the doorway between the hall and the living room and went upstairs to my own bed, which felt very fine by then. The next morning when I awakened I couldn't stand up, my tongue was swollen, I couldn't see well, and I was covered with hives. I crawled to the top of the back stairway and called Nellie and she came up, took a look at me and telephoned Dr. Kirtley. But at my request she didn't tell Mother. In the rest of this paragraph the things I quote as having been said by Mother were told me later by Nellie. When Mother, from her bed near the living room windows, saw the doctor get out of his car in front of the house and start up the walk with his black bag she rang the little dining-table bell she kept by her bedside to summon Nellie; and when that lady stepped in from the next room Mother pointed through the window at Dr. Kirtley and said, "Good Heavens, Nellie, this isn't his day to see me is it? I haven't combed my hair." Nellie mumbled a noncommittal reply which Mother didn't hear but typically didn't admit she hadn't. She watched the doctor walk past her doorway to the front hall, heading for the stairway, and said, "He must be going to the bathroom." Upstairs after a quick examination he told me he thought my trouble was a severe reaction to the horse serum but he wanted me back out at the hospital to be sure there was nothing else wrong; and from the upstairs extension he phoned for an ambulance which pulled up in front of the house within five minutes. When Mother saw the ambulance attendants heading up the walk with a stretcher she rang her bell and said to Nellie, "Mercy, they aren't coming for me, are they?" She watched them troop past the hall doorway and head for the stairs. "Well, that's a relief," forgetting I was up there, I hope. When they came downstairs a few minutes later, with me on the stretcher between them she watched the procession go by the hall doorway, rang the bell and inquired with a frown, "Mercy, Nellie, where are they taking Billy?" Keeping the faith with me, Nellie replied loudly this time that she didn't know but was sure I'd be all right with Dr. Kirtley. This seemed to reassure Mother completely.

Back to earlier days:

In the higher elementary school winters in Sullivan—fourth, fifth and sixth grades—the Mix-Mixers spent a great many rainy Saturdays in the basement of 250 West Washington Street. The term "Mix-Mixers" was pretty much reserved for our gang's football team in the fall; our winter hours in the basement were spent as the "50–50 Club," named in recognition of our boyhood ideal of sharing. The inner sanctum of the Club was a large corner room of the house's full basement, lit by a couple of bulbs hanging by their wires from the first-floor joists and further brightened by a couple of small windows near the top of one side wall, their sills level with the ground outside. When Dad first saw the Club room on one of his trips home he told me that for a while after the house had been built a middle-aged black man named John Wells had worked for Mother and him and had slept down there. Among other things, John had been the fastest bricklayer in the county and was addicted to strong drink and had died in a gunfight on an island in the Wabash River one Saturday night. The Wabash was about ten miles west of us. Dad said John had been very loyal to Mother and him and, when sober, had worked hard maintaining the house and yard. I guess in a sense he was Ray's predecessor, although different entirely from my pal.

Ray kept a long, heavy workbench in that basement room; and when he let us take over the room for our Club we recognized his prior right to keep the workbench and his tools there. Also of course he was a member of the Club—the ranking one. In fact he invented its secret handshake: three-part, successive grippings of the right hand, similar to the "high-fives" of today but not overhead. The Club room was adjacent to the furnace room, but there was no opening in the brick wall between the two, although there must have been one in the past which had been sealed off, because there was a door-size portion of the wall made of thick wooden planks. Maybe John Wells had been bothered more by the dust from the furnace room and its coal bin than by the absence of its over-flowing warmth. Anyhow, on cold days we found the 50–50 room chilly, and also, as a properly occult organization, we needed a secret door; so Ray sawed out a five-foot section of the plank wall and put hinges and a latch on its Club-room side to allow the initiated to enter after giving the secret knock.

The 50–50 Club did more that just have meetings where important matters were discussed like when the next meeting was to be held; it encouraged membership participation in intra-Club sports events, including B-B gun target shooting, wrestling, boxing with huge gloves Dad sent, and indoor (outdoor, with the coming of spring) track and field competition. I wasn't good at the latter, but excelled with the B-B gun and later the .22 and I was pretty confident about boxing after some lessons my first summer at Culver until my life-long close friend Brandy Dunlap caught me with a couple of head-ringing punches I didn't see coming. Helen Fischer cut out of felt some winged feet and other sports logos which she sewed onto our sweaters or jackets as victory emblems in the various events. The girls at school admired those.

Membership in the 50–50 Club and the Mix-Mixer football team didn't mean our voluntary or involuntary exclusion from extra-curricular activities generally at school. We played mumblety peg and leap frog, shot marbles and sailed kites in their various seasons along with everybody else. And certainly we became aware of and then fascinated by girls at the same age that all boys always have. We simply fell together as a group with no implication of elitism, and liked each other and had a lot of good times together.

Chapter Ten

BILLIE HAYS
250 WEST WASHINGTON ST.
SULLIVAN, INDIANA

(10-18-25)

Dear Father:

Yesterday I went to Indianapolis to have my lower brace poot on
... I did not go to church because my brace hurt so, but I went to sunday-
school. I feel all right now. I am having lots of fun. Some times my pal
Maurice Lee coms over and we had a football game day before yesterday
and the score was 73–73 a tie.

I love you

Will H Hays Jr.

* * *

Nov. 2, 1925

Dear Miss Fischer:

Don has been up here all afternoon he is behaveing fine Mother
is not a bit cross and I am getting along fine. He is watching me with most
interest.

I love you very very much. Say hellow to Eugen for me.

I love you very much +++ ooo

Bill.

P.S. Don is asleep now.

W.H.H.

I love you

P.S. I hope you got back to Crawfordsville safe. Hurry back here.
I love you

(11-8-25)

Dear Father:

I got the quirt and pencile you sent me you know. I just have written to Grandfather Thomas. I hope his broken leg feels better soon. Don is here in the room looking at me so funny, I wish you were here to see him. I hope you will come home soon.

I love you

Billie H Hays

P.S. I told Grandfather his grandog sends his love too.

* * *

Wednesday Evening

Dear Mr. Hays:

About seven o'clock this morning, Billie broke the silence with "Miss Fischer, see if these are all right, Wisconsin, the capital is Madison, Michigan is Lansing" and so on, naming the Central States. His dressing was some what prolonged because of the jig-like steps he learned from Harold Lloyd in *The Freshman*, which he saw on Thanksgiving afternoon. He greeted Ella the cook, Don and Ray with these same dance steps. After breakfast he and Don had a ten minutes visit, until the school bell rang.

"Robber and Police" is the present game at school, while football is the home game. This evening Charles, Maurice Lee and Bill had a fine game until Maurice Lee wasn't tackled just right, and his absence made the game a duet. However Maurice Lee couldn't stand to leave a good game and was back with only a few minutes out. Right now Billie is at work on long division problems for tomorrow. He is in an extremely good frame of mind. This can't always be said at the same time arithmetic is mentioned!

Sincerely, Helen Fischer

* * *

(11-29-25)

Dear Father:

I am having a very good time.

Jiggs, Ray's little five year old nephew came down to see me a little while ago.

One time you told me you were going to take me to Calif this winter. I wrote to Bill Hart that you said I could come, he will feel very disapointed if I don't come. I would like Miss Fischer to go to.

I love you

Will H Hays Jr.

P.S. Don is just fine, but he likes to taste everybody.

* * *

December 9, 1925 [1]

Dear Billie:

... You will be ten years old on the eleventh and it has been a pretty important ten years since you were born ...

I have been studying your report for last month and am delighted, indeed, to note that you have advanced from G plus to Excellent in spelling, reading, geography and history. In arithmetic I note that you have held your own. To hold your own is good, but not as good as you can do ... Anything that is worth doing at all is worth doing well and we will have to jump on that music thing just as hard as you tackle Maurice Lee in football.

The only thing in the report that worries me a little is the self-control which seems to have slipped back from G plus to P plus. If a man can't control himself, he can't control things and to succeed he has got to control things ... and I know you will, just as I know you are going to: (a) Stand up straight; (b) Get fat quick by drinking a lot more milk and eating a lot more green vegetables, etc.

I will be home in a few days again for Christmas and we will have a great visit ... You are and will continue to be always the source of my greatest happiness.

Affectionately yours, Will H. Hays

---

1. *From Hollywood*

(12-12-25)

Dear Mr. Hays:

Billie had a happy birthday yesterday . . . As soon as the "crowd" gathered after school Billie asked them to the dining room. He sat at the head of the table, Marion Giles at the foot, Charles H. and Sammy Lindley to the right and Junior Henderson to the left. Your telegram to Billie was given to him and he took on an important look and "sat up"— you know how—and said, "Business matter, boys, just business" in his droll way and read it . . . After refreshments the five had a game of football, then we went to a movie, and the day was ended with a good phone talk with you. He really appreciated that . . . After he was "tucked in" and his prayers said we talked over lots of things. He is going, as your telegram said, to make the most worth while man in the world.

Sincerely, Helen Fischer

* * *

WILL H. HAYS, JR.[2]
BILLIE HAYS [3]
250 W. WASHINGTON ST.
SULLIVAN, INDIANA

Dear Father—(Santa)

For Christmas I would like more that anything a pair of football shoes a football helmet and football pants. I have football socks.

I love you, Will H. Hays Jr.

P.S. Don#wants#a###########
Y E A S U L L I V A N

* * *

2. *Handwritten*
3. *Print crossed out by pen.*

December 15, 1925

Dear Mr. Hays:

… Billie came into the house about five oclock this evening after some football in the back yard, and … by six oclock had done almost all of his arithmetic problems and had written Christmas cards to three friends. As he was sitting down to dinner he said enthusiastically, "Perfect! Simple problems, good food, then an hour of Dr. Doolittle." A few days ago we heard "Red" Grange over the radio, who said an athlete should eat lots of potatoes and spinach. Billie's comment: "Boy, I'm glad it wasn't oysters."

He and Don are the best little friends ever.

Sincerely, Helen Fischer

* * *

December 19, 1925.

Dear Billie:

I have your letter here in Hollywood and will just go out and see if we cannot find the football paraphernalia. I note the postscript which you erased and can read nothing of it but "Don wants a——." Anything Don wants you have to get him. You are running Don; I am running you.

I will reach Terre Haute at noon of Christmas Eve. I wish you would bring the other guinea pigs, John T. and Charles, and come up to meet me.

Love to all.

Affectionately, W.H.H.

Private
(1-17-26)

Dear Father.

Ray has a barn in his back yard that he says he can keep the pony we talked about. He sayd he can build a stall and bring the pony to my house every day and take it back in the evening …

I love you.
Will Hays

January 18, 1926

Mr. Will H. Hays, Jr.,
Sullivan, Indiana.

Dear Billie:

Herewith is the program of the game between Red Granges's Chicago Bears and the Los Angeles team they played here in Calif. this past week end . . . The Chicago Bears are the fastest team anybody ever saw and Red Grange is a great player. He had number 77 on his back.
Love to all.

Affectionately, Father

(1-24-26)

Dear Father—

I saw the show *Clothes Make the Pirate* and the Captain Dixie Bull was funny. Leon Errol I mean by Captain Dixie Bull . . . I have been playing pirate with charles and John and Joe and Lee in the basement this last week.

I love you very much and I mean it.

Will H. Hays Jr.

* * *

February 2, 1926

Dear Billie:

. . . I am pleased that arithmetic has gone from P plus to G . . . I wish you could do a little better in music. I realize that music is not a necessary equipment of a good lawyer or a hard boiled business man, but music helps the soul, improves the taste, softens the disposition and has been an inspiration through all the ages. Particularly, do I want to call your attention to the slipping of self-control. A man who cannot control himself cannot control others—he could not even control a pony . . .

I appreciate your splendid grades and assure you of my absolute knowledge that you can and will clean up the few weak places.

Affectionately, W.H.H.

February 5, 1926

Mr. Leon Errol,[4]
315 Central Park West,
New York City.

Dear Mr. Errol:
Herewith is a letter from Billie Hays, aged ten. You will get a laugh. You are entitled to one—you have helped the world immensely with the ones you have given others.

Sincerely yours, Will H. Hays

* * *

(2-14-26)
Dear Father–
. . . I just wrote to Mr. Howard Christy and thanked him for the book he sent me, *Done in the Open*, with drawings by Frederic Remington. I am going out to Ray's house to play for a little while this afternoon. How do you like the Valentine I sent you?

I love you
Will H. Hays Jr.

HAYS & HAYS
Attorneys-at-Law
Sullivan, Ind.

Dear Miss FISCHER[5]
I love you very much. I have always loved you and I always will, you are my best friend when I am in destrest. I love you

. . . SSS###   ---
Bill

---

4. *From New York*
5. *Typed by W.H.H., Jr.*

102

(2-21-26)

Dear Father—

Don and I have just been having lots of fun. I would tie him to the wagon and take a whip and drive him and he would go like a real Eskimo dog.

Next Thursday and Friday the "Iron Horse" will be here and you and I can go if you come home then.

James Collins is coming over to play with me if he can this afternoon and we can have lots of fun playing "Dog Team."

Don is as black as ever.

> I love you
> Will H. Hays Jr.

* * *

March 11, 1926

Dear Billy,

I have just received here in Hollywood from Miss Fischer your report and am returning it herewith ... This is progress, and progress or improvement is the great essential thing. I note with particular pleasure that in self-control you have increased the grade from P to G. A performance like that makes a pony and other desirable things come a lot easier.

Fine work, my boy; keep it up.

> Affectionately yours, Father

* * *

BILLIE HAYS
250 WEST WASHINGTON ST.
SULLVAN, INDIANA

March 14, 1926.

Dear Captain Dixie Bull— [6]

I accept the commission you sent me as First Mate on your pirate ship *Sea Tiger*. I've been wanting to be a pirate all along but I never got

---

6. *Name of character played by comedian Leon Errol in the film,* Clothes Make the Pirate.

a chance. We'll have Father for Official Deck Washer. I'll bet he will make a good one. I've got a little black dog, Don, who will be a good mascot. He will keep the rats out of the cupboard.

Thank you very much for giving me the honor of being your first mate of your pirate ship *Sea Tiger*.

> Ye First Mate
> Bill Hays

* * *

April 11, 1926.

Dear Father,

Ray has a little baby named Morris Ray Russell. He is a new member of the 50–50 Club and a good one too. He is four days old. Don is fine and is having a good time I hope. He has good eats too.

I went to Dr. Jones in Indianapolis on the train yesterday and my teeth hurt like 60 today.

There is a dove's nest out here in the yard. Mrs. Dove is sitting on her eggs and she don't want me to tell any boy so they won't come down and tear it up. You will keep it a secret so I am telling you.

> I love you
> Will H. Hays Jr.

* * *

April 13, 1926

Will H. Hays, Jr.,
250 West Washington St.,
Sullivan, Indiana.

Dear Billie:

I sent you this morning from New York by parcel post a new spring overcoat. Sunday when I get there I will see how it looks. Also, I went today to the big toy store to see if I could pick up a mechanical toy for you . . . I didn't do anything, there were so many. You will have to give

me some more dope on Sunday. Besides, with a new overcoat and maybe sometime a pony we don't have to hurry about mechanical toys.
Love to all.

Affectionately, Father

May 16, 1926

Dear Father–

I received the trunk you sent me and Uncle Hinkle is going to give me the victrollo this afternoon.

I am the main actor in a play at school of which the name is George Rogers Clark that is who I am . . . We took in a new member to the 50–50 Club the other day by the name of Edward Moody . . . I am having lots of fun with my bicycle. I hope you are well and will be home soon. Thanks for the trunk and victrollo.

I love you
Will H. Hays

* * *

May 20, 1926 [7]

Mr. Will H. Hays, Jr.,
West Washington Street,
Sullivan, Indiana.

Dear Billie:

I wonder if you received the little clothes tags which I sent you with "Will H. Hays, Jr." on them. I want you to use these because I want you to be Will H. Hays, Jr., up at Culver this summer, including signing your name "Will H. Hays, Jr.," instead of "Billie Hays." Big boys when they get out in the world use their real name and I bet you sign it "Will H. Hays, Jr."
Love to all.

Affectionately, Father

7. *From Hollywood*

May 30

Dear Father–

Boy, Buster sure is a good pony, I like him dandy. He sure is a good one and I would like to have him very much instead of renting him. The book I am reading now is *The Last of the Chiefs*. I am promoted to 6B now.

Mother won't let me sign my name Will H. Hays Jr. to letters. She sent for some more tapes for Culver they are like this, "WILLIAM HAYS JR" instead of "WILL H. HAYS JR." It's not as bad as Billy but I would like to have like you.

The parade went past just a little while ago on the way to the Cemetary. The Boy Scouts were the first ones in the parade and I'll sure be glad when I am a Scout.

I love you
Bill

May 31, 1926.

Dear Billy:

This is Decoration Day.

. . . We wouldn't have a country with all its liberties and privileges if good men and women hadn't worked for it and been willing even to fight as they did and die for it . . . The good things don't just happen in this world—they are brought about and you have to work hard for them.

I am looking around for a good pony and I think it would be better not to actually buy this one before Culver. We will work the pony thing out some way, be sure of that. I will leave here two weeks from tomorrow for home for two or three days and then on to California, and while I am there, we will cover a lot of things.

Affectionately your Partner,
Father

* * *

(6-14-26)

Dear Father–

I sure have been having fun this week in Crawfordsville with Eugene Fischer[8].... It is awfully hot here today and has been for several days. I am sorry you cannot be here Tuesday! Don is having a good time here too. I hope you are well.

> I love you
> Bill (and Don)
> B.D.

* * *

June 24, 1926

Dear Billie:

I am writing this as I am approaching Los Angeles... I have been impressed, as I always am, by the vastness of the country and the privileges of living in it....

I just read in the paper that Lieutenant-Commander Byrd arrived in New York yesterday. He flew to the North Pole after years of determination to do it... It is a splendid example as you are now about to enter Culver... I know you will do well always wherever you are, because you are an honest boy; you would not lie; you will do the very best you can always... You are clean and keep your mind free from evil thoughts. Someone once said "You cannot keep the birds from flying over your head, but you can keep them from building nests in your hair." You are going to succeed, too, because you are a healthy boy. This is of paramount importance.

I will stop to see you on my way back from California. I can't tell when that will be... I am engaged in this work because I think it ought to be done for the benefit of yourself and all the other boys that are

---

8. *Helen Fischer's brother.*

around now and will be around in years to come. You are the principal reason for about everything I do.

> Affectionately your Father,
> Will H. Hays

P.S. I am not unmindful of the fact that I have promised you a trip to California. I expect that the better the persimmons are knocked at Culver, the quicker it will come and the better it will be. Go to it!

* * *

Billie, Miss Fischer, and "Don" on West Washington Street in Sullivan.

Ray Russell, his first son Morris Ray, and W.H.H., Jr., in the Russells' yard in Sullivan.

Chapter Eleven

I went to Culver Military Academy for parts of four summers. The summer school was divided into three main parts: the so-called Navy, the Cavalry and the Woodcraft. The Woodcraft section, in turn, was divided into two parts, the very young boys being "Cubs," and the somewhat older ones "Woodcrafters." I was a Cub at ages ten and eleven, and a Woodcrafter at twelve and thirteen. I think the summer sessions each lasted a month or six weeks in the very hottest time of each summer. It was in the northern part of the state, and Ray drove me up there. Sometimes we were accompanied by Helen Fischer and at least once—probably the first time—by Mother. It was a four or five hour drive then, and on about half the drives we had a flat tire. In those days a flat had to be replaced by prying the punctured tire and its inner tube off the rim and prying the spare back on, rather than replacing the whole wheel. This process alone took Ray an extra forty-five minutes, and the sweat poured down his face and dripped off his chin onto his hands or tools or the dusty road where he squatted on his heels. When Miss Fischer and I were his passengers we got out and sat in the shade of a tree beside the road—not having the strength or skill to help him—but the times Mother went, she sat in the stifling car's back seat, regally stirring the air against her face with a bamboo fan while Ray hammered and grunted and raised the car and her up and down with a shaky jack. She didn't complain or urge Ray to hurry, but it was clear that her acceptance of the situation was gorged with a sense of its absurdity.

The Cubs amounted to Cub Scouts with close-order drill and the Woodcrafters to marching Boy Scouts. Both were military-woods-men combinations; we fell in on company streets for fingernail inspections and jumped off on butterfly-netting patrols. Indian touches were added through things like the Saturday night council fires in dark woods. All kinds of boys were sent to Culver, as to Riverdale later: incorrigibles for discipline, kids under foot in divorces or whose parents were in Europe, over-sensitive ones to be hardened, bullies to be taken down some notches, indoor types for tastes of the outdoors, bed-wetters to let others deal with that problem, scions of wealth, poor relations' offspring (atonement surrogates), big and little kids, fat and skinny and smart and dumb ones. Some—at least at first—were homesick generally, others specifically for one parent or both or buddies or dogs. Not a few of the twelve and thirteen-year-olds had begun to fantasize about girls and indulge in the immemorial rite of adolescent ferment. (I never heard it regarding Culver, but there was a rumor later at Riverdale that they put saltpeter in the oatmeal to lessen that pressure.) Culver wasn't a bad place at all. I learned to make a bed off which you could bounce a quarter and to shine my shoes and clean up my room to hell and gone. I've been uncomfortable ever since in sloppy surroundings. Most cowboys are the same way, I learned in other summers, although because of frontier not military traditions.

My memories of Culver are another kaleidoscope of activities and people: marching to the mess hall, to the Friday movies, to the swimming pier and in Sunday parades; the leaping strides that a funny, short kid named Fietelbaum took to keep up with the rest of the company; Fietelbaum's muttering "Eeek-a-freak!" as we marched past any staff member, requiring my shouting the cadence—I was first sergeant—more loudly than normal to cover the disparagement; the morning and evening roars of the French-75 on the lake shore as it cannonaded reveille and retreat with blank shells, except for the morning when somebody put a billiard ball in its muzzle, resulting in a satisfying hole in the Naval School's thirty-foot flagship moored offshore; the scratchy wool dress uniforms in the mid-summer heat; the early morning just after I had formed up our company for its march to breakfast when a red-faced lieutenant with a crew cut and an Irish name, yelling obscenities, chased a huge, black-haired lieutenant with a German name down our tent-lined street, shocking even Fietelbaum into silence; another lieutenant sending for me on another morning and my finding him standing by his tent's narrow bureau in his undershorts, the front of those sticking out from his body weirdly, and my telling him I recalled having to be somewhere else and getting out of there fast and avoiding him after that; taking boxing lessons, learning classy moves and being whipped by a classier-moving Cuban kid; "Fort Chimo," the only solid building in the Woodcraft area (our tents being canvas-covered, wooden frames with wooden floors), which served the sanitation needs of several hundred boys with its long unpartitioned rows of toilets and lavatories, its vaulted interior presenting surely one of the state's bizarre sights every morning after breakfast; the frustrated pet raccoon in its cage near the mess hall trying to wash in its water pan the ice cream offered it by Cubs and Woodcrafters.

I increased my swimming skill during those Culver summers, passing life-saving and other tests required for merit badges, and competing in some races. In fact, I won a race one afternoon that was very special for me, because Dad was there. His few visits excited me and also caused a good deal of stirring around on the part of the lieutenants and other staff members. I've always thought of swimming as more than a healthful pursuit, prescribed at another time by doctors for my back; it often has been almost a mystical experience for me, making me feel like dolphins look as though they feel as they slide and turn through the water in seeming weightless dreams. Later, in my Riverdale years—especially in the one after a long hospitalization and body cast for my back—Dad's matchless New York chauffeur and my good friend, Tom White, drove me every afternoon for months from the school on 252nd Street in the Bronx to the New York Athletic Club on Manhattan's Central Park South to work out in the pool there; and the summer after that I drove every morning in a rented convertible from our also rented beach house in Santa Monica, California, to the Hollywood Athletic Club to swim. Incidentally, it was at the latter place in 1932 that I had the invaluable training and the thrill of swimming alongside multi-event world's champion Johnny Weissmuller and his friend Buster Crabbe, as Johnny helped Buster train to win an Olympic Games Gold Medal that year. (Johnny was then, and Buster was to be, the movies' Tarzan.)

One Culver incident was not pleasant. Colonel Harold Bays was Commandant of the Woodcrafter-Cub summer school and was a kind man whose family had a long friendship with the Hayses, except for my Uncle Hinkle. One of his brothers was a Sullivan attorney at whose funeral years later I was to be a pallbearer and after attending which Uncle Hinkle was to send his suit out to be cleaned; and another brother was Democrat state chairman (Indiana politically was his fiefdom in those days) who also toured with his lady friend without as much success in an acrobatic dancing act and was chauffeured around Indiana by a state policeman. One day I was summoned to Colonel Bays' headquarters office, where he told me the examining board for the "Silver C"—one of the Woodcrafter awards which should bring great pride to Dad if I earned it—had noticed that the Luna moth in my insect collection seemed pretty bedraggled. The Colonel asked me if I personally had caught the one in my collection. In great, swallowing shame, which it hadn't occurred to me until then to feel, I said that indeed I had borrowed it from another boy, a friend of mine, because I had spent a large part of the twenty-four hours ahead of the board's deadline unsuccessfully trying to net a Luna of my own. I'm sure Colonel Bays felt bad, too, when he told me that under the circumstances my Silver C would be withheld. As I've said, he was a kind man: he didn't use the word "cheating." It almost didn't make me feel better when he added that I had a chance to win the medal before the encampment's end by completing satisfactorily a number of additional requirements that he and the board would think up. I managed to thank him and grope my way, blinking, out of his office, feeling that I'd let him and Dad and Ray and Miss Fischer down. I did make it up to them, I hope; I completed the additional requirements and was awarded the Silver C before I left Culver that summer.

A more pleasant Culver memory is of the lakeshore Maxinkuckee Inn where generations of Culver boys—and nowadays girls—have been fed Sunday dinners by their visiting families and friends. A special feature of dining at the Inn was the spectacular filling of water tumblers by an elderly, black waiter in a white coat who swooped his pitcher upward at least a foot and a half as water poured from it and then lowered it precisely in time to keep the tumbler from running over, all without spilling a drop on the white tablecloth.

Chapter Twelve

(7-5-26)

Dear Miss Fischer—

    I am gitting along fine at Culver. I am just back from drilling. My tent mate is John Frazier Giller. How are you getting along. I have recieved a letter from Mother, Father, Aunt Cile since I have been here . . . Excuse my rotten written letter because I am expecting the whistle to blow any time now and I am in a hurry.

    How is Eugene!

I love you, Bill

xox xox xox ooo
xox xox xxx

P.S. and don't forget it

"W.H.H."

* * *

WESTERN UNION TELEGRAM

July 11, 1926

CULVER CUB WILL H. HAYS, JR.,
TENT 191, PACK 4, DIVISION 5,
CULVER SUMMER WOODCRAFT SCHOOL,
CULVER, INDIANA.

    VERY CONFIDENTIALLY I HAVE JUST HAD A TALK WITH TOM MIX STOP HE HAS A PONY NAMED TONY JUNIOR THAT HE WANTS TO GIVE TO YOU STOP . . . SOMETHING MAY HAPPEN TO PREVENT IT BUT I THINK IT WILL PROBABLY HAPPEN STOP IF HE DOESNT WE WILL GET A TONY JUNIOR OURSELVES STOP HOPE TO SEE YOU NEXT

SATURDAY AFTERNOON STOP KEEP UP THE GOOD WORK
THERE OLD PARTNER . . . LOVE.

W.H.H.

* * *

Dear Father—

I have just come back from permit with miss Fischer. John my
tent mate is playing my victollo. We had Garrison parade and we each
had a peice of candy for the best line or that is the men in the second
patune. We beat the first patune, they didn't have any candy.

Hurry up and come up here.

I love you.

W. H. Hays Jr

* * *

(7-26-26)

Dear Father.

I am just back from permit with Uncle Hinkle. I had a good time.
I am going to take Wilson Robinson, Dick Sellers and Jack Kittle and
Frazier out on permit next Saturday. I wish you were here now.

Consil fire was good last night. Every thing is all right here
I love you very much

Bill.

(8-13-26)

Dear Miss Fischer

I am out of the Hospittle now and am feeling good. I ate supper
there. You told me the other day to write you but there is nothing to tell.
I haft to go now.

OXO   OXO   OXO   OXO
XOX   XOX   XOX

Bill

XXX OOO XXX OOO

* * *

August 16, 1926.

Dear Will:

I just have your pen note about Bill's little difficulty a week ago at Culver. My first inclination was to climb Helen Fischer, but when I called him the boy properly resented that. The investigation seemed to disclose that Helen Fischer had little Bill back at 8:30, the only mistake being that, in his excitement to write you before taps at 9:00, he forgot to stop at the guard tent and check in. After thinking about it very much, I didn't mention it to Helen Fischer, because I knew that her purposes were altogether good, and her execution was not subject to enough criticism to justify how badly this would have made her feel, given her very great affection and her splendid discipline in everything else, while she is away on her vacation.

I feel very satisfied that you will be perfectly happy with the result of Bill's experience up there and the honors he has won . . . remembering, always, that he is just ten years old, and that this is his first summer away from home, mixing with a crowd of new boys and men. It is altogether a pretty hard-boiled situation for a little pup to be in . . . I know it sounds funny for a horse thief to preach a sermon against larceny, but if the horse thief knows that stealing is wrong, from his own experience, he ought to be able to preach a good sermon on that subject. Accordingly, you will pardon the suggestion that there really is nothing for you to worry about.

Affectionately, H.C.H.

* * *

WESTERN UNION TELEGRAM

DAY LETTER — NEW YORK, AUGUST 20, 1926

CULVER CUB WILL H. HAYS, JR.,
TENT 191, PACK 4, DIVISION 5,
CULVER SUMMER WOODCRAFT SCHOOL,
CULVER, INDIANA

UNCLE HINKLE HAS JUST ADVISED ME THAT YOU SWAM FOUR HUNDRED AND TWENTY FIVE YARDS STOP

MY GOODNESS THATS FURTHER THAN I COULD RIDE IN A BOAT . . . LOVE

W.H.H.

* * *

September 3, 1926

Mr. Will H. Hays, Jr.,
Sullivan, Indiana.

Dear Billie:
    . . . The fact that you did a splendid job at Culver this summer is the best proof that you will be a success in whatever job you undertake. You went up there without any experience away from home, into a group of new boys, and you took the hurdles as fast as they came up and you cleared them all splendidly. I was a little distressed, of course, about the fact that you failed one Sunday night to check in. I haven't heard the details yet about the court-martial but I know that the reason you forgot to check in was probably because you were waiting to write to me . . . Colonel Bays and the officers treated you splendidly because you were honest and had been a good boy theretofore. That shows how valuable it is to have a good record and do right.
    . . . I am pleased with your development physically . . . That is the reason more that anything else that you went to Culver. I am enclosing herewith a United States Government bond for five hundred dollars which is a token of appreciation for your winning your cub Bronze and Silver "Cs" the first year and your swimming "C" and the Hubbard Award and getting to be a lance corporal. You told me in the automobile it is not necessary for me to give you anything because you did that, but I want to . . .
    I am sending you by express the Rocky Mountain sheep's head. It will be a fine decoration for your room at home. I want you to furnish that the way you want to. You must remember you're my full partner. What you want, I want, and what I want, you want.
    As you start back to school, I know you will buckle right down and do the job that has to be done at school, and . . . drink a lot of milk, eat the green vegetables, stand up straight, play football, play baseball, learn to box, wrestle with Ray, and gain a couple of pounds every week.

Affectionately, Father

Dear Miss Fischer:

1926

I have missed you so much this time more than any other time in my life. I love you dearly dearly dearly dearly.

Don't tell Uncle Hincke I said so but you are my best friend. I love you.

Bill.

From Culver

(9-5-26)

Dear Father—

I received the letter you sent me from the White House. School starts tomorrow I will be in Miss Neal's room this year again I think. She's a dandy teacher . . . I have not yet received the thinges from Buck Jones. He was sure good in the movie Friday night.

I love you dearly, Bill

* * *

Chapter Thirteen

IN Sullivan in those years the biggest meal of the week was Sunday dinner at noon. The noon meal every day was "dinner," not "lunch"—I didn't learn about "lunch" until Riverdale—and the evening meal was "supper." As I recall, either chicken or a roast invariably was the entree, in whichever case with all the trimmings. Normally our meals were served as well as cooked by the lady of the kitchen—Ella Shaw or later Mrs. Adams—except when Dad was home for a few days, when Ray served them. Occasionally we were invited for Sunday dinner to Uncle Hinkle and Aunt Lucile's house, which was down the street a way initially and then across the street after they built their big brick one. There was a question whether Uncle Hinkle's house was bigger that the Bays' at the edge of town. Eating at Uncle Hinkle and Aunt Lucile's was not as relaxed as at our house. I got the impression rather early in life that Mother didn't get along well with Hinkle and Lucile. I think their dislikes were reciprocal. Incidentally, some time after Dad hired Ray, Uncle Hinkle hired a young white man named Cy Curtis as a chauffeur, and in later years Cy was succeeded by a nice black fellow named Louis Granger. The Hayses across the street also had a gardener, an elderly Scot named Mr. Forbes, who was the father of the only cook I remember at their house, Rachael.

Sunday was the day in those years when I wrote to Dad—Miss Fischer saw to that. I used to do this chore sitting at my small desk in my bedroom—the former sleeping porch—beside a big window which looked out on the backyard with the huge tree in its center, footed by a bench made of stones brought from some ancient Hays homestead, with the sandpile and later Sawdust Park on beyond that. From the bedroom window I also could see "Stratton's Hill," the rear-sloping portion of our neighbors' backyard on one side of which we sledded in the wintertime; and across our neighbors' yard on the other side I could see Jennings' Lumber Yard, over and through the lumber piles and culverts of which I climbed with the gang after school in the first and second and third grades. Writing to Dad wasn't always a chore; sometimes I wanted very much to tell him something or ask him for something. I'd rather have talked to him personally and smelled his not-unpleasant morning breath, as I did when I was really little and he was home on visits and I got into bed with him to hear stories about grizzly bears in the Washington Zoo.

I'm sure I missed him in the years of my life before my first at Riverdale, after which we were together at least most week ends; and I remember hating to see him leave Sullivan after his two-or three-day visits, first from Washington and later from New York and Hollywood, which were great galas of excitement. But except for those bittersweet times I can't recall consciously grieving over his absence or wondering why he wasn't home or why Mother and I weren't with him or exactly what he was doing. His being away was a fact of my existence; it never had been any different and I didn't spend time brooding about it, although I realize now Ray's and Miss Fischer's being there certainly had a bearing on that. I also realize that it must have been much harder on Dad. A couple of decades later on one of his visits to my adult home to see how our first baby daughter was doing—he had sat in the hospital waiting room when my wife Virginia bore Kathy while I was off on an Army assignment—he looked up from playing with the child on the floor and with tears in his eyes said to her mother, "Babies are wonderful, they're just wonderful. I can't remember Bill when he was this small a human!" Not infrequently there was an aura of sadness about him.

Just a few years ago Helen Fischer told me that my mother's stepmother had put an announcement in the Crawfordsville paper of her stepdaughter's engagement to Dad, knowing he'd fallen in love with another girl from a nearby town, and that he had felt obliged to marry Mother to avoid shaming her publicly. I believe that Mother didn't help plan or even know about the entrapment.

After the early distemper death of my first dog, Glen, and then weeks of my pestering Miss Fischer and Ray and Mother and, in letters, Dad about getting another pup, the arrival one day of a black Scottie in a crate from the West was a jubilation. Ray drove Miss Fischer and me out to the railroad station in Depot Town and there we uncrated Don and brought him home. I think he lived with us as my good companion (but not everybody's) for a couple of years, snapping at Postman Walter Criss (who, Realtor Bill Borders said at Walter's retirement dinner at the Elks, had "either been bit or pissed on by every dog in town"), barking at passersby and, when nobody passed, just barking, and chasing cars until he was hit accidentally one day by undertaker Ed Billman's new Nash and died in my lap in the gutter. Don's replacement, Byron, a second beautiful Scotch collie, lived for a long time. In fact, I left town for Riverdale before he died and I really don't remember how much later that was; he just wasn't there on one of my vacations home. He was a loving, lovable animal like the others, and my own last one—although I've shared a number of fine dogs since then with other people, including my children. During my early life, almost until the time I left Sullivan for Riverdale, Mother had a strange conviction that meat and especially pie were bad for me; and I remember Byron sitting beside me on the back stairs which led from the kitchen to the upper floor while I ate after-supper helpings of meat and pie sneaked to me by Ella or Mrs. Adams, and Miss Fischer kept Mother occupied with conversation in the living room.

More than once, I think, during the Sullivan years I moved into Uncle Hinkle and Aunt Lucille and Chuck and John T.'s home for reasons and lengths of time I don't remember exactly, although I'm pretty sure it was because of Mother's hospitalization at least once in Chicago and other times maybe to let Miss Fischer have vacations.

Chapter Fourteen

Sunday
(9-5-26)

Dear Father

Last night I went to the show. As soon a it got out I came straight home at 20 after eight. As soon a we get in the door mother begins raising the deivle because we were late. I go to bed at 8:30. She says I can't go to the show any more on Saturday and chases me half way up the stairs.

Please do something

Love, Bill

* * *

New York City
469 Fifth Avenue,
September 8, 1926

PRIVATE

Master Will H. Hays, Jr.,
Sullivan,
Indiana.

Dear Billie:

I have your personal letter of Sunday and will endeavor to solve the problem you mention at a very early date. I will get busy on it right away. In the meantime you be a nice, good boy, just like you always are, and depend on me working it out along the lines we agreed.

I love you.

Affectionately, Father

* * *

HAYS & HAYS
Attorneys-at-Law
Sullivan, Ind.

September 11, 1926.

Mr. Will H. Hays,
Apt 12-C, 300 Park Ave.,
Newyork City, N.Y.

Dear Mr. Hays:
Work is progressing on re-building the sleeping porch into Billie's room. However, it is very difficult to explain it to Mrs. Hays without telling her it is to be permanent and not just temporary, as she was led to believe. Just such as this and many more things make it very difficult to handle sometimes . . .

Sincerely yours, Paul Kester

Sunday
(9-12-26)

Dear Father:
Yesterday a big box came It was the goats head. There were 6 fellow's in the back yard, they all ran to see what it was. Don Howard got the first look at it. I got the first feel. Ray was completely surrounded with boys when he was opening it . . . We went to see Tom Mix in *Hard-boiled* and it was sure good.
I love you

Bill

* * *

September 13, 1926

Mr. Paul Kester.
Sullivan, Indiana.

Dear Paul:
I don't think you need to try to have Mrs. Hays understand that the work is not permanent. It is permanent while it lasts, but it will all

124

be torn out and put back into the sleeping porch when Bill gets through with it as his room. I will write her.

Best wishes.

Sincerely yours, W.H.H.

* * *

Dinner time, Monday
September 13, 1926

Dear Father,

Mother won't let me eat any dinner today without wearing a bib and by heck I'm not going to eat any dinner. Please fix it father you don't know what I haft to go through.

I love you, Bill

September 18, 1926

Dear Billie:

About that bib business.

I can understand how you feel about it exactly. You are too old to wear a bib usually and you shouldn't have to . . . However, the important element in this situation is that Mother asked you to use a bib and . . . you should give careful consideration to the suggestion of your mother. A wise man never has a showdown on non-essentials. A wise man never yields on principal either . . . You are a generous, big boy and one that will always be generous in your opinion as to whether or not a thing is right which Mother or Miss Fischer asks you to do.

You are exactly right about the matter of the Saturday shows. You can go the movie either on Friday or Saturday nights and stay until they are out if the show is the kind of a show that boys ought to go to. Most of the movies are that kind of shows now. I am going to talk to Mother about the shows as well as the bib business . . .

I love you.

Affectionately, W.H.H.

* * *

Sullivan, Ind.
September 20, '26

Dear Mr. Hays:

This is not a pleasant task. I would rather tell than write you my version as you've asked.

Since Bill has been home he has tried to ward off the bib question—and has done it well. But it is not an easy thing to eat while having critical and unpleasant, fussy remarks made most of the time. At noon the other day, Mrs. H. got the bib and told B. to put it on. He said "No, father said I didn't have to wear a bib any more." Mrs. H. jumped up, grabbed the bib and started to tie it. B. held it so that it couldn't be tied. Then she slapped him and jerked him several times. His eyes filled and he said "Mother, I don't want to wear it." She said, "It doesn't make any difference what you want, I want you to wear it and you are going to." He said, "I won't eat any dinner then." She said, "All right. Nobody cares." He had let her tie it on in the meantime. Then he untied it. She told him to leave the table. He said "All right" and went upstairs.

He came down after a while, stood at the table, looked at his plate of baked beans and potato, and said "I'll go to the kitchen and eat." She followed him out and told him he couldn't eat anything out there. He went in the back yard . . . Always before when he was sent from the table we have given him food some way. This time I gave him some money and told him to stop at The Black Bat cafe on his way to school.

That evening at the table Mrs. H. said, "I have been thinking it over and have decided you will only have to wear your bib morning and noon. In the evening your waist is soiled and you won't need it." Bill objected, but has been wearing it mornings and part of the time at noon. When he doesn't, he is fussed at and it's hard to eat without spilling something; then she remarks about that.

I am adding some extras, while I'm on the subject

1. He is treated as he were five years of age—but really gets along better now than he did then because he takes so much and doesn't object as he did even then.

2. His food has a little more variety, but very little, than before he went to Culver.

3. He was forced to put on knit underwear (cap sleeves) the second day of school—instead of wearing the athletic suits the boys wear until cold weather.

4. He has to wear a sweater indoors and out. He is not allowed to decide for himself whether he is too cold or too hot.

5. There is nearly always an unpleasant time when Bill asks to eat with Charles and John T.

6. Pie is served to him in a sauce dish, taken out of the crust.

Mr. Hays, I am under a nervous strain always, and I want you to know—frankly—that I am going thru this only for my love of Bill, and I adore him. He is the sweetest, dearest and most precious thing in the world to me.

Sincerely, H.V.F.

* * *

FOR

Will H. Hays, Jr.

Dear Billie:

This, the first copy[1] off the press, is for you from

Your friend, Reginald Wright Kauffman
Geneva, Switzerland
Sept. 21, 1926

* * *

(9-26-26)

Dear Father

I am going to write and thank Mr. Kauffman for the book he sent me. Yesterday was a fair day Ray and I made a piece of furnisher for my room and it got its first coat of varnish. I made a sword and shield out of wood and had a good time with them. Lee was over for dinner and he and I had a good time playing together in the back yard.

Gee! when are you coming home? I wish you would hurry. Every thing has been going all right since I saw you last.

I love you

Bill.

* * *

---

1. *The book* Seventy–six. *An excerpt of the* Chronicles of the Rowntree Family *was written by Kauffman and illustrated by Clyde O. DeLand. The author dedicated the book to W.H.H., Jr.(see following pages 128–31).*

189

FOREWORD AND DEDICATION

SOME months ago, Billie Hays, I asked you to help me in my new work of writing books for boys. I had seen what the grown-up critics kindly said about " The Rowntree Chronicles," but the important thing was to find out what boys thought about them, and so, my own children being still a bit young for consultation, I appealed to you. I wanted you to tell me why you, as a " regular boy," liked or disliked my endeavors, for then I would know what to put in and what to leave out hereafter. Well, here reproduced, is your answer:

December 13, 1925.

BILLIE HAYS
290 WEST WASHINGTON ST.
SULLIVAN. INDIANA

Dear Mr. Kauffman—
I have finished the
book "The Ranger of the

v

FOREWORD AND DEDICATION

Susquehannock" that you sent to me. I like it very much and the reason is because it is adventurous. Right when you think Nicholas Rowntree will get caught he slips out and gets away. The night when Nicholas warns the stranger and almost gets caught at it is very exciting. Then when Sir Geoffrey and he are at the inn in the last of the the story and he walks into the tap-room

vi

170

FOREWORD AND DEDICATION

and sees ferret-faced I was
very much excited.

When Sir Geoffrey jumps
out of the window and breaks
his leg and they almost
get caught is exciting too.

I like your book too
because it is about history
and history is my favorite
study in school.

Then boys that play foot-
ball and are real boys like
it because it has a lot
of life in it.

vii

FOREWORD AND DEDICATION

I will read the new story that is coming with much eagerness,

Your friend

Will H. Hays Jr.

That has been a real help, and I hope I've profited by it in the consequent revision of " Seventy-Six! " I trust you will find herein the same elements that made " The Ranger " attractive — the same and more of them — and of course, as a small return for your assistance, I dedicate this unit of " The Rowntree Chronicles " to you.

Sincerely your friend,

REGINALD WRIGHT KAUFFMAN

VILLA DES ROSES,
5, Avenue Calas,
Champel, Geneva,
Switzerland;
Feb. 25, (N. S.) 1926.

viii

October 4, 1926

Dear Billie:

I had lunch Friday with Gene Tunney, the world's champion heavyweight boxer, and Fred Thomson, the Western cowboy motion picture actor, both good men.

While he was in France in the war Fred had a great deal to do with the athletics of the boys in the army, and he met a buck private in the Marines and became very much attached to him. That buck private was a fine boxer. After the war, Fred Thomson lost sight of the buck private.

Last winter Tunney was in Hollywood, making some serials, and a friend said, "There is a motion picture actor out there that knows you. He is a top cowboy actor." Tunney said, "I don't know any cowboy actor. What's his name?" "Fred Thomson," he was told. Tunney said, "I knew a man named Fred Thomson in the war, but he was a college graduate, a postgraduate, a minister, a great speaker, a chaplain in the army." "That's the man," said his friend. So Tunny went to see him, and it was the same Fred Thomson . . .

I will be home next Sunday unless I go to Philadelphia to make a speech at the First Presbyterian Church for the Pension Fund, in which case a few days after.

Love to all.

Affectionately, W.H.H.

* * *

(Billy's answers to your questionnaire of September 28 - H.V.F.)

1. How is school going generally? *All right.*

2. How do you like your teacher? (Usually if a boy doesn't like his teacher he is not getting along well but if he likes his teacher it is usually true he is getting along all right.) *Fine.*

3. Are you giving special attention to concentration? This you should do. *Yes.*

4. How is your self-control? This should be better after your time at Culver. *All right.*

5. Are you eating some green vegetables every day? *Yes.*

6. What food do you eat particularly at your three meals:

    a. Breakfast—*bakon eggs or French tost or cakes.*

  b. Dinner—*Meat, vegetables dessert.*

  c. Supper—*Vegetables mostly A glass of milk at each meal.*

  7. Are you eating more than you did when you went to Culver? *Slightly.*

  8. Are you having a larger variety of food? This is important because you now should eat pretty much what a big boy eats for you are a big boy. *Slightly.*

  9. Are you playing hard every night after school? *Yes.*

  10. Are you getting your lessons all right? *Yes.*

  11. Do you study any at night? *Not yet.*

  12. What time are you going to bed? *8:30*

  13. Do you catch cold easily or are you free from colds? *Free*

  14. Are your clothes heavy enough and not too heavy? *Some times I have to wear my sweter and it makes me to hot.*

  15. Do Charles and John T. come over and play with you and how often? *Everyday*

  16. How often do you go over there? *as often as I want*

  17. How often do you eat over there? *Mother lets me once a week.*

  18. How often do they eat with you? *When ever there asked*

  19. Are you going to the movies? *Yes*

  20. What nights do you go to the movies? *Friday or Saturday*

  21. What are some of the movies you have been to see? Give names. *"Flaming Frontier." "Poker Faces" "Hard-Boiled" "My own Pal" "The blind godess" "For Hevens Sake" is coming this week "The Sea Beast"*

  22. How is Don? *Fine*

  23. Do you take a good deal of care of him yourself? *Yes*

  24. Have you talked to William Jamieson about the pony? *Yes, He don't know yet but he'll see.*

  25. Are you playing football yet? *Yes and have been for a good while*

  26. Have you plenty of heavy clothes? *Yes*

  27. Does your overcoat fit you now? *Yes*

  28. Do you have a raincoat? *yes would like a pair of leather High top Shoes that come to my knees and knot the kind I had last year. Size 4.*

* * *

Sunday
Oct 24, 1926

Dear Father

  Yesterday Ray and I went squirrel hunting and brought home a rabit which we had for dinner to-day . . .

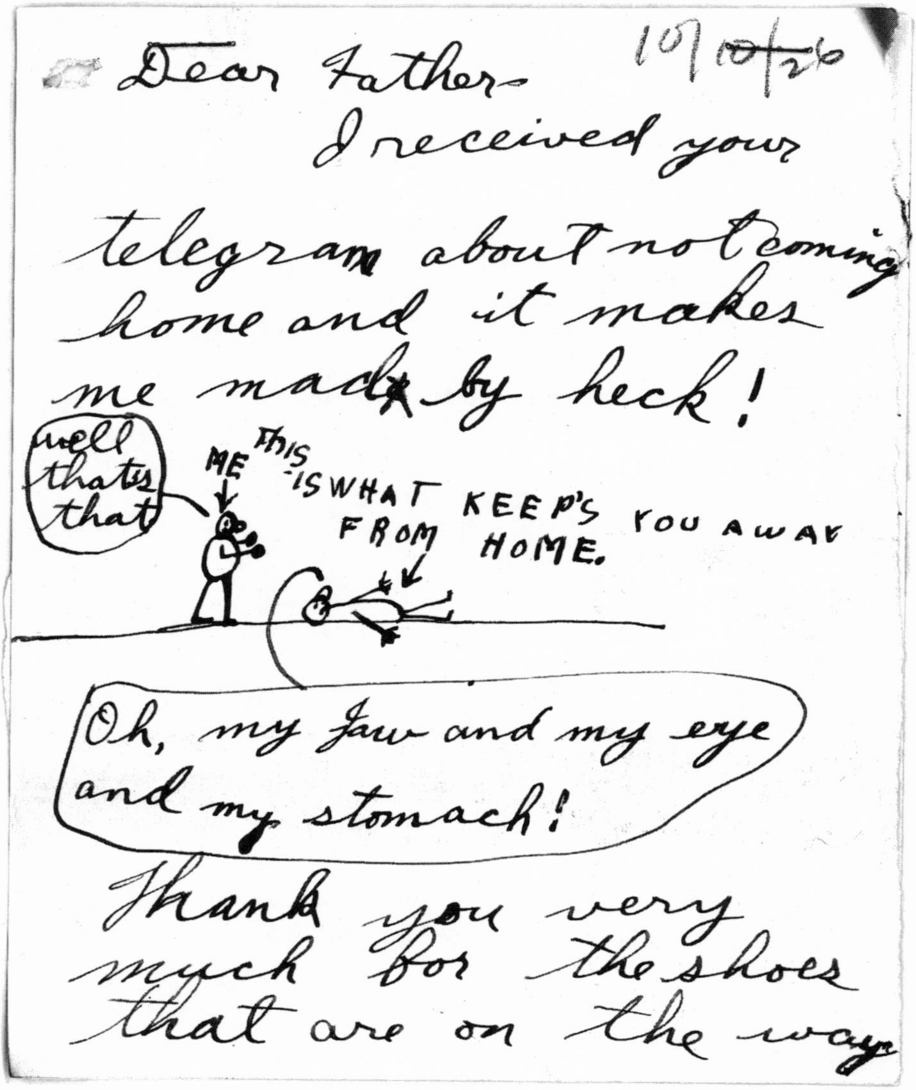

10/10/26

Dear Father-

I received your telegram about not coming home and it makes me mad by heck!

Oh, my Jaw and my eye and my stomach!

Thank you very much for the shoes that are on the way

John, Stewart Hart-
felder, Lee and I we
had a game of foot-
ball. Lee and I stood Stewart
and John. They beat us
be three.
Well please come
home next week
and be sure about it.
I love you
Bill Hays.
H

I can't hardly wait to see you for this is the longest time you have ever been away.

Enclosed are some pictures of Rays baby which you will like.

I love you

Bill

P.S. I <u>must</u> go to "behind the front" Saturday night.

* * *

WESTERN UNION TELEGRAM

OCTOBER 27, 1926.

WILL H. HAYS, JR.
250 WEST WASHINGTON ST.
SULLIVAN, INDIANA.

HAVE JUST LEARNED THAT THE PICTURE BEHIND THE FRONT IS GOING TO BE SHOWN IN SULLIVAN NEXT SATURDAY STOP YOU MUST SEE THIS STOP IT IS THE FUNNIEST THING YOU EVER SAW STOP WILL BE HOME SUNDAY AFTERNOON STOP HOT DOG

WILL H. HAYS

* * *

WILL H. HAYS, JR.
250 WEST WASHINGTON STREET
SULLIVAN, IND.

Dear Father—

I am writing to the best father on earth to congratulate him on his birthday.

Very lovingly, Will H Hays Jr.

I love you   Nov. 3, 1926

* * *

(11-7-26)

Dear Father—

This is my first letter to you in my new room. This is the fourth year of the 50–50 club. The other evening we elected presedent, Seckutary and football captian. Ray went hunting the other day and got 7 rabits and one squirrel. When I go we'll get 21 rabits and 14 squirrels

I love you

Will H Hays

* * *

Nov 14, 1926
Sunday

Dear Father—

I have invited 20 people to my party including myself.

This morning at church we had a new preacher. I thought he was very good.

Here, nearly all the trees are bear of leaves and I have been having a big time playing in the leaves. Latly the gang and I have been playing foot ball. One game the whole gang divided up and the score was 56 to 63 in the favor of the side I was on.

I love you

Will H Hays Jr.

* * *

November 20, 1926

Dear Billie:

. . . I wouldn't be surprised if the gun and hunting knife you asked about were found by December eleventh. December eleventh is a good day for you to find things . . .

Don't forget the hard work at school (including self-control), hard play, green vegetables, more milk, standing up straight, etc., etc.

Love to all.

Affectionately, W.H.H.

* * *

December 19, 1926
Sunday

Dear Father—

Ray and I went hunting yesterday. We had a good time but didn't catch any thing... Boy I can hardly wait till next Friday evening when you come. I'll meet you with a new chauffeur at Terre Haute.

I love you.

Will H. Hays, Jr.

Boy that gun is swell, Father.

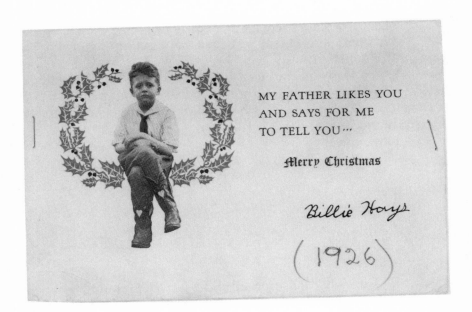

MY FATHER LIKES YOU
AND SAYS FOR ME
TO TELL YOU ···

Merry Christmas

Billie Hays

(1926)

Jan. 9, 1927

Dear Father

I went hunting with Ray and John. We got one rabit. Ray got that one. One jumped right up in front of me. I shot at him but missed him. Don went with us but he stayed in the car with Miss Fischer.

I am going to make a steam engine. It began to snow again this morning. I have been playing with my meccano, it is all right. Tell Tom Mix hellow for me, do the same to Doug Fairbanks and Bill Hart. We are reading *Last Of The Mohicans* and boy its good.

I love you very much.

Will H. Hays, Jr

Written in Hollywood
6331 Hollywood Boulevard.

January 24, 1927.

Dear Bill:

Herewith I am returning the report which I received this morning from Miss Fischer. I am delighted with it. I note with special pleasure that your self-control has gone from "G" to "G plus" . . .

Now then, I want to tell you what happened Saturday. I saw Tom Mix and he told me he had your pony, that he had been training it and by spring it would be ready to send to you . . . I would not say anything about it yet around there because something might happen— he might go lame or he might turn out to be too wild, but it looks mighty good now for "Tony, Jr."

I went to the polo game Sunday afternoon with Hal Roach, who was one of the players. One of the reasons I want you to be a still better horseback rider is that sometime you can play polo . . .

Love to all.

Affectionately, WHH

* * *

(1-30-27)

Dear Father—

The ice has all melted here and its just like spring out-of-doors.

Boy! when I heard about Tony Jr. I nearly busted with delight. I wish spring was here so that he would come now. Boy! I cant hardly wait. When he gets here I'll be the happiest boy in the world. Friday night I saw Tom Mix in *The Canyon Of Light.* Is Tony, Jr. the real son of Tony? . . . I am getting along fine in school and working hard and getting better in Arithmatic.

I love you very much,

Will H. Hays

* * *

Dictated en route
February 14, 1927

Dear Billie:

Here's a fifty-cent piece of the Oregon Trail . . . This is sent to you by Ezra Meeker. He is ninety years old and drove a wagon over the Oregon Trail, probably one of the first ones.

Love to all.

Affectionately, Father

February 28, 1927

Dear Billie:

. . . Back here in New York, I got your letter asking permission to whitewash the walls of the 50-50 clubroom and have wired you it was all right to do this, because you want to keep the club clean in every way . . .

I want you to keep track of all expenses incident to Tony, Junior. He will be your pony, but there is some responsibility goes with this. It costs money to keep a pony . . . and you will have to pay these bills . . . I will help you provide the money but you have to handle it all and watch the expenses and keep track of everything.

Love to all.

Affectionately, Father

* * *

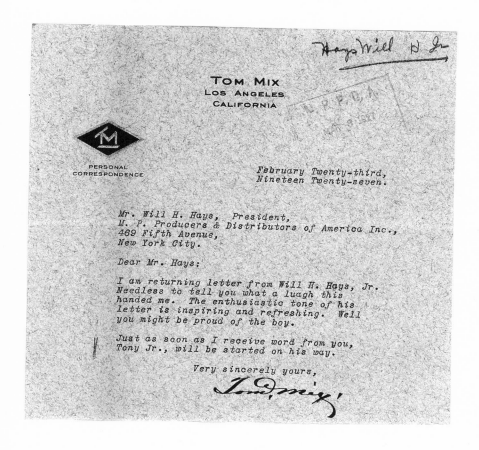

TOM MIX
LOS ANGELES
CALIFORNIA

PERSONAL
CORRESPONDENCE

February Twenty-third,
Nineteen Twenty-seven.

Mr. Will H. Hays, President,
M. P. Producers & Distributors of America Inc.,
469 Fifth Avenue,
New York City.

Dear Mr. Hays:

I am returning letter from Will H. Hays, Jr.
Needless to tell you what a luagh this
handed me. The enthusiastic tone of his
letter is inspiring and refreshing. Well
you might be proud of the boy.

Just as soon as I receive word from you,
Tony Jr., will be started on his way.

Very sincerely yours,

Tom Mix

Monday March 7

Dear Father:

Everybody is fine including Don. Hope you are . . . When Tony comes I won't be able to thank you and Tom Mix enough. I'll be so happy.

I am first baseman on our baseball team. Wayne Lloyd, pitcher. Lee Gray, fielder. Brandy Dunlap, catcher. and Dave Giles, Third Baseman. Its some team I tell you and so is our football team. The basketball goals are up fine. Saturday a few of us boys had boxing and wrestling matches.

I love you

Will H. Hays, Jr

* * *

WESTERN UNION
1927 MAR 9 PM 28

INDIANAPOLIS IND 9 21 5P
WILL H HAYS
8TH FLOOR WINFIELD BLDG 4689 FIFTH AVE

PLEASE SEND WIRE TO LITTLE BILL TO SHOW HIS MOTHER REQUESTING HIM TO GO TO INDIANAPOLIS SATURDAY WITH LUCILLE AND BOYS TO SEE YOU IN FIRST SOUND VITAPHONE FILM.

HINKLE HAYS

Dear Father —
Every time I want to wear my long pants mother raises hell and says I can't wear them? All the other boys do and I ought to do it too.

I love you
Bill.

Chapter Fifteen

INCIDENTS and people I recall from Sullivan in the early days stir lots of emotions, making a whirling jumble of memories. They're so fleeting it's impossible to express them chronologically or in detail; like dreams, they recede or collide or accelerate away as I try to tell them. I guess I'll seize some of their fragments as they wheel past and give words to them as quickly as I can:

Playing with Lincoln Logs and Erector and Mechano sets and electric trains on the living room floor for weeks after Christmases.

Pants legs caught in the bicycle's chain and sprocket.

Bicycling past that black-haired Colleen's house on South State Street without glancing at it, hoping she might be looking out of a window, pretending I didn't realize where I was.

Hearing that Dad had gone to Hollywood, California, to be in the movies—not act in them, do something about running them, some kind of "Czar," Miss Fischer said.

Maurice Lee Gray and Dave Giles and I after school one winter day coming upon the body of an elderly lady who obviously had slipped on the icy sidewalk, the blood from under the back of her head frozen in a dark, glassy puddle—the first time any of us had seen a dead person except at a funeral parlor.

Dave Giles with even a slighter build than mine eating three candy bars a day.

The blood gushing from a boy's split lip at recess.

My asking Ray when we were alone in the basement what a girl looked like "down there," his thinking seriously a moment and then saying, "Sort of like the hairbrush on Miss Fischer's bureau," my mulling over that for several days before asking him which way the handle went, and his still-serious reply that he hadn't meant to include the handle; and my subsequently looking up "ovaries" (which I'd heard from someone had to do with sex) in the big study-hall dictionary and noting the margin's diagram of what looked like a plant's thick stem and two delicate pear-bearing branches and being more confused than ever.

The lovely scents, like Aunt Lucile's, of the lily-of-the-valley bed on the morning side of our house in the sun.

The spidery cool under the back porch, the time my rabbit got loose and Ray had to remove the lattice-work below the elevated floor's edges to get him out.

Hearing within our household of first trans-Atlantic flier Charles Lindberg's visit to Dad in New York, at the suggestion of Dad's friend Dwight Morrow (to be the flier's father-in-law), to ask advice about a movie-starring offer from some big production company, and Dad advising Lindberg against commercializing his heroic image. (If that company had learned of such "disloyalty," I wonder what its head honcho might have said to Dad!)

The six-inch silk American flag Admiral Richard Byrd had carried on his flights across the Atlantic and both poles and sent to Dad as thanks for fund-raising help.

Christmas Eve recitation at church of a forgotten poem; candy-nuts-and-oranges (the words always were run together) in dime-store red-net stockings; the smell of freshly waxed pews and of lighted candles and of the great Christmas tree strung with popcorn and cranberries and paper chains; Dad walking into the church, just off the train at Terre Haute from Washington or New York, my heart pounding with excitement and fear there shouldn't be time to tell him everything before his departure.

A footrace in our driveway with Chuck, normally less coordinated than I, which Dad staged and which unaccountably I lost; and my sense of bitter frustration, my hot, tearful chagrin.

The early Sunday morning when I answered the phone and it was Dad, and I interrupted his dramatic greeting to tell him excitedly that I'd got my First Class badge the previous evening and he switched from whatever he'd started saying to congratulating me on that accomplishment; and it wasn't until later I learned he'd been calling from Paris over the new transatlantic cable and had written down some impressive things to say about the advances of man and the greatness of America, but had decided the First Class badge said it all and had torn up his notes.

Aunt Lucile blowing cigarette smoke in my ear to ease my earache when I was very young—her first and only cigarette.

With the coming of spring, changing from leather shoes to Keds and, with summer, from Keds to barefootedness; the difference under roller skates between rolled asphalt and tingling, coarse-grained concrete.

Sitting on a board across the barber chair's arm for my first haircut, hearing-feeling the clippers and smelling the bay rum.

Fall's brown walnut stains on farm boys' hands, which had to wear off because soap couldn't do the job.

Fishy cod-liver oil; cloying yeast; cold, sweet milk; all good for bones—but forget the first two!

Staying overnight twice with "Hindu" Henderson, once at his and his brother's and sister's two rooms and kitchen over the fire station, once at my house after seeing *Gorilla* at the Lyric (the less "grand"—Mother's words—of Sullivan's two movie theaters).

The night the movie at the Sherman was stopped in the middle and the house lights went up and the manager walked onto the stage to say in a strangling voice that part of a nearby mine had caved in.

The emptiness of half my school classroom's seats the day after the terrible fifty-one-death local mine explosion, each empty seat signaling that a father, an uncle, an older brother had been destroyed the night before; the week-long pall over the town as a half-dozen funerals daily rolled silently down West Washington Street toward Center Ridge Cemetery.

Seeing my name at the end of the short list of Hays and Hays law partners lettered on the firm's frosted glass door in the Sherman Building; hearing that it had been painted the day after my birth—and incidentally never questioning whether I wanted to be a lawyer until I'd started practicing years later, when it was almost too late.

A Wabash fraternity man across the street from Grandfather Thomas' house in Crawfordsville, where I was visiting with Mother, taking me for a spin in his Stutz Bearcat, the wind pressing my eyelids shut; the over-head toilet tank in the Thomas' upstairs bathroom flushed by a long pull-chain; the hollow ticking of the tall clock there at night; the story of Grandfather's only drink of whiskey years before when he was bitten on the hand by a rattlesnake as he turned over an old bucket in the garden; my falling scared but unhurt down the stairs from his warm kitchen to the dark cellar.

Sullivan elementary school teacher June Bollinger, a lovely woman, whose boyfriend we understood played semi-pro baseball. I recall the hot flush of seeing bare flesh above her rolled stockings from my desk near the front of the classroom and the blissful time she held my hand for a block as she took her class for a walk to the cemetery.

The parlor Victrola's scratchy but still nape-raising version of John Phillip Sousa's *Stars and Stripes Forever*.

Visiting the Nehi bottling plant in Depot Town with another school class and being far less awed by how they got the orange pop into the bottles than by the guts of the Depot Towner who'd climbed the nearby water tower to paint "Murph loves Mary" eighty feet in the sky.

Depot Town's dirt streets and scaling-paint houses and few tar-papered shacks and West Washington Street's affluent near distance.

"Apple rolls" at school on teachers' birthdays and the one in particular when a few of the hard cases in the back row threw the fruit they'd brought at the blackboard instead of rolling it down the isle—all in the "spirit of fun," as loyal Miss Maple recounted to Principal Hadie Sinclair in fruitless defense of them, ahead of the enema tubing.

The smell of homemade flour-and-water paste wafting up and around the elementary school room from paper doilies and scissored poster stock the week before Valentine's Day; the same smell of another week's relief maps of the Rockies, Alps and Andes inspired by an "Introduction to Geography."

The numbness of high-topped feet and hands in mittens caked with ice particles on the way home from school through snow on winter afternoons; at school recess, running and jumping onto an iced strip of sidewalk and sliding a dozen feet and going back to get in line for the next sliding.

The night when—as surely a very little boy—I laughed so hard at Buster Keaton in *The Electric House* at the Sherman Theatre that I lost control of my bowels and immediately started walking the uncomfortable two blocks home; and since it was the last night of that movie's showing I didn't get to see its end.

In maybe the fifth grade stamping Ruth Buck's name on a pencil with a machine at the corner news and soft-drink stand, and an hour later sliding it onto her desk in study hall on my way ostensibly to consult the atlas.

Raising the hinged top of my homeroom desk and stuffing into the resulting crack the end of Catherine Furgeson's pigtail as she leaned back in her seat in front of me, so it would give her head a tug when she tried to stand up; that was because I liked her, even though her penmanship, using the Palmer Method, was perfect.

Sitting at dusk in the apple tree in our backyard watching the setting sun and humming *Look for the Silver Lining*, which felt good in my ears on a summer evening.

The windowless loft of A. B. Gray's grocery store on a rainy day, playing in the big empty cardboard boxes with Maurice Lee.

Fantasizing in my bed at night about having an automobile wreck in front of Joan Crawford's house and her running out to me as I lay in the street and my being carried into her house by her butler, where she put me to bed and nursed me back to health.

Being driven in Uncle Hinkle's car—by Cy Curtis, I suppose—with him and Chuck and John T. for a long morning up to South Bend to watch Notre Dame play a home game; and sitting there in a box with a man whose photograph was the only one in Notre Dame's locker room besides Knute Rockne's: Harry Miller, All-America of about 1910, I think, an older brother of Don Miller, one of the Four Horsemen.

Thick phonograph records, played with bamboo needles on bureau-size or table-size Victrolas which had to be cranked up to run.

A wooden cigar whittled for me exactly like a real one by my paternal grandfather, John T. Hays, whose doctor had warned him to stop smoking them but who, Grandmother Hays discovered when she was helping him pack for a trip, kept a stock under a false bottom of his trunk; my earliest memory of him—and one of my very few—sitting in his tilt-back, leather armchair in his living-room down the street, folding the Sunday paper into boats and hats for Chuck and John T. and me; the snapshot somewhere of him and my maternal grandfather, Judge Albert D. Thomas of Crawfordsville, both ramrod straight and with moustaches, standing unsmilingly together like a couple of old-time frontier marshals.

The coming of spring at the same time as the coming of marbles, tops, kites, baseballs, and hoops rolled by T-ended laths.

Another elementary teacher on whom I had a crush—not as beautiful as Miss Bollinger, but pretty and nice—named Eva Shepard, sympathetically rubbing my neck as I rested my head on my crossed arms on my desk with a pretend headache so she should do that.

Ignoring an old man in an alley uptown who offered two of us friends fifty cents apiece to see us fight.

The after-school bread and butter and sugar sandwiches of Aunt Sallie Cain, sister of Dad's and Hinkle's mother, youthful seventy-year-old retired school teacher with an unquenchable love of life and of lively youngsters who interrupted her nephew's bawling out of Chuck at a Sunday dinner table, sternly, "Hinkle, don't be a martinet!"

Watching two highschool boys having a bloody fistfight in a weedy plot behind Giles' livery stable—scary, sickening, fascinating.

Ray tapping maple trees in our backyard and boiling the sap into syrup.

Brandy Dunlap telling the Mix-Mixers he had heard somebody uptown say a movie was coming called *Damn She's Good*, which turned out, on investigation by Ray, to be *Damaged Goods*—not too different, in a way.

Awakening night after night with aching legs, which Miss Fischer thought were "growing pains" and probably were, whatever those are, although this began and lasted for several months after Tony had fallen on me and Ray had picked me up and set me in the seat of an old buggy nearby until feeling returned to my legs so we could walk home.

Dad finally getting mad on one of his trips home at Mother's exaggerated frugality and stalking through the house, turning on every light in every room until it must have looked from the outside like a great, silent party; his trying patiently at first when he was home and then with some controlled irritation and finally giving up trying to persuade Mother to buy stylish dresses and abandon the high-button shoes she wore for years after the style had become extinct, even after I entered Riverdale and she visited me there.

The quiet way Dad's lips, tongue and barely audible sigh relished his morning coffee; and the house painter's reply to Dad's invitation to come in and have breakfast with him: "Done eat!"—and Ray's wincing at that.

Halloween trick-or-treating with the Mix-Mixers, which didn't involve vandalism but used up a lot of soap and shelled corn and energy on some crisp late-October nights; eating plates of ice cream on upended barrels at a Halloween party that Dave Giles' mother gave us in their basement; only minimally pestering the Strattons, because Cuppy (a sweet four-and-a-half-foot hunchback) and Mrs Stratton welcomed us and our sleds every winter to the hill back of their house. (It was in Cuppy's newly tilled front yard many years earlier, according to neighborhood legend, where Dad had sown turnip seeds and Cuppy had watched for weeks in amazement as vegetables had grown with the bluegrass he had planted.)

Ray and I listening on the parlor Victrola to a record by "The Two Black Crows" which he brought to the house one morning, and his delight in mimicking their Southern Black accents for months afterward; and listening to "Amos and Andy," Ray's favorite radio program, and his mimicking their drollery too; long talks with Ray about his past, including his boyhood on his father's farm near Terre Haute and his job at Kingan's packing plant in Indianapolis, where he killed incoming animals with sledgehammer blows between their eyes, and his religious conversion—his obviously joyful "finding Jesus"—and my questions about how it felt, whether it was like a light flashing, or suddenly seeing

148

Jesus like in stained glass at church, or hearing organ music, and his smiling and tilting his head back and saying with love, "You'll know, Pal; you'll know."

Nicknames reflecting physical characteristics: Skinny, Shorty, Sissy, Fatty, Gimpy, and nicknames reflecting other attributes: Greasy, Meat-Head, Fussy.

Parties for me by what must have been twenty-five kids at Bob Bradbury's house—a surprise one—and a few days later at Mary Dix's farm before I left for Riverdale, Ray driving Ruth Buck and me into town from Mary's (Ruth and I in the back seat by Ray's grinning arrangement) and my not letting him down, by kissing Ruth—actually, bumping teeth with her.

Chapter Sixteen

March 25, 1927

Dear Billie:

...As you know, Uncle Hinkle and Aunt Lucille are going to go to Los Angeles, California in May and take John T. and Charles... They invited you to go along and I told them you could... Too, Uncle Hinkle proposes to take you all to San Francisco so you will be there when I make my report to the General Assembly about the $15,000,000 Pension Fund for the Presbyterian ministers.

Love to all.

Affectionately, Will H. Hays

* * *

(3-27-27)

Dear Father—

... Boy I can't wait till we go to California and see Tom Mix and Bill Hart and all the rest of the movie actors. I sure will thank Uncle Hinkle for asking me to go with them on this trip ...

In the 50–50 club initiation you have to sign your name in blood. I have done this. I did it when I cut two of my fingers. Don is fine and black as ever and a little blacker. The 50–50 club motto is this— "Hang on as long as you can and then a little longer." Pretty good, eh?

Here's a hot one: A mule met a ford. Mule: What are you? Ford: An automobile, what are you? Mule: A horse—and they both laughed

I love you very dearly,

Will H. Hays, Jr.

* * *

March 29, 1927

Dear Billie:

I know you have to have long trousers for the trip to California because all the boys have them. Every time I see boys who live in New York at church, or on the street, or in the movies, they all have long trousers.

With love to all, I am

Affectionately, Father

(April 10, 1927)

Dear Father:

I would like to go to the show *Casey At The Bat* at the Sherman on Thur. and *Tin Hats* on Saturday. Please write to mother about this but do not tell her I sent this.

I love you.

Will H. Hays, Jr.

* * *

April 13, 1927.

Dear Billie:

I wired you last night to be sure to see *Casey At The Bat*, with Wallace Beery. It's a great laugh. If there is something else you want to see on your regular Friday or Saturday night you should go to that, too. You will meet Wallace Beery when you are in California . . . I am delighted with the improvement in Arithmetic, notwithstanding the fact we slipped back just a little in Reading and History. You will hit these two between the eyes this month, I know. Another fine thing is that Self-control was kept up to a G-plus . . . Nothing succeeds like success. Keep it going all the time. And when you get home in the evening, play as hard as you work in school.

Love to all.

Affectionately your Father

* * *

Miss Martha Hays,
1301 North Alabama Street
Indianapolis, Indiana.

Dear Martha:
 . . . I will appreciate it if you would plan to go down and visit at Sullivan the week end that the folks start to the Coast. I think it would be nice for you to be with Helen then so she would not miss Billie so much . . .

Affectionately, W.H.H.

* * *

May 1, 1927.

Dear Father—
 . . . I think that I will ride Tony Jr. home from California . . . I love you very, very much,

Will H. Hays

* * *

(5-16-27)

Dear Miss Fischer—
 The Chief was some train coming out here. Boy! We spent a lot of time in the observation car.
 California is wonderful . . . We saw Charles Ray making the picture called *Betty's the Lady*. We also saw Lara Laplant making, *A pair of Silk Stockings*. We are going out on "location" with the Dunken Sisters . . .
 I love you,

Bill
XXX OOO
XXX OOO

* * *

(6-12-27)

Dear Miss Fischer—

Tom Mix presented me with Tony Jr. Boy he is a keen pony! With Tony he gave me a saddel, Bridel, and rope. We are going out to Will Roger's Ranch today. How is every body at your home and all around there? . . .

I love you,

Bill

xxx   xxx   ooo   xxx   ooo

* * *

June 26, 1927.

Dear Father:

Tony got here to Sullivan Friday morning and had kicked his crate apart but was in fine shape. He is the best little pony I have ever seen. He is sure fine riding too. He is a plum good horse just as Tom Mix says. I just wrote to Mr. Mix and thanked him. Every body is fine here including Don and Tony. I hope that you feel fine after the trip. That was sure some trip.

I am going to ride Tony this afternoon out on the farm where he is kept.

I love you,

Will H. Hays, Jr.

(EDITOR'S NOTE: Later in this day, Tony, Jr. reared and fell backward on W.H.H., Jr. Ray Russell picked up the latter and set him in the buggy of the farmer who temporarily was "boarding" the pony, until feeling returned in twenty minutes or so to Bill's legs. They went then to the Hays home, without—at W.H.H., Jr.'s insistence—telling anyone about the accident. Several years later, it was a New York doctor's opinion that the animal's falling weight may have caused the compression fracture of a lumbar vertebra which became apparent during x-rays of W.H.H., Jr.'s gradually developed curvature of the spine, and that the fracture may have contributed to the curvature.)

* * *

W.H.H., Sr., Tom Mix, and W.H.H., Jr. (on his pony, Tony, Tony, Jr.) at Mix's California ranch the day of Tom's gift of the pony to his young "pardner."

The Mix-Mixers on the steps of Will Hays' Sullivan, Indiana, residence in 1927, sporting the brand-new sweaters just received from the Movie Czar. Judging by their determined expressions, the team members were geared to whip the Depot Towners, come Saturday's game in Sawdust Park. But everybody, including the townspeople, knew that the east-enders were no pushovers! W.H.H., Jr., stands third from left, front row.

WILL H. HAYS, JR.
CULVER SUMMER CAMP OF WOODCRAFT
CULVER, INDIANA
(7-11-27)

Dear Miss Fischer—
...I am acting as Top Sargent and I hope I keep it. Frazier is my tent mate again this summer and I sure am glad. How is every body? I am having a fine time here and I am going to get my Cub gold C.

I just got through writing to Mother. Gee! I can hardly wait till you come up soon. Uncle Hinkle is going to come up later too. John T. and Chuck are fine.

I love you.

xxxooo xxx ooo xxx ooo

Bill

* * *

August 29, 1927

Will H. Hays, Jr.
250 West Washington St.,
Sullivan, Indiana

Dear Bill:
I got back to New York yesterday and am working hard this morning trying to have "best tent" at my office . . . As I told you in Sullivan, sitting back on the stone by Don's house, I very, very much appreciate the fine job you did at Culver this summer.

. . . I am enclosing herewith a bond for five hundred dollars. I am not sending this to repay you for your fine work because you did that work because you wanted to . . . It means more to me than anything in the world for you to be the fine partner which you are. <u>I have absolute confidence in you</u>.

Affectionately yours, Will H. Hays, your father

(9-2-27)

Dear Father—
Today mother wouldn't give me my allowance so I came over to Uncle Hinkle's and he gave me my allowance. She wouldn't give me my

allowance last week either. Yesterday I wrote to Miss Fischer at her home in Crawfordsville[1] and sealed the letter and mother made me tear it up. And when I want to go to the show on Saturday she won't let me. and all she does all day long is to fuss—fuss—fuss. I wish you would see about it please. These are some of the very many things that happens while you are away.

                    I love you, Will H. Hays, Jr

                    * * *

(9-5-27)

Dear Miss Fischer—

        ...I am getting along terribly here without you. I wish you didn't have to leave Sullivan. Don is up at the Dr's office and boy Tony is swell. He sure has changed. It is awfull hot here today. How is Eugene and all the rest?

        Well Good-by, I love you

                    xxx   ooo   Bill

                    * * *

(9-5-27)

Dear Father—

        ...I was down to see my girl Ruth this afternoon. Boy she is some girl too. I sat with her in the show the other night.

        Don is fine.

        Well good-by

                I love you

                        Will H. Hays, Jr.

                    * * *

---

1. Helen Fischer had left the Hays' employment upon W.H.H., Jr.'s departure for Culver in July. She moved back to her hometown of Crawfordsville, Indiana, where she resided, unmarried, for the rest of her life.

September 30, 1927

> Mr. Courtland Smith
> Fox Film Corporation,
> 850 Tenth Avenue,
> New York City.

Dear Mr. Smith:

    ... You will recall that your newsreels had some beautiful shots of Tom Mix presenting the pony to Billie, entitled "The Luckiest Boy in the World." Mr. Hays had the thought that he would like to have this film. I want to place an order also with your company for one of last year's newsreel about Billie at Culver ...

> Sincerely yours,
> Julia Kelly
> Secretary to Mr. Hays.

Dear Father—

    We played one team this week and beat them 41–0. And the next day we played a team with fellows bigger than we are and got beat 12–18. Tony is fine as ever I am on the tract for a good natured airdale pup. They would die for their master. How is every thing, partner? I wish you would write mother and inforce the rule about shows Friday or Saturday. She wouldn't let me go to the show Saturday. It's all right when your there but when you go—

        I love you,

> Will H. Hays Jr.

* * *

(10-13-27)

Dear Miss Fischer—

    I sure have been having a fine time here at home but not as good a time as I would if you still lived here ... Boy we sure have a good football team if I do say it ... Brandy is our 50–50 club editor and a good one to he uses big words and uses them right at the righttime.

    Tony is fine but little old roughneck Don is in dog heaven now.

Old Don "kicked the bucket" some two weeks ago. I'm going to get a new airdale pup as soon as possible.

How is everything? Say where did you put my hunting knife? Hope you are well and happy.

I love you

xxx ooo xxx ooo xxx ooo

/III/ /lll/oooo/vvv/eee yyy/ooo/uuu

Bill

* * *

(11-6-27)

Dear Father,

We played another game and got beat but the guys we played were big and one fellow was past highschool. Boy our sweaters are dandy, two big M M's on the front and a number on the back. I am number 11, center. It is a nice day here and there was ice on the puddles of water this morning. "Sawdust Park" is what everybody calls the back lot you had sawdust spread over where we play. Tony's shed is there . . . The gang sure appreicates the donation of sweaters you made and are trying to pay you back.

Well Good-by

I love you

Will H. Hays, Jr.

HAYS & HAYS

Attorneys-at-Law

Sullivan, Ind.

November 21, 1927.

Mr. W. H. Hays, Jr.,
250 W. Washington St.
Sullivan, Indiana.

Dear Bill:

Yesterday you were to stop and see me at my house to discuss certain things I told you I wanted to talk about . . . I am still waiting for an explanation as to how it happened that you broke this engagement, which is very unusual for you . . . I wanted to talk to you about the following: (1) Swearing; (2) Writing bad stuff on Tony's barn; (3) Boys

159

trying to imitate westerners to the extent they seemingly become tough
... I wish you would stop at some early date.

Affectionately, Hinkle C Hays

* * *

(11-21-27)

Dear Father.

I went to the Wabash depaw game up in Crawfordsville yesterday. Wabash won 13–7 count. Our team is going to play our last game
Thanksgiving. When are you coming home?

... Tony is all right and I wish I could say Don or some dog is all
right too. How would a St. Banard dog be?

I love you

Will H. Hays, Jr.

* * *

November 28, 1928

Dear Bill:

I was mighty glad to hear on the telephone that you had been
elected captain of the Mix Mixers football team ... I bet you nobody on
the Mix Mixers got mad at anybody else on the team. When that
happens, a team does not win.

... St. Bernards eat as much as a couple of horses, and a lot of time
has to be spent cleaning them, and maybe it would be a big job for you
with all your other duties.

I love you.

Affectionately, Father

P.S. With further reference to the St. Bernard, if my partner
wants a St. Bernard, then a St. Bernard it shall be. However, before
finally deciding, I want you carefully to think over the several things I
said above. Also, St. Bernards do much better in a cold climate, and
because of that, just when we got your pup grown and trained and got to
loving it, then it is liable to die. Remember I love you.

* * *

12/4/17

Dear Father-

I relise that a St Banard dog is too big so I will get a collie.

I have just finished dinner over here at Uncle Hinkle's; boy its fine to have Nancy here, and say, I can hardley wait till you get here, Boy I love you and I miss you.

I sure am having a fine time lately.

Yes, I am Captian for next year.

There isn't much doing lately.

I'm all right and hope you are the same.

For Christmas if you have time I would like a Lionel electric train, if you please.

I love you

Will H Hays Jr,

161

December 7, 1927

Dear Bill:

    . . . I think you are right about the St. Bernard being too big. You are a wise kid. A collie would be much better.

    In your Sunday letter you struck out the suggestion about a Lionel Electric Train. I will be glad to hunt around and see if I can find one. You must let me know the things my partner would like to have for Christmas . . .

    I love you.

Affectionately, Father

* * *

WESTERN UNION

NDA660 48 NL. SULLIVAN IND 9 1927 DEC 10 10 AM

WILL H HAYS.
300 PARK AVE NEWYORK NY.

    YOU ARE INVITED TO M M PARTY AND MAKE IT SNAPPY GET A MOVE ON . . . THE CAKE IS WAITING AND THERE IS NO FAKING WHO WINS WE WIN OH BOY HURRY COME ON 2 TO 5 SATURDAY DEC 10 LETS GO

BILL HAYS

(12-12-27)

Dear Father—

    Boy I sure had a fine time at my birthday party yesterday. I am very sorry you couldn't come too but bissness is bissness and has to be done before pleasure . . . I do not want an electric train. I just thought I did. I dont think of any thing for Christmas now unless its a scotch collie pup . . . Well partner is there any thing I can do for you? I am going to join the scouts on Monday night and try to get my tenderfoot badge. Well I hope you are all right.

    I love you very much,

Will H. Hays, Jr.

December 21, 1927.

Dear Billie:

All right, you get a collie dog.

On Christmas day we will decide on what kind of a collie to get and where to get it . . . I believe he ought to be past the distemper age. However, this is an order on me for one collie dog, just the kind and age you want, and also this is a promise to get if for you.

I love you.

Affectionately, Father

(1-1-28)

Dear Father—

. . . As soon as I finish this letter I am going to change clothes and slide on Stratton's hill with Lee. Aunt Sally was here for dinner and talkitive as ever, I think she is just finishing dinner now if she can stop talking long enough . . . Boy I can hardly wait till the collie comes.

I love you, Will H. Hays, Jr.

* * *

January 9, 1928.

Will H. Hays, Jr.,
250 West Washington St.,
Sullivan, Indiana.

Dear Bill:

. . . I wish you were going with me to California. Didn't we have a fine time out there? . . . I haven't had a chance yet to buy the collie, but I am looking all around for it . . . Study hard, play hard and continue to be the same square shooter that you are.

I love you.

Affectionately, Father

January 25, 1928.

Mr. Hinkle C. Hays,
Sullivan, Indiana.

Dear Hinkle:

I have read with care your full letter about the incident in Sullivan in connection with kidnapping. While that turned out to be nothing more than a lot of loose talk the fact remains that a number of people over this country have been kidnapped . . . I did not go to Mexico to visit Ambassador Morrow on my way out here to Hollywood, as you know, because of that very possibility . . . The boys and you should talk to no strangers whatever. The boys should not answer anybody's request to leave school. This wave will pass and pretty soon they will be old enough to put up a pretty stiff fight if anybody starts anything.

Affectionately yours, W.H.H.

* * *

Chapter Seventeen

HINKLE Hays was an intelligent, very authoritarian, highly—really neurotically—organized man. I may have got some of my over-organization from him although I'm sure Dad had most to do with that. It's a Hays trait. Lucile also was intelligent, but she had more of a sense of humor; she was a softer person than he, not abjectly subservient to him, but aware that the easiest way to live with him was to let him have his way most of the time. They were basically a loving couple, although his characteristically limited patience obviously was strained by her at times, as it was by just about everybody in varying degrees, from mildly and seldom with Dad to harshly and frequently with the law office secretaries. Lucile's own more flexible patience was stretched pretty thin by him occasionally, if less obviously, especially when he rode Chuck and John T. and sometimes me too hard. He was less severe with me than with his sons, maybe in part because he felt more responsible for their conduct than mine—he considered them more representative of him than I was—and in part because he didn't want to offend Dad, whom he regarded with a mixture of near-reverence and perhaps unconscious envy. He used to express despair, even faint contempt, over his older brother's tolerant, forgiving nature, saying as only a half compliment that Dad was the nearest thing on earth to Jesus Christ. He smoked expensive cigars and wore tailor-made suits and custom shoes, although I was aware simply that he smoked cigars and always wore suits and kept his shoes shined. The things I remember most about dinners at his house were the formality of those compared with ours and my wanting to get back outdoors or across the street as soon as possible. As for my longer stays there, I recall having fun with John T., Chuck, cook Rachael Forbes, successive chauffeurs Cy Curtis and Louis Granger, and somewhat more sedately with Lucile, but being unrelaxed around Hinkle and a little scared of him, at least apprehensive of his temper. He had red-faced, cussing fits of anger over John T.'s and Chuck's and my giggling in bed early in the morning while he was trying to sleep, once on the train to California after Dad had left President Harding's Cabinet to become the so-called "Movie Czar," and another time when one of the Mix-Mixers yelled up at me from Hinkle's driveway when I was staying there overnight. The latter time Hinkle lurched out of bed to the window and bellowed down for the boy to get off his property and the boy, Don Howard, squinting up at him calmly, said, "Go to hell"—which was comparable to telling Napoleon that.

Hinkle shared with my dad a veneration of their mother and father; and John T. and Mary Cain Hays' two sons loved each other and I know Dad loved their half-sisters by John T.'s previous marriage, Martha and Bertha. My Aunts "Mattie" and "Bertie" always were good to me. The former never married, but the latter was Mrs. Hurley Drake. I know Hinkle loved me, for all his temper.

Chapter Eighteen

January 28, 1928.

Dear Bill:

. . . Spelling is . . . a hard nut to crack. Your grandfather Hays always used to divide his words in syllables . . . It is a great report, my pardner . . . Remember you are to: study hard and play hard, and remember about standing up straight. Don't forget this a single minute.

I love you. Father

P.S. I am delighted to see you are still G plus in self-control. That is just the most important thing of all.

* * *

HAYS & HAYS
Attorneys-at-Law
Sullivan, Ind.

February 6, 1928.

Dear Will:

Very confidentially, I had a funny, but a sweet, experience this afternoon. Bill was in a quiet conversation with my secretary. I found he wanted his allowance three weeks in advance. He told me, confidentially, that Charles had not made the Mix-Mixers team last year and, therefore, didn't get a sweater, that he wanted to give Charles a sweater as a present and he wanted to get the money tonight for their "coach" Waldo Wheeler to order a sweater.

I told him it was never wise to spend money before it was made, but the best way for him to do was to punch his ticket with his Uncle . . . Accordingly, we settled the matter by him getting the sweater money from his Uncle, so that he is still in good shape on my secretary's books, and at the same time he has learned a little lesson on not drawing in advance . . .

> Affectionately, Hinkle C. Hays

* * *

(2-16-28)

Dear Father:

> . . . Byron I think I will name my collie when he comes. Byron is a Scotch name. Any of the following are all right. Tige, Darkey, Bum, Ask-Him, Terry.
>
> I hope you come home soon. I love you <u>very much</u>.

> Will H. Hays, Jr.

* * *

February 27, 1928.

Dear Bill:

> Since I got back to New York every day and every night many times I have thought of you. How I loved the visit with you last week in Sullivan. Some of these days we are going to have a real long one, when neither of us have anything to do but play with each other . . . I am going to begin now to look around carefully for the collie and I think I will get Albert Payson Terhune on the job.
>
> Keep up the good work that you are doing. Study hard, play hard, eat lots, drink lots of milk (please do this because I want you to get fat) and be sure to go to the bathroom at least once a day.
>
> I love you.

> Affectionately, Your father

* * *

(2-29-28)

Dear Father

I had a picture of Tom Mix, Bill Hart and Hall Roach which were all autographed to me, also a lot of very pretty nature pictures, and all of the above things are thrown away by mother, torn up and burned. Just think a picture that bill Hart autographed to me, the only painting of him he sent me. A lot of my toys were thrown away too and boy I'm mad. Sir won't you please look into the matter with me please.
<u>I love you very much</u>.

Will H. Hays, Jr.

* * *

(3-4-28)

Dear Father:

. . . Gee father, you are working to hard because I saw your picture in the paper and I could tell by your eyes. If you had sense you would quit killing yourself and come home.

You are sure are fine for getting me a dog and I sure appreciate it too boy!
<u>I love you very much</u>!

Will H. Hays, Jr.

* * *

(3-5-28)

Dear Miss Fischer:

. . . I'm going to have a dog very soon, boy. Byron a collie.

The other night I went to a basket Ball game (I'm in the Scout Band) and got home at what time do you guess. At 10 minits after eleven. That aint so late for you but it was for me. Well I love you as much and better than before.

I love you

Bill

xxx   ooo   xxx   ooo and a million more

WESTERN UNION
MARCH 30, 1928

WILL HAYS JUNIOR
SULLIVAN INDIANA

NO BUILDINGS IN PARIS ARE OVER THREE STORIES HIGH STOP IT IS SPRING HERE . . . WROTE YOU A LONG LETTER FROM BOAT STOP AM AT HOTEL CRILLON . . . LOVE TO ALL

DAD

* * *

April 9, 1928

Dear Bill:
. . . I went to dinner the other night at the oldest restaurant in Paris. It has been a restaurant since 1582. They have kept a record of the number of ducks served, and the duck they gave to us was 91,604.
I love you.

Affectionately, Father

* * *

April 22, 1928

Dear Bill:
I have just talked to you on the telephone away over here in Paris and heard you just splendidly. Congratulations on being a First Class Scout. Keep up the good work, old pardner . . .
We have been here three busy weeks now and are getting along pretty well on the job we have to do, though haven't seen much of Paris yet.
I love you.

Affectionately, Father

* * *

SULLIVAN DAILY TIMES
4-19-28

JUNIOR HIGH ROLL OF HONOR

Principal Harry C. Gilmore of the Sullivan Junior High announced today the honor roll for the past six weeks' work . . . 7A . . . Bill Hays . . .

* * *

Paris, France
April 29, 1928

Dear Bill:

. . . The blossoms are all out . . . Gen. Pershing, who is in France arranging to build monuments here to the American soldiers, invited me to go with him yesterday out to the battlefield and it was a splendid experience . . . He took his maps and books and showed me all about how they fought the battle of Belleau Wood and Chateau Thierry in detail . . . Today I went to the American Church where all the Americans in Paris always attend.

I love you.

Affectionately, Father

* * *

(5-13-28)

Dear Father—

Well, I sure am glad you are back the U.S. again, that means you will be home soon; <u>hurry</u>! We were out in the woods yesterday and Junie Henderson and I killed a black-snake; Junie slammed him on the head with a brick and I stabed him with a sharp stick and then cut his tail of to take home and prove it . . . This year the scouts are having a week camping trip and I'm going, I'm a first class scout now.

Well, be home soon.

I love you

Will H. Hays, Jr.

* * *

171

May 17, 1928.

Dear Bill:

I am delighted that you are going to the camp with the Boy Scouts . . . I know that when you are there you will conduct yourself as a real Scout. You will eat enough of the right things, you will play hard, obey orders and have a fine time all around. I wish I could be with you.

I love you.

Affectionately, Father

* * *

May 23, 1928.

Dear Bill:

. . . I have told Tom Mix that you are sure coming to New York next Sunday and he is very happy about it. At the theatre last night I saw his act with Tony and it's a dandy . . . Come on you guinea pig!

I love you.

Affectionately, Father

* * *

May 31, 1928.

Dear Bill:

I am giving you herewith the report of the examination the osteopath made of you in New York yesterday because of the tenderness in the lower part of your back . . . You have a slight curve in your spine . . . I am attaching two copies of the paragraph concerning your exercises which will help correct that, one copy for you and one for Ray. I want you to begin your exercises right away.

It made me very happy to have you here on the visit.

I love you.

Affectionately, Father

* * *

(6-2-28)

Dear Miss Fischer:

...I went to N.Y. last week and I sure had a fine time to. We saw Babe Ruth play and I won a shooting match. We also saw Tom Mix...

I love you,

Bill

xxx   ooo   xxx

* * *

June 13, 1928

Dear Bill:

Here's a funny thing: Sunday I met a friend...who was starting out to put his son on a ranch in New Mexico where the boy is going to go it alone with the cowpunchers the rest of the summer...That is the same kind of a program you and I talked about after you finish the Woodcraft next year, when you'll be fourteen. The only difference is that I would stay with you out there because you have got to show me a time.

I have been getting data about prep schools. I got your letter of Sunday, suggesting that the school be about 50% "book larnin'" and 50% physical exercise . . . I am much impressed with one called Riverdale Country School and am going out there soon to see it...It just happens that Mr. W. B. Ward, the friend who was taking his boy to New Mexico, sends him to this School . . . Also if you went to Riverdale, of course, I could see you frequently.

I will see you at Culver on my way to California the first week in July.

I love you.

Affectionately, Will H. Hays

* * *

HAYS & HAYS
Attorneys-at-Law
Sullivan, Ind.

July 6, 1928.

Dear Will:

You asked me to fill out a school application blank in regard to Bill . . . and I have listed in it, as "traits to be improved," the following things: (1) A slight tendency to be stubborn . . . in an argument, if Bill finds another boy to be right, he is sometimes slow to admit it; (2) A pronounced tendency to forgetfulness . . . e.g., his hat . . . ; (3) I have only given him second rate when speaking to the ladies, etc.; (4) I have, also, given him second rate credit in studiousness. He has never had occasion to work, because he is so smart and the school work does not require it . . . While you, of course, want to tell the school the things you want to have remedied, still you must not fail to tell the boy's merits, including his most wonderful disposition, his very unusual alertness, his most mature discrimination, and his most perfect thoughtfulness of others.

Affectionately, H.C.H.

* * *

(Dictated en route to Hollywood)
July 7, 1928

Dear Hinkle:

. . . In your letters to Bill at Culver, urge him to get his tests all behind him quickly in order to show his officer and me just what a son of a gun of a kid he is.

Riverdale is really a crack school for what we want. W. B. Ward has his two boys there, Charles Evans Hughes his two grandsons, etc. It is no sense a hothouse school but a real he-boy arrangement.

Love to all.
Affectionately, W.H.H.

* * *

(Dictated en route to Hollywood)

July 7, 1928

Mrs. Will H. Hays,
College Hill,
West Wabash Avenue,
Crawfordsville, Ind.

Dear Helen:

Arriving at Culver on July fourth on my way to the coast, I found Bill seemingly well and happy. His roommate seemed a nice boy. I met the mother and father of his roommate who are very nice indeed . . .

. . . I explained to him regarding winter school that we were very anxious he "go to school" and not be "sent to school." . . . I also explained to him that Riverdale was less than an hour out of New York and that I could more or less keep an eye on him when I was in New York which would be, of course, a considerable part of the time.

. . . He said he was perfectly willing to go to a winter school. He did suggest, however, if he went to school in summer, then went to school in winter, that he wouldn't get to play very much. I suggested that the Culver arrangement was more or less of a "camp" but he replied promptly that a camp was a school, all right. I explained that he would get about three weeks vacation at Christmas, two at Easter, and a month between summer school and winter school in the fall and spring . . . and he suggested that summer after next he would either like to go to some "ranch out west" or just stay at home . . . He mostly certainly intends to go the Wabash College. That was covered fully.

I will be glad to have a letter from you further approving of this program . . . If the arrangement does not work out to the obvious best interests of Bill, it can be changed.

Affectionately, W.H.H.

* * *

(7-8-28)

Dear Father—

I just got back from Garrison parade. I am going to get my Woodcrafter Bronze "C" Saturday. I am well satisfide with the Winter Proposition.

I love you, Bill Hays

Hollywood California
July 10, 1928

Mr. Will H. Hays, Jr.,
Tent No. 2 - Division No. 1
Culver Summer Schools,
Culver, Indiana.

Dear Bill:

. . . .I have been reading some of Bill Hart's novel *Whitey and the Injun* each night. Whitey's father said to him when they started, "I don't feel sorry for you, Whitey; I feel sorry for the grizzly bears out there." The way you shot at the target in New York makes me feel like Whitey's father. When we make that ranch trip, I feel sorry for the bears, not you.

I love you.

Affectionately, Father

* * *

Tuesday
(7-23-28)

Dear Father—

Well, one more week gone and not many more to come.

I am going to (or know why) get my woodcrafter silver C very soon.

Well it won't be long til I'll be with you in New York. I wonder what my dog will do, and Ray. Gee! I hope Byron don't forget me and Ray don't quit work at our house, ever, like Miss Fischer. I received your letter about Tony coming to New York to ride on week ends. I think that would be pretty hard to do and if Tony leaves Byron will have nobody to play with.

Its about 5:00 in the morning now, I am going on an early morning bird hike in a few minutes . . . I am a corperal, I got my cheverone the other day, yesterday it was. Well good by.

I love you

Will H. Hays, Jr.

* * *

WESTERN UNION
1928 JUL 28 PM 7 42

NDC 1098 132 DL=SULLIVAN IND 28 500P

WILL H HAYS=
BLACKSTONE HOTEL CHICAGO ILL=

ON LEAVING CULVER FOR CALIFORNIA JULY FOURTH YOU WROTE ME YOU WERE AFRAID BILL WOULDN'T WORK HARD ENOUGH STOP LITTLE BILL HAS BEEN MADE CORPORAL AND WILL PROBABLY RECEIVE HIS SILVER C MONDAY NIGHT STOP THIS IS GREAT SUMMERS WORK AND WHILE HE CAN GO AHEAD WORKING ON HIS GOLD C HE SHOULD NOT BE DRIVEN TO TRY TO WIN IT THE FIRST SUMMER BECAUSE HE IS ENTITLED DURING THE REMAINING THREE WEEKS TO A LITTLE PLEASURE BY WAY OF DIVIDENDS ON THE FINE JOB HE HAS DONE SO FAR STOP JUST WANT TO RECOMMEND YOU NOT FAIL TO BE PROPERLY APPRECIATIVE OF A KID LIKE THAT STOP LOVE=

H C H.

* * *

(Dictated en route to New York)
July 29, 1928

Mr. Will H. Hays, Jr.,
Culver Summer Schools,
Culver, Indiana.

Dear Bill:
What a happiness it was for me to be with you today at Culver on my way East! I never saw you look as well. You are brown as a berry, and <u>very much straighter</u>. I am very happy about the way you are doing in your tests and that you are a corporal. I know you will get your silver C this week and I want you to have the finest kind of a time. It is a great thing to be happy in one's work . . .
I love you.

Affectionately, Father

CULVER, INDIANA
LAKE MAXINKUCKEE

August 22 ,1928

Mr. W. H. Hays,
250 W. Washington St.,
Sullivan, Indiana

My dear Mr. Hays:

This is a resume of Bill's accomplishment during the summer . . . He has won the following awards: Woodcrafter Bronze and Silver "C's", Sharpshooter Medal, Swimming "C", Culver Honor Award, five Notches, and two Merit Badges.

Bill's interest also extended into the field of athletics, taking part in track and swimming, but didn't win in the divisional competition . . . In boxing he put up an exceptionally good fight in the finals yesterday but lost.

There were five boys in the Second Division who exchanged butterflies for Silver "C" butterfly collection. The boys confessed to the misdemeanor, and their "C's" were taken away from them. As a penalty they had to win five extra points on their Silver "C" card. All of them accomplished this without the least bit of difficulty and their "C's" were returned to them. I think this taught all of the boys a real lesson not to try to use some one else's articles for themselves . . .

Yours sincerely, Orin K. Noth,
Commander, Div. II.

* * *

August 27, 1928

Dear Bill:

I am sending this letter to Sullivan because I think you will be there Wednesday. I hope to get home on next Saturday afternoon . . . If there is anything which I don't know about and which you have not had a chance to tell me, I want you to tell me about it when I get home. I want to know all about the details of everything . . .

I love you.

Affectionately, Father

Remember this—Dear Miss Fischer—I did love you, I do love you, and I'll always love you. You Pal.XXXOOO Bill [1]

* * *

(9-16-28)

Dear Father—

I sure had a fine surprise last night . . . Ray said Bob Bradbury [2] was going to the show with us so we went past for him in the car. When we got up to Bob's House, Mrs. Bradbury came out and said he wasn't quite ready and for me to come in. Well I went in and there was a bunch of girls and Boys and everything was all decorated up and a girl came up to me and handed me a gift and on the card it said "Hope you a pleasant winter" and then it gave all their names. Some surprise party!

Well Byron is in fine shape. I went to church this morning. Well Good-by.

I love you

Will H. Hays, Jr.

* * *

September 18, 1928.

Mr. Will H. Hays, Jr.,
250 W. Washington Street,
Sullivan, Indiana.

Dear Bill:

By this time you are getting ready to start here to New York. This start is not as big an adventure as when you started to school in Sullivan, nor as important as when you started to Culver, which was really the first time you went away to school, but it is another start and you are going to like it fine . . . I have written Uncle Hinkle telling him to make certain the "Mix-Mixers" feel free to continue using the back lot while the Captain of the Team is down here to get some special training . . . I am looking forward with the greatest pleasure to meeting you. I love you.

Affectionately, Father

---

1. *Entry in H.V.F.'s diary in W.H.H., Jr.'s handwriting, August 28, 1928, evidently in Crawfordsville en route from Culver to Sullivan.*
2. *A Sullivan "Mix-Mixer."*

RIVERDALE COUNTRY SCHOOL
RIVERDALE-ON-HUDSON
NEW YORK CITY.

September 27th

My dear Mr. Hays—
　　I have Billie all unpacked and he seems very happy and contented. I asked him last evening, how the first day had passed, and he replied "All right, I like it fine."

　　You asked me to let you know any thing he needed. Last evening he said, "When my Father comes out, I want to show him my table and ask him to get me a desk set like the other fellows have."

Cordially Yours, (Mrs.) Frances W. Welch[3]

* * *

September 29, 1928

Mrs. Will H. Hays,
250 W. Washington Street,
Sullivan, Indiana.

Dear Helen:
　　Bill is here at the Ritz Tower and is entirely all right . . . He is anxious, of course, to get his room decorated. I remember how homesick I was because I did not have any pictures of the folks. Bill wants a picture of you framed and I will send him one of mine. In addition he wants a kodak picture of Ray and of Byron. He also wants a kodak picture of Tony. I have written for banners of Culver and Wabash College.

Hastily, Bill

* * *

---

3. *Dorm "mother."*

October 1, 1928

Mr. Will H. Hays, Jr.
Riverdale Country School
West 252 Street & Fieldston Rd.,
New York, N.Y.

Dear Bill:

It was great fun for me to have you with me over the weekend. Enjoyed it thoroughly. I sent out to get some hooks and wire for you to hang pictures with; also I am getting an American flag.

I will probably see you during the week and on Saturday sure. I love you.

Affectionately, Father

* * *

Dear Bill:

I just have your note. You bet, old partner, I can understand. Oh boy, I've been through it and I'll never forget it. Homesickness is like the measles, everyone has to have it and get over it. Stick it out and in a few days you get interested in other things and the real pain of homesickness has passed. So, don't be discouraged and don't be ashamed of it.

You are going to like it out there soon. I am going to get out if I possibly can one evening this week in time to see the football practice, but if I don't I will see you Saturday sure and we'll have a lot of fun over the week end.

Remember, "the battle is won in the heart of the soldier" ... You have plenty of spirit, old kid, and now is the time to trot it out. Jump into football. Jump into the studies. Jump into everything . . . Theodore Roosevelt was supposed to be a very brave man, but he used to have to fight when he was a boy more to bolster up his spirit than to build his frail physical body. I am right here if needed, but you won't need me.

I love you.

Affectionately, Father

* * *

181

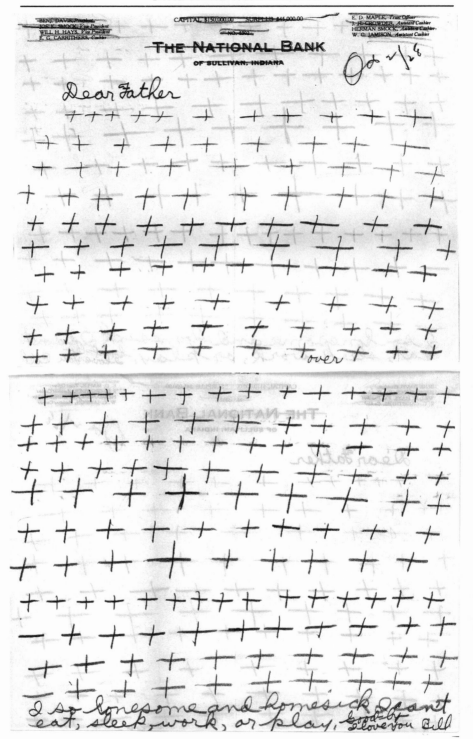

Dear Father

over

I so lonesome and homesick I can't
eat, sleep, work, or play. Good-by I love you Bill

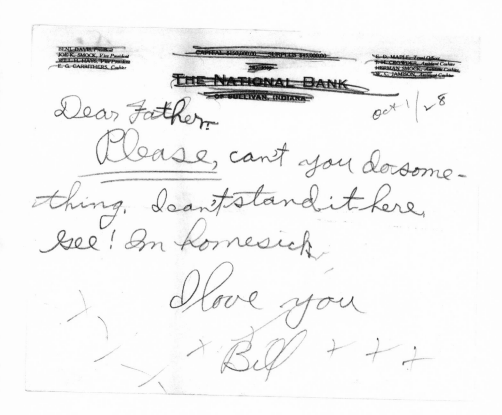

Dear Father:

Please, can't you do something. I can't stand it here, see! I'm homesick.

I love you

Bill

702 N. Court St
Sullivan Ind
Oct 3. 1928

Dear Mr. Hays:

Mrs Hays just showed me a letter which she received from Bill today, and this is what it said:

> *"Dear Mother:*
> *I am Homesick and want to come Home, please write father.*
> *I Love you, Bill."*

This is the second letter she has had from him this week. She says she is pleased that he is Home sick, and is writing him to tuff it out until she comes, at which time it may be discussed. I have no authority to write this to you, aside from the fact that I want to be of any possible service to you in helping to make Bill happy to be there with you, which is unquestionably the best place for him. I have written him two letters and am trying to encourage him to stay and be happy.

Bill Loves his Dog so much, do you suppose if we would send the Dog up there, he would be satisfied? Anything I can do along this or any other line, let me know.

yours truly, Ray Russell

* * *

October 5, 1928.

Dear Bill:

Here's a picture of a funny old fellow. He is supposed to be about a hundred years old and came up from the Arizona Indian section. I thought he might hand you a laugh. He is a little bit cross-eyed and looks like he had been eating green apples, but he is kind of a nice chap. Don't you think so?

Affectionately, J.K.[4]

---

4. *Julia Kelly, W.H.H.'s secretary.*

Chapter Nineteen

MY first weeks at Riverdale were the most traumatic of my life until then. I had not been previously, and have not been since, homesick in what must be the clinical sense of that word. I existed for a time in a depressed state characterized by unpredictable, irrepressible seizures of crying; it seemed unreal that I was where I was; I felt trapped, alone, foreign, afraid of the places and the people around me. Against my nature and despite trying I couldn't respond to the friendly words and gestures of the few boys who, to my embarrassment, noticed my illness; their very overtures seemed to increase my panic. I don't recall clearly how long this lasted, probably not as long as it seemed at the time, but I'll never forget the boys whose innate kindness caused them to try to free me from my self-exile and eventually succeeded in doing so.

Ed Hubbard and Colin Lofting and Pedro Suau and Bobby Gibson and Jack Ward—those beautiful New Yorkers (expect for beautiful Puerto Rican Pedro), with backgrounds so apparently remote from mine, will occupy for the rest of my life their special warm room in my heart. I don't know exactly why Riverdale hit me so hard this way at first; Culver hadn't done it to me, and later other changes in my life like Yale Law School and the Army and strange new jobs, including among others eight years as Crawfordsville's mayor, weren't going to depress me. Maybe it was because I knew the separation from my Sullivan childhood was to be permanent, a divorce for all time and not just another step in the progress of my existence.

Anyhow, I came out of this condition after a while. Wrenching thoughts of Ray, the Mix-Mixers, Miss Fischer, Byron, the backyard, Sawdust Park, leaf-smoking fall, Sullivan County's woods and fields, those images gradually melded with and then receded beyond (not in love but in immediate activities and people) the daily goings-on and new friends at Riverdale. I listened and learned and began to join in. I found, for instance, although they lived in a two-floor apartment on Park Avenue with their folks, a butler, maid, cook, and uniformed chauffeur, Ed Hubbard and his brother Bob simply were Manhattan versions of

Brandy Dunlap and Hindu Henderson. Their mother was as kind as she was beautiful; her second husband, withal his seat on the New York Stock Exchange and the family yacht, was friendly, and their lovely debutante daughter Virginia was as outgoing and fun-loving as Ruth Buck. Colin ("Skipper") Lofting turned out to be the son of Englishman Hugh, whose *Doctor Doolittle* had enchanted many of my boyhood hours; and Skipper's almost unnerving thirteen-year-old maturity, arising from and defending against his being very much on his own, somehow was simultaneously a stabilizer and a stimulus to adventure for the rest of us. Pedro Suau was my first friend with a foreign accent; his nature combined kindness with a volatile temper; and he required of me only that I pronounce his first name "Pethro" rather that "Peedro"—I can still hear him saying vehemently, "No, no, Beely, not *Peedro*; Pethro, Pethro!"

Bobby Gibson, whose father I think was among other things a wealthy backer of heavyweight boxer Gene Tunney, played center on Riverdale's good football team and I heard later became at least All-Ivy League and maybe All-America at Dartmouth; and he was as gentle as he was big and rugged, so often the case of course with men who don't feel they have to prove their manhood.

Jack Ward, older than I, didn't stay at Riverdale long after I got there—we overlapped just my first year—but it was his father who had brought the school to the attention of mine originally. Besides being a nice guy he probably had been clued in by his dad to help me get started. In fact, I remember on one of my earliest Sundays in New York going with Dad for brunch at the Wards' big house in Westchester County or maybe on Long Island—Dad told me Mr. Ward was head of the big company which later became Continental Baking—and sensing that the purpose of the excursion was to help me overcome my homesickness by giving me a feeling of a family tie in the area. Maybe Dad felt visiting him on week ends wasn't family enough, which should have been too bad because I lived then for Saturday noons and hated Sunday evenings. I knew everybody was being very nice; but in those early weeks that seemed perversely to accentuate my loneliness.

Dad tried to be helpful in more ways than the Ward visit. He wrote "buck-up" letters to me from his office on week days and gave me pep talks at the Ritz Tower on week ends. He told me that he'd "nearly died" of homesickness during his first weeks at Wabash College (first nights away from his family, all of a hundred miles). He even got me laughing at the story of his Christmas homecoming—the day-long train ride by way of Indianapolis, the hours of waiting there, the chugging on down the snowy land—when he figured that maybe not the Elk's band, but surely all his family and friends should be waiting for him in Sullivan. When the train screeched to its brief stop, nobody but the station agent was visible, and that man was busy with a message for the engineer. Then it dawned on Dad: the folks were going to surprise him at home! Grabbing his straw suitcase, he hurried toward the town square and his home two blocks beyond that. Reaching the square, he literally ran into Mart Farley, the blacksmith whom he'd known since childhood, and of course paused to let Mart welcome him home. Dad set down the suitcase and they shook hands; and Mart grinned at the suitcase and back at Dad and said, "Howdy, Willy. Goin' somewheres?" (Dad used to say that was his first lesson in humility.)

My adjustment to life at Riverdale never metamorphosed into affection for the school itself, although over the years there I made a good many friends, both students and faculty, and even then recognized its academic excellence. There wasn't anything bad about the school— it traded a superior education for very hard work—it simply wasn't a warm environment, at least back then. Maybe it was too far from Sullivan grade school and the Mix-Mixers. It was institutional. I suppose the students' feelings accounted at least in part for that; I think many of them felt they'd been sentenced to do time there rather than enrolled for a challenging and rewarding life-experience. Perhaps that attributes too much of my own reaction to others; maybe they look back on going there with the same affection and nostalgia with which I remember my Wabash College days. Of course, a boarding school is more confining and regimented than a college and deals with a younger, more dependent person. On the other hand Culver was confining and regimented and I don't remember it as though it were painted gray. The fact it was always summer at Culver may account for my image of it as at least somewhat brighter.

Academically it was a big jump from Sullivan grade school to Riverdale's second form; Riverdale was about a year ahead in its requirements. I flunked first-year Latin and had to take it again my second before going on to Caesar my third. Mr. Gardner, who taught both courses, kept that from being a humiliation for me by his combined toughness and patience. I almost flunked algebra but managed to scrape by it with some intensive tutoring; and my first encounter with French resulted in only a conditional passing, the condition being that I tutor in that subject with a Wabash professor the following summer in Crawfordsville and pass a second final exam before school started that fall. I finally made up the lost ground and got into the swing of German and physics and chemistry and the other courses along with everybody else. My favorite courses were two given by Mr. Clough—pronounced "Cluff"—and Mr. Thompson in literature and composition. With them I left *Tom Swift* and *Roy Blakely* behind and turned to *Ivanhoe* and *A Tale of Two Cities* and *Tess of the D'Urbervilles* and *Shadows on the Rock* and other memorable happenings; and with their exuberant proddings I let my urge to write hang out, and turned in paper after paper which they took apart and helped me reassemble. Under a couple of teachers named Callisen and Pratt I eventually even got to liking algebra and became half-way good at it. I think Mr. Callisen's success particularly, not only with me but with the rest of his class, was abetted by the combination of his flair for showmanship and his old-Navy-man requirement of discipline—he had been a submarine captain—often taking the form of a flying, skull-whopping blackboard eraser. German I took under a German giant whose authentically guttural accent was fascinating and somehow faintly confusing to hear from such a friendly person. American history was taught by a nice floorwalker-looking man who appeared to have a thing for a lady teacher. She also was nice enough, but she walked and sat around with a handkerchief pressed to her mouth as though she were stifling grief or bad breath. The man who had started the school and ran it with the imported English title "headmaster"—the teachers were "masters"—was a ruddy-cheeked, super-scoutmasterish man with an over-hearty voice and an underappreciated, or at least almost invisible, wife. I don't know what the faculty thought about him but the students, when they thought about him at all, considered him at minimum a character. He was by no means unfriendly or unapproachable; he just struck us as windy. He conducted the daily convocation in the gym, and on one of those occasions he spent the whole twenty minutes demonstrating his recommended use of only one paper towel in the students' bathroom. We held our breaths for his ideas about toilet paper, but those weren't forthcoming.

One of the masters I remember most and incidentally to whom I was very grateful lived at the end of the dorm floor on which my first year's room was located. He was a young man just out of college, clean and slender and crew-cut, and kept his maybe twenty boisterous charges at that end of the floor under reasonable control by firm but fair and understanding rule. He had his hands full doing it along with teaching some math classes, but he found time to tutor me in algebra (paid for by Dad) a couple of nights a week after the lights-out bell; and he pulled me through Mr. Callisen's course. I remember one morning after a late-night session he came into my room as I was dressing for the breakfast bell and asked me if I had looked at the bottom of my feet, and when I said I hadn't he smiled and suggested I do that. Surprisingly, because I'd taken a shower before going to bed, they were dirty. He said he'd read for an hour after our tutoring session and so had seen me in my pajamas turn the corner from the direction of my room into the main hall and walk toward the stairway to the outside. Realizing I was walking in my sleep he'd put down his book and followed me down the stairs, outdoors and along a hundred yards of asphalt driveway to the classroom building, where I'd tried unsuccessfully to open the locked door, turned around as he'd ducked behind a tree, and headed back to the dorm building—jumping over a puddle left by the earlier rain—and, with him still following, climbed the stairs to our second floor, walked down the hall to my room and got back into bed for the rest of the night. When he told me what had happened I remembered vaguely jumping over the puddle in what I thought had been a dream. I think that's the only time I've ever walked in my sleep; and he said he never had followed a sleepwalker before and was fascinated by the phenomenon. His name was Nathan Pusey and many years afterwards he served with great distinction as president of Harvard University.

Mr. Pusey and the other masters who lived on the dorm's various floors during the years I was at Riverdale probably knew more than we thought they did about the students' activities, troubles, families, and aspirations. They knew about some of those because they could see and hear and others by deduction and educated hunch. There was no trick to recognizing frustration or unhappiness or rebellion when it took such an outward form as—and each of these things happened—running away, or carrying every owned book everyday to class whether needed or not and enroute carefully not stepping on cracks, or throwing a two-hundred-dollar dental retainer into the oatmeal vat so it should surface in somebody's (hopefully the headmaster's) bowl at breakfast. Sometimes I'm sure that recognizing the nature or cause of a problem wasn't easy, which undoubtedly was why a psychiatrist interviewed each student at least once a year and was on call the rest of the time. A lot of the shenanigans sprang from boredom, or just exuberance, or their combination, such as Bobby Halsey pulling himself up and down the dumbwaiter—his father became a famous World War II Pacific-fleet admiral—or a boy named Bean galloping down the hall unreeling the fire hose, or Joe Kennedy, Jr., "frenching" a master's bed, or somebody hanging a pair of girl's panties on a horn of Mr. Callisen's wall-mounted African trophy.

Helped by my Mix-Mixers experience, I made center on one of

the school's junior varsity football teams next to guard Joe Kennedy, Jr., a fine boy who later was killed in World War II and whose younger brother became President of the United States. I'm not sure I remember young Jack, who should have been in a lower form; at those ages a few years make a great difference. Neither Bobby nor Teddy was around. After about a year they transferred to Choate, I guess because their father wanted them to end up at Harvard, and Choate was the route there. Joe Kennedy, Sr. and Dad, who were good friends, came up together from Manhattan once to watch us play football and another time to watch a baseball game in which I played first base and young Joe the outfield. Joe got some good hits and I struck out more than I got on base; I remember feeling embarrassed but not as miserable as I had back in Sullivan when I'd lost a foot-race to Chuck. Maybe it was because Dad had seen me play well in football.

Mentioning Mr. Kennedy's and Dad's friendship brings to mind an incident that happened years later, during World War II, related to me by Hernando Courtright, at the time manager and part owner (with Dad and Loretta Young and Irene Dunne and some others) of the Beverly Hills Hotel. That hotel's famous, wheeling-dealing, movie-star-littered watering hole, the Polo Lounge, ran out of Scotch whiskey and couldn't get more—a tragedy second only to the War, itself, by Hollywood standards. In desperation, Hernando appealed to teetotaling (but provenly resourceful) Will Hays for help. A week later, a truckload of Scotch was delivered to the Hotel. Hernando said he'd found out afterward that Dad simply had phoned Joseph P. Kennedy, with the magic result.

Chapter Twenty

CULVER, INDIANA
(LAKE MAXINKUCKEE)

5th October, 1928.

Mr. Will Hays,
469 Fifth Ave.
New York City.

My Dear Billy:
        In compliance with your request I asked the Sales Store to ship you a Culver banner for Billy Jr . . . Give my regards to the young scout.

                                Sincerely yours,
                                Harold C. Bays
                                Commandant

                        *   *   *

WESTERN UNION
INDIANAPOLIS IND
8 OCT 6 PM 10 40

HON WILL H HAYS=

        RITZ TOWER 465 PARK AVE AND 57TH NEWYORK NY=
WILL COME WHENEVER SUITS BEST NOTHING COUNTS
SO MUCH TO ME AS BILL BEING CONTENTED HE MUST
MAKE THE GRADE WOULD IT HELP HIM FOR ME TO STAY
NEAR HIM FOR A WHILE REMEMBER HIS WHOLE FUTURE
DEPENDS UPON THIS LETS ALL PULL TOGETHER COUNT
ON ME LOVE=

                                MARTHA

Monday—October Eighth

My dear Mr. Hays.

As soon as you left yesterday I went right in to see Billie and he told me enthusiastically of the good time he had with you—of Al Jolson and Joe Cook and "It was great." Then Jack Ward returned and I got him to go to Billie right away and so there was no chance to be lonesome.

Sincerely, Frances W. Welch

* * *

October 8, 1928

Mrs. Will H. Hays,
Sullivan, Indiana.

Dear Helen:

I was very happy to learn that you plan to arrive here in New York on Thursday and spend the next week end with Bill. I am leaving on Thursday or Friday for Cody, Wyoming, to be gone about ten days with some men on a hunting trip.

Bill said yesterday he was making a lot of friends out there and I am sure he is getting pretty well over his homesickness. He is planning already about your visit . . . I will arrange for you to have my automobile and chauffeur at the hotel whenever you want one to go out there or anywhere else . . .

With love to all,

Hastily, Bill

* * *

(10-9-28)

Dear Father—

I am writing this letter to wish you a very happy trip. Please be careful, because although you may have a fine hunter[1] he might not be able to stop a charging grizzely.

Gee, I love you, father and hope you have a wonderful time.

Well Good-by,

I love you, Bill

---

1. *Leonard Morris.*

October 10, 1928

Dear Bill:

Thanks a thousand times for your fine letter wishing me good luck on the trip . . . It is going to be a great pleasure to ride horseback each morning and see the wild game . . . I may get out to the school before I go, but I hardly think so. However, Mother will be out Saturday morning to bring you down for Saturday afternoon and Sunday with her here. I will bring you something from the West which will be interesting.

KEEP HITTING THE BALL, KID.

I love you.

Affectionately, Father

* * *

October 29th 1928

For: The Head Master, from the Assistant Headmaster.
Re: William H. Hays, Jr.; 2nd Form; age 12 years, 10 months.

. . . From the Stanford achievement test it was found that in reading William has a mental age of 16 1/2 years; in Arithmetic, twelve years, seven months; in Nature Study and Science, 14 years, 11 months; in History and Literature, 16 years, three months; in the Uses of English Grammar, 15 years, 11 months; in Spelling, 12 years, 11 months . . .

In our judgement the proper solution of his scholastic difficulty is a lightening of his schedule . . . Billy is a winsome little fellow and his attitude has from the first been the finest. He is conscientious, eager to do well, and co-operative in every way.

* * *

October 30, 1928

Dear Bill:

I called Prof. Hackett[2] this morning to find out what day this week you play your football game and he said Friday. I am going to come out Friday afternoon and see it . . . I think what we want to do Saturday is go straight from there to West Point and see the Depauw–West Point game . . . Then we will get back in time to do something Saturday night. On Sunday we will go out to the Hudson River Country Club and fly

2. *Headmaster.*

your Silver Ace model plane. A week from Saturday we will see the Army–Notre Dame game here . . .

Work hard, old pardner, and play hard.

I love you.

Affectionately, Your father

* * *

(11-1-28)

Dear Miss Fischer—

Well, everything is all right here and gee, how are you and everybody at your house? I sure wish I was home with you now. I bet your having a good time in Crawfordsville. I am all fixed here but of coarse not as happy as I would be at home or with you . . . Tell Eugene hello for me and the same to your Mother, brothes, and all the rest. Mother has been here lately. She is leaving tomorrow.

Well good-by

I love you, Bill

XXX OOO XXX OOO

* * *

December 12, 1928

Dear Bill:

I think it is fine for you to go up to Colin Lofting's for the weekend . . . I know that you and Colin will be very careful not to miss the train and will be sure to be back to school by 5:30 Sunday afternoon. With the enclosed $10 buy your railroad tickets up and back and otherwise have what you may need to spend there. What you do not spend you can keep to buy Christmas presents with or other emergencies.

Be sure to take along your sweater and a white shirt, pajamas, tooth brush, bath robe and slippers and everything you would wear here. Be sure to wear your heavy overcoat. The important thing is not to catch cold. I know you will have a fine time and I am not going to worry a bit about it because you are a fine boy and an absolutely safe partner. Give my best wishes to Colin's father . . .

I love you.

Affectionately, Father

(12-30-28)

Dear Father—

Well I have just one more week here in Sullivan, gee the vacation goes too fast, I think. How are you, I'm fine. I am going to have Junior Henderson down to stay over night Tuesday and we are going to see *The King of Kings* that night; oh boy. I went to Church this morning and this afternoon I'm going to play with Byron . . .

Well Good-by

I love you

Bill Hays

alias Will H. Hays, Jr.

* * *

Dear Bill:

I am glad you had a good vacation . . . Now that you are back in school, hit'em hard, Partner, but remember to avoid colds. You do this by not getting cold immediately after getting too hot . . . Also, be sure always to have a clean handkerchief . . .

I love you.

Affectionately, Father

* * *

Mrs. Will H. Hays,
Sullivan, Indiana.

Dear Helen:

I am leaving New York today and will be at the Beverly Hills Hotel, Beverly Hills, California. I will be gone only two or three weeks. Mattie is all set to stay here until I come back. I talked to Bill last night and he is feeling great and jumped right into his work in fine shape.

Love to all.

Hastily, Bill

* * *

RITZ TOWER
(1-13-29)

Dear Father—

Well I'm back again here in the Ritz Tower, having just finished my Sunday dinner. Everything is fine and Aunt Mattie and I are well and happy and hope you are too and having a good time.

When you come back through albuquerque N.M. would you see if you could scrape up some old Indian or cowboy relic for my room at home? Thanks. If you see Tom Mix will you tell him hello for me? Say father you know My scout master at home Mr Don Maple? well somebody shot him through the head the other day in the bank, here are the evidences: Mr. Bolinger of Shelburn came down the day he was shot to get some money from the Sullivan bank and then after the shooting dissapeared and was found later trying to committ sucied. He confessed he had forged $80,000 worth of money to run his Shelburn bank. I think Bolinger shot Mr. Maple. (This is very confidential, I mean my suspicions.) If I ever get hold of Bolinger it will sure be too bad.

Hot dog it won't be too long till you come back. Oh boy. Well good-by.

I love you

Bill Jr.

* * *

(3-6-29)

Dear Father:

Gee I have good news. Today Mr. Gardner [3] in class said, "Bill I'm not worrying about your Latin as much as some others because you are working. I don't care how rotten a boy is just as long as he is put all he has into it—(hot dog)—I wish I had more time to give you." Boy I'm going to work. You have done so much for me! Say Father, may I bring Colin home with me next week end? I hope so.

Well Good-by,

I love you (and working for you)

Bill.

* * *

Hollywood, California
April 8, 1929

Dear Bill:

Hope your spring vacation at home was a happy one and you got a good rest and ate lots, too.

---

3. *Assistant Headmaster, as well as Latin teacher.*

I just have your report cards for the last two weeks of last term ... making an average of 81 and putting you in Group 1. Hurrah! This is really fine. Now we are going good ... I bet you do not fail in a single thing any more. Keep up the good work, kid.

I love you.

Affectionately, Father

* * *

May 1, 1929

Mr. Will H. Hays, Jr.,
Riverdale Country School
Riverdale-on-Hudson
New York.

Dear Bill:

Just as with John T. and Charles, I am offering ahead of time no special reward for your performance at Culver again this coming summer, either on behalf of your father of myself, but I am just merely stating that we are going to turn you loose up there and watch what you do.

Remember to watch your bowels and teeth and take deep breaths daily. Also, do not forget your prayers each night. "Remember now thy Creator in the days of thy youth" ... I know you will do your best and if a fellow tries his best, he can do no more, and when you have done that you will find no kicks—ever—from

Your affectionate uncle and pal, who loves and trusts you more than you will ever know.

Hinkle C. Hays

* * *

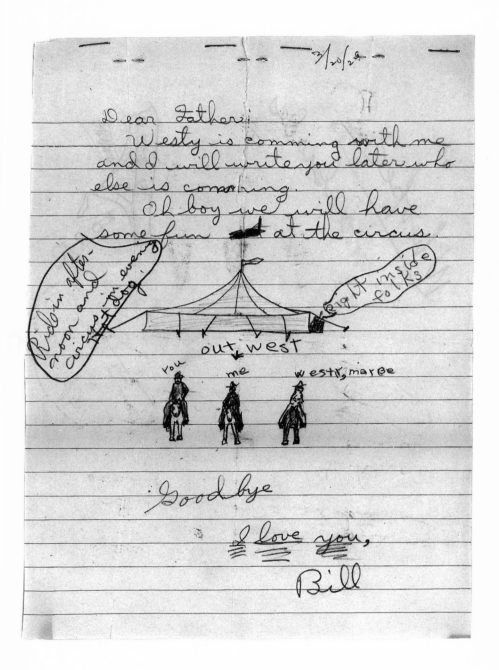

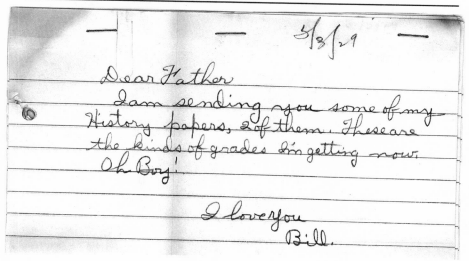

5/8/29

Dear Father

I am sending you some of my History papers, 2 of them. These are the kinds of grades I'm getting now. Oh Boy!

I love you
Bill.

Will H. Hays, czar of the motion picture industry and former chairman of the Republican National Committee and postmaster general, has sued his wife, Helen Thomas Hays (above) for divorce, charging incompatibility. The suit was filed in Sullivan, Ind., Mrs. Hays' home. The petition states they have not been living together for many years. The movie magnate asks custody of a 14-year-old son. Attorney for Mrs. Hays announced a settlement has been agreed upon and she will not contest the suit. The Hays were married in 1902.

The report of the Hays divorce as it appeared in the Breckenridge Tex Amer *on 8 May 1929.*

Chapter Twenty-one

THE finest all-around athlete at Riverdale was a kid who had the best build I've ever seen on a boy anywhere near that age; he could have been the model for Michelangelo's David. Something happened fleetingly to my emotions in relation to him which I never had felt before or have since; I developed a kind of crush on him for a couple of months one spring. I don't know whether it was hero worship or had sexual undertones or was some kind of wishful identification with a physique like his in place of my skinny one. I've read since that this isn't an unusual phenomenon of adolescence with entirely heterosexual individuals. He certainly never was aware of my fascination as I followed him around in awe from one interscholastic track meet to another; and I didn't have any conscious desire to touch his body. I simply wanted to watch his graceful, powerful actions and be recognized by him as a friend.

This David or Adonis or whoever he was certainly made a striking impression on me that spring; but so did the twenty-year-old Slavic girl whose job at the school was to change the linen on all our beds once a week. She and her high, firm breasts and sturdy, well-shaped legs pushed full-blown into my consciousness with my opening door one morning when I was lying in bed through breakfast because of a sore throat and temperature. I got up and stood in the corner while she wordlessly stripped—an exciting word under the circumstances—my bed and remade it; and when she'd left and I'd got back into bed again I lay there with a higher fever and a forgotten throat while I let my thoughts sort through every moment and motion of her recent presence. When I mentioned her later to Ed Hubbard and Bobby Gibson and some of the others they all said they had felt her full impact. In fact another of the boys said he'd felt more than that of hers but I doubted it. Her ardent breasts and legs didn't return the next year although fantasies of them did; maybe she got a better job or got married, or the headmaster heard about her.

There was a neighborhood drugstore about four blocks from the school in the otherwise residential neighborhood, called "Doc's," and some of us often walked there to buy ice-cream cones during the forty-five minutes between dinner's end and the study-hour bell. One night I didn't walk. I ran with three "townies" after me. They sometimes laid for Riverdale boys, and that night they spotted me alone. There were a few street lights along the way and I figured my best bet was to head for darkness; so I cut between two houses and then parallel to the street and raced toward Doc's across one barely discernible back yard after another with what might be called reckless abandon if that didn't imply a certain fearlessness. I was scared as hell. Luckily I lost the townies but just before I reached home base an invisible clothesline nearly tore my head off—or felt like it. My neck ached for a week. That was the last time I went to Doc's without company.

The passage of time around school was punctuated by abrupt shifts in action and location propelled by bells—not tolling bells, buzzers. And in our pajamas, or subdued sports jackets and slacks, or Rogers-Peet blazers with the Riverdale emblem, or team uniforms, we switched what we were doing and where we were doing it with the sound of buzzers ringing in our ears. The least offensive buzzer was the one marking the end of Saturday morning's eleven o'clock class and thereby of school week; the most dismal one ordered the beginning of Sunday night's two hours of study. Within a half-hour after Saturday noon all the chauffeured limousines and somewhat lesser family conveyances had departed the parking lot with their offspring, mostly in the direction of Manhattan from the Bronx suburb of Riverdale but in some cases toward Westchester County or Long Island or Connecticut. I don't recall ever having to stay at school over a weekend but I do recall thinking how grim it must have been for the very few who occasionally, for one reason or another, may have had no escape. My buddy Tom White always was waiting for me in Dad's so-called "town car," the model first of a Packard and later of a Cadillac in which the chauffeur sat outdoors. I always threw my already packed suitcase into the back seat and climbed into the uncovered front one beside Tom; and Tom always said something in his Brooklyn accent like "Jeese, Bill, how'd it go this week?" and tugged down the brim of his black chauffeur's cap and set the big car smoothly and happily into motion toward thirty hours of freedom.

When Dad was in New York on weekends, Tom drove me first to his office at 28 West 44th Street, a half-block west of Fifth Avenue. If Julia Kelly ("JK"), his secretary since Washington days who always called him "General," told me he could spend the rest of the afternoon with me, I hung around talking to her and some of the other people in the office—mostly his second fine secretary Earl Bright (whom he "loaned" later for the duration of World War II to General Eisenhower at the latter's request), his assistant Maurice McKenzie, former sports-writer Walter Trumbull, and Lamar Trotti, long afterward to become an Oscar-winning screenwriter and producer at 20th Century-Fox studio who invited me to collaborate with him on the musical movie, *You're My Everything* in 1948. (It won second in the annual Screen Writers Guild competition.)

I remember one time while waiting for Dad I watched a lady in an office across the street and one floor down take off her clothes above the waist and sit in a contraption like a dentist's chair for a half-hour while a man in a white coat did something to her breasts, which I finally decided must have been tweezing hairs from around her nipples; whatever he was doing it was pretty exotic and made me feel hot all over.

Dad's and my Saturday afternoons when he could get away included things like looking at the big-game rifles in Abercrombie & Fitch and riding horseback in Central Park, although that usually was on Sundays, and going to matinees of the circus and of the rodeo when those were in town and of Broadway shows, the latter however much more often on Saturday nights. Then we went back to his apartment—the top floor of the Ritz Tower at 57th and Park during the first several Riverdale years and 28-A of the Waldorf Towers after that—and dressed for dinner and went out to some restaurant like our favorite Le Voisin with its proprietor's great German Shepherd lying in the cloakroom and its even greater waiters and after that to the theater. Speaking of those apartments I don't recall the names of the bellman or two at the Ritz Tower but several of them at the Waldorf Towers became my friends: Kelly, Tony, Barney, Eddie; and Eddie Breslin of the main hotel lobby.

Most Broadway shows we went to were musical comedies and we always sat on the front row right over the orchestra pit eight or ten feet from the footlights, at least when just the two of us went, before Dad married Jessie Herron after his and Mother's divorce. I think Jessie liked the fifth row. I remember shows like *Sunny, Sons-o'-Guns, Kid from Spain, Scandals, Ziegfeld Follies, Red-Hot and Blue,* and people like Marilyn Miller, Jack Donahue, Eddie Cantor, Willie Howard, Bert Lahr, Bea Lillie, Ethel Merman, Will Rogers, and Bob Hope. I'll never forget Joe Cook, starring in a long-running musical revue, sitting down in the middle of his show to talk across the footlights with his fellow Indiana native Will Hays. Joe was from Evansville. I'm sure it was the only time a Broadway show has been stopped while a couple of Hoosiers jawed about their home towns. Dad introduced me to Joe as the audience and showgirls and musicians craned to watch.

I remember vividly going backstage after another show to visit with Jimmy Durante in his dressing room while he took off his makeup and changed into street clothes, so we could tell him how much we enjoyed his performance. Dad overcame my hesitation at going backstage for fear of bothering Mr. Durante or any performer by telling me he'd heard a number of them say it was a compliment which, if unpaid, might as well have been a slam. He said that to be moved to laughter or tears by an actor and not tell him so was like welching on a debt.

After those shows we always found Tom White parked at the head of the limousine line, often talking with the mounted policeman who patrolled the theatre district, and usually he drove us back to the Ritz Tower or the Waldorf but sometimes in the fall or spring we walked together to the apartment and turned out all its lights and looked over the glowing city and drank a glass of milk before going to bed—at least before Jessie became a part of Dad's life, or I should say our lives. One of those nights we stopped at the New York Times building to see the paper put to bed and talk to the editor, a Mr. Ochs I think was his name. On Sunday mornings when Dad was in town he and I went to the Madison Avenue Presbyterian Church to hear Dr. George Buttrick preach—my all-time favorite in the pulpit—and on those afternoons went horseback riding in Central Park; we kept our horses in a stable about half a block off the west side of the Park somewhere in the 70s. Dad's horse, Powder River, had been sold to him by the fine old-time actor Fred Stone; and the latter's lovely actress daughter Dorothy had sold him her mare, Alicia, when her dad had been hurt badly in an accident and they'd had to give up their own Sunday rides together.

Incidentally, Fred and Dorothy were appearing in a successful Broadway show—I believe it was called *Lightnin'*—at the time of his accident, and their and Dad's close friend, Will Rogers, came back to New York from California to substitute in the lead role for Fred until he recovered sufficiently to return to the play.

Alicia was a lot better mannered than Tony of Sullivan. She was as gentle as little Brownie of Estes Park and even better neck-reined. I had many good week-end rides on her, both on Central Park's bridle paths and in the fields around Pawling, New York, where Dad and Jessie rented an old farmhouse one fall as an occasional retreat and to which he had Powder River and Alicia trucked. (Dad's friend, Lowell Thomas, who I'm proud to say became a friend of mine, first told him about Pawling.)

If I had to name a couple of my most memorable rides in those years, I'd say one was the October Saturday evening when I rode with the cowboys in Madison Square Garden's opening parade of that year's World Championship rodeo, and another was the Sunday afternoon in the Park when Dad and I reined up at our car which Tom had parked beside the bridle path and Will James—whose famous books *Smokey* and *The Lone Cowboy* I'd read recently—stepped out of the back seat so Dad could surprise me with an introduction.

On a future day Will James was to visit my room in the city's Hospital for the Ruptured and Crippled (dismal name) and to give me the original of his oil painting of the horse Smokey which was the frontispiece of the boxed Christmas edition of his book. A third less exciting but still good ride I remember was one around Central Park's reservoir when Dad gave me his version of the classic father-to-son sex lecture; and the reason I remember it was his version's almost wistful emphasis on the beauty of physical love. I sensed he was as passionate a man sexually as in his work, and it didn't take any sophistication on my part to know he and Mother hadn't shared even a bed for a long time, and that saddened me without understanding a whole lot about those things.

Chapter Twenty-two

May 13, 1929

Dear Bill:

We had a fine "vacation" week end up in Connecticut with Colin and Ed and Bob and Westy. I hope you are all right this morning.

One of the great advantages of a vacation like that is that it enables one when he comes back to work to jump into his work with renewed vigor . . . It is pretty important now that we work awfully hard during the week so as to round up things all right for the end of the term.

I love you.

Affectionately, Father

* * *

WESTERN UNION

W H HAYS ESQ=
469 FIFTH AVE=

NO LETTER FROM BILLIE THIS WEEK HAVE HIM WRITE IMMEDIATELY . . . AM ANXIOUS ESPECIALLY ON ACCOUNT OUTING . . .

H.T.H.

* * *

WESTERN UNION

May 16, 1929

MRS. WILL H. HAYS
250 W WASHINGTON STREET
SULLIVAN INDIANA

...THEY HAD A FINE TIME AND HE IS ENTIRELY ALL RIGHT STOP WILL TELEPHONE HIM TONIGHT TO GET OFF HIS USUAL LETTER TO YOU ...

B.

* * *

(5-21-29)

Dear Father:
Sam wants me to come to his house next week end but I can't hardly do it because I got to study and also talk to you about home and Colin maybe visiting there before I go to Culver. Shall I tell Sam I have a lot of work to do and not all school work, either? (and that is true, you know: talking about Colin).
Gee Father, thanks an awfully Lot for the dandy week-end for all of Us. Gee we had fun! I saw you and your towel waving in the apartment window quite plainly when we drove away, could you see me?
Well Good-bye.
I love you

Bill

* * *

Dear Bill:
I appreciate what you say in your letter about the invitation to spend next week end with Sam. I have a plan for Sunday which will enable us to study some and do another thing ... What I refer to is going by train to New London, Connecticut, where Fred Stone will meet us with his car and drive us to his ranch, which is about eight miles out of New London. He will take us over his ranch and show us some horses which we may want to buy.
I love you.

Affectionately, Father

May 28, 1929

Dear Bill:
Speed and Flash the turtles are in fine shape . . . When I went in the other bedroom at the apartment this morning, Speedy was lying on top of the big rock in the bureau drawer, all spread out, and Flash was racing around all over the lot. I put in a little fresh water. They are both feeling fine.
See you Saturday.
I love you.
Affectionately, Father

* * *

June 15, 1929

Mr. Bill Hays,
250 West Washington St.,
Sullivan, Indiana

Dear Bill:
This time last week you and the other Peanuts, John T. and Chuck, were eating lunch on the S. S. Leviathan in New York harbor. And some lunch that was. O, Boy! . . . I am glad we went to Coney Island, too. That trip was not as instructive but it was fun anyway . . . Finally, I am glad you are having a good time at home before you go to Culver, too, and I know you will remember to get your Woodcrafter Gold "C" and swimming "C" and get all your other tests just as soon as possible . . .
I love you.
Affectionately, Father

* * *

Mrs. Will H. Hays,
250 W. Washington Street,
Sullivan, Indiana.

Dear Helen:
. . . As to Bill's failure in Latin I am not concerned as I knew he was going to. We discussed with the Master the advisability of having him tutor some and try to pass it. It was decided to let him take it again and then he will always be in the front rank of the Latin procession. He

was up in the front rank in all student activities and was liked by everybody. He has learned to study and I think will make a good record next year.

With love to all.

Hastily, W.H.H.

* * *

June 25, 1929.

Dear Will:

Pardon my frank suggestion, but while you were only in Sullivan for a few minutes last Thursday, you certainly spilled some beans . . . Young Bill understands you authorized him learning to drive Aunt's Ford, which, of course, should not be since he is three years under the legal age and so short that he cannot even see over the cowl unless he has a box underneath him. Now uncle Charles thinks he should learn also . . . I got to them very vividly what a jury could do to their fathers if any accidents happened under such law violation of thirteen year old boys driving cars.

The second thing I discussed with them was the fact that I am having Bill's and Charles' immediate officer at Culver . . . punish whichever one does not present a perfect score in partnership behavior toward the other, as I will also . . . I used you as an illustration of an ideal partner.

Affectionately, Hinkle

* * *

June 29, 1929

Mr. Bill Hays
Tent #117,
Culver Woodcraft School,
Culver, Indiana.

Dear Bill:

I have rented a farm in Pawling, N.Y. for us to spend weekends on next fall and early winter and where the horses we bought from the Stones are going to be kept . . .

Remember what I told you about hitting the Culver work between the eyes the first few weeks . . . I have no concern about the way you are going to knock the persimmons. Also enjoy it and have some fun . . .

I am going to start to California on next Tuesday and I am hoping to stop off at Culver on Wednesday.

I love you.

Affectionately, (WHH)

*   *   *

(7-1-29)

Dear Father:

Well, I'm started in Culver O.K., & am going to work hard for Gold "C" . . . Jack Cawley my tentmate, wants to beat me out for top Sargent. We are friendly enemies . . . Boy, listen father, If you don't make this California trip partly a vacation I'll Come out and make you. Please have a good time.

Good-bye

I love you

Bill

*   *   *

(dictated on the "Chief")
July 4, 1929

Dear Bill:

I was delighted with the way things looked at Culver yesterday . . . I am very certain really that you are going to knock the highest persimmon this year.

. . . I've decided to stop off tomorrow at that New Mexico ranch we talked about . . . and if you want to get me all you have to do is ask for long distance and then say you want to get me at "Vermojo Ranch in New Mexico, through Trinidad, Colorado" . . . I can have a week on horse-back and sleeping in that mountain air before I do the work that has to be done in California.

I love you.

Affectionately, Father

*   *   *

210

Hollywood, California
July 20, 1929

Dear Bill:

Maybe tonight you will get your golden "C" . . . I am glad you got knocked off the canoe by a limb on the way down the Tippecanoe and had all that fun. It doesn't hurt anybody to get knocked off the boat occasionally . . . Have a good time and do your work and I will take care of the rest.

I love you.

Affectionately, Father

* * *

(7-28-29)

Dear Father —

Lt. Noth just told me you had not heard from me lately but I don't understand it, because I wrote you every Sunday. Thank you very much for wiring me back that you are sending my Woodcrafter friend Duain McKinney and his parents a permit to go into some Studios . . . I sure hope you are having a dandy time, You had better!!! . . . Well good-bye

I love you, Bill

* * *

Dear Bill:

Congratulations!

I'm back in New York now but my thoughts are with you. I am really delighted the way that you are hitting the ball at Culver. You looked fine yesterday. You are standing much straighter. Keep it up and you will be as straight as Gene Tunney . . . Keep looking after your digestion; be sure you go to Fort Chimo once or twice every day . . . I am mighty proud of you . . . Do everything there is to do, obey the rules whatever they are, as you always do, and just laugh your head off . . .

I love you.

Affectionately, Father

(8-10-29)

Dear Father.

Well It will be over here at Culver before very long now . . . How are you? Gee I'm glad you were so happy about my Gold "C" and being top-kick. It made me happy to make you happy.

Ill be seeing you pretty soon in New York, after Crawfordsville.
Hot Dog

I love you.

Well good-bye

Bill

* * *

Mr. Ray Russell,
702 N. Court Street
Sullivan, Indiana.

Dear Ray:

To make Bill's month between Culver and Riverdale as pleasant as possible for him and for his mother, I think it would be good for you stay in Crawfordsville a while after you bring him back there from Culver. Bill will be very happy, I know, if you will do this . . . He has a great deal to do at Crawfordsville besides have fun, in that he must go to Indianapolis to see about his teeth, etc., but I have no doubt his mother can figure out his month in such a way as to let you take him down to visit Charles and John T. and Tony and Byron in Sullivan for a few days . . .

Sincerely yours, Will H. Hays

* * *

August 19, 1929

Dear Bill:

. . . I went up to see the horses that I bought of Fred Stone, Saturday, and they are great (just as you are doing at Culver!). You'll remember one horse is a little mare named Alicia, the one ridden always by Dorothy Stone, and the other a stud named Powder. Believe me,

Powder is some horse. You may get good enough to ride him before the year is out, but you would have to be awfully good . . .

I just have a letter from Ray that he surprised you camping at Turkey Run[1] a while back, and I am glad that worked out all right. I thought that would be fine for both of you.

I love you,

Affectionately, Father

* * *

August 28, 1929

Dear Bill:

I am delighted that you and Ray and Miss Fischer and Eugene have been having fun in Crawfordsville, playing horseshoes and shinny and swimming in Sugar Creek, and that you had the good visit in Sullivan . . . If it is not too cool, there is a swimming pool at the Crawfordsville Country Club that ought to be some fun . . . Perhaps there are some good movies there, too. I think they have a sound machine at one of the movies there. You will want to go to the early show so that you will not be up too late but no doubt it will be all right with mother if you leave right after the first show.

I was particularly pleased to read that you not only did not lose any weight at Culver but gained 6 pounds, up to 85. There is nothing so important to you, with football ahead of you, than gaining weight.

I love you.

Affectionately, Father

* * *

August 28th 1929.

Dear Will:

After pitching horseshoes, little Bill complained here of his back hurting . . . I want to suggest that when he comes down East you have that gone over again by the doctor who looked at him last year . . .

There are certain other observations of interest growing out of his quick visit in Sullivan. First, he is thoroughly sick of the Crawfordsville

---

1. *An Indiana State Park near Crawfordsville, on Sugar Creek, down which the Culver Woodcrafters canoed for several days.*

end of the situation, and states a strong case: two crackers and a little milk for Sunday supper; refusing to let him stay out but for a few minutes after sundown; continued criticism; having his way in nothing; and from ten to fifty others which he told me have produced a very deep and inevitable resentment . . . It will make you very happy, as it did me, to find how he loved his home here . . . He made one beautiful crack about being happy to go back to New York, which, though not complimentary to the city, embraced a father's greatest encomium. He said, "I would rather stay in Sullivan than go back to New York to school, except that I want to be with Father" . . .

Affectionately, H.C.H.

* * *

Aug. 28

Dear Mr. Hays:

Please excuse any (cuss) words that I might use in this letter in expressing myself to you about the way (our Bill,) is being treated here in Crawfordsville. If he was a boy of mine, the only time He would ever get to come to Crawfordsville would be when I was right with Him, and that would only be one Day at a time.

Mrs. H. T. Hays asked me to get Bill acquainted with the better Boys here, and to do everything I could to make it pleasant for Him, so He would get to feeling at Home here. This I agreed to do, principally the seeing to it that He had a good time, while here, which is also in line with your instructions to me in a letter of recent date. This evening when I shook Bill's Hand, and left Him pleading with his Mother to let him go to a Show and stay until it was over, and she would not, I could have cried. She said He could go, but He must be Home by 8:30 o'clock. I called to see what time the 1st show was out, and they said 9:00, or 9:15, and of course He would have to get up and leave the show by the time it was half over. As I say I left Him pleading with Her to let Him go, and told Him that I would call Him on the phone in half an hour to see if He had won the case. This I did, and He (crying) said He could not go. Mr. Hays, if Bill was an ordinary Boy, I would not feel as I do about these things, but He is such a darling Boy no sane person could help loving Him and doing things to please Him. He was crying before we arrived here in Crawfordsville on our way from Culver. I am sorry to worry you with this, but I think you should know how Bill is being treated.

Hoping that something can be done in Bill's favor in this regard, I am yours very sincerely,

Ray Russell

August 20, 1929.

Dear Will:

You suggested over the phone that you thought Ray had a wrong idea about the situation at Crawfordsville. I think you are wrong. I told Ray that he and I must keep Bill pepped up so that the young man understands that he must go through the period at Crawfordsville and so he does it with grace and with as much pleasure as possible to himself, and constant respect to his mother . . . However, this thought for you. There is nobody that thinks taking castor oil is having a good time. Accordingly, in fairness to the kid, isn't the best procedure not to try to get him to think that things are either pleasant or normal, but merely admitting those facts and showing him that his duty to his mother is to go there whenever that is required, and at all times be sweet and respectful?

. . . Let us not forget that in a very short time this boy will have reached, my dear brother, such a degree of discretion and judgment that, if he is not already there, he will interpret his own duty, as well as his own pleasures, and where he will have an inevitable amount to say, properly, as to where he spends his time, and what he does with it . . . and the great love he carries for his father, and I think for other relatives, possibly should not be allowed to become involved in the exercise of his judgment and discretion. Eventually he will not be prevented from doing about as he pleases in such matters, and the law takes cognizance of that fact and gives him exactly such rights . . . I trust I will be pardoned, for you know my love for him, which is an independent thing with which neither of his parents have to do. This little brief can accordingly be accepted from me as guardian ad litem.

Affectionately, H.C.H.

* * *

(H.V.F. Diary)
Crawfordsville,
August 31, 1929

> *Bill and Ray came to see me in afternoon. We went riding. Bill not well.*

* * *

(9-2-29)

Dear Father—

Well, I'm fine and having a good time in Crawfordsville. I hope you are too. Fine I mean. I hope very much to be able to go to the state fair this week at Indianapolis. Enclosed are some pictures I drew of the fair. I shure had a lot of fun at Sullivan the last trip. Boy, I just can't express in words how dandy the house there looks.

... Well it won't be long now till I'll be with you again, Hot Dog. Well good-bye,

I love you.

Bill

* * *

Dear Hinkle:

... I note what you say about Ray and Bill and for all of this I am far more grateful than you have any idea, for all your suggestions and help on this particular subject matter.

With love to all.

Affectionately, W.H.H.

* * *

September 3, 1929

Dear Ray:

I appreciate your frank letter about Bill's situation in Crawfordsville. I realize the difficulties, of course. Your job and mine is to make it just as happy for him there, or wherever he is, as we can. I know you will work at this just as I do . . . I appreciate your being up at

Crawfordsville with him and know that will contribute much to his pleasure.

With best wishes always, I am

Sincerely yours, Will H. Hays

* * *

September 7, 1929

Dear Bill:

....I wish you would talk to Mother and write me right away the things you have been inoculated against, and when, and whether or not they took, so I can fill out a blank here for school. Also, let me know what things you need to wear that have been worn out. Also are you getting the "Bill Hays" markers for your clothes there, or shall I order them here at Rogers-Peet?

I love you.

Affectionately, Father

* * *

WESTERN UNION
Sep 7 1929

HON WILL H HAYS=
469 5 AVE=

MRS H INSISTS THAT I GO HOME TODAY AND RE-TURN SEPT SIXTEENTH BILL INSISTS THAT I STAY HERE WHAT SHALL I DO=

RAY RUSSELL.

* * *

MARTHA HAYS
1141 NORTH DELAWARE STREET
INDIANAPOLIS, INDIANA

Thursday
(9-12-29)

Dear Will:

. . . You know Bill has only had three days of real vacation (that was while he was in Sullivan). It is only reasonable to believe he should have some real rest. I wish you would find a good sanatorium and put him in for a week's rest cure before school . . . This will prevent any trouble this winter. That is that.

Love—Martha

September 17, 1929

Dear Bill:

There is going to be a fine chance this fall to do some good target and pheasant shooting on the farm where we are going to ride horseback on Saturdays. I therefore think it would be a good thing for you to bring your guns with you on the train when you and Uncle come on. You can assure your mother that there will be absolutely no chance for you to get shot or any boys to get shot . . . Any old bug ought to hit a pheasant; certainly an "Expert Marksman from Culver" ought to be able to.

On next Sunday when you get in here and you can have a big, fat vegetable dinner that night. We may make Uncle Hinkle eat milk toast.

I love you.

Affectionately, Father

* * *

Chapter Twenty-three

WILL Hays' life didn't seem to alternate between ups and downs, happy and sad times, good and bad ones, but to form a continuum of those. For every upbeat a downbeat chimed in. I really didn't give that thought at the time; but in retrospect, I'm sure it must have occurred to him, at least now and then.

He'd made a brilliant success of a United States presidential campaign—withal a less than brilliant winner—and had been rewarded with a job he didn't really like. He'd played an eminently constructive role as the nation's postal chief, but he'd wanted to be a well-paid industry executive. He'd wanted to be happily married, but he wasn't— the first time, at least. He'd resigned as United States Postmaster General to accept one of America's highest paid jobs—president of the big motion picture companies' brand-new self-regulatory association— and found himself so regulated by its uniquely frustrating demands that he almost had no other life, not to mention family.

The movies had got themselves into trouble with the public over what was deemed films' obscenity and over personal scandals of some of the biggest stars; and state legislatures and Congress were threatening to pass censorship laws which in effect should have required the making of forty-eight different versions of every film, ruining the business. Taking their cue from the professional baseball clubs' hiring of a nationally respected federal judge as "Baseball Czar"—Kenesaw Mountain Landis—after the "Black Sox Scandal" to make them police themselves, the movie companies formed a production and distribution association and hired the nationally respected and incidentally persuasive cabinet member as the policeman of their self-regulation. The press gave all this tremendous hullabaloo, dubbing Dad the "Movie Czar" and ascribing to him absolute power to allow or disallow the production or exhibition of any and all movies. Actually, this power later was delegated by him to an assistant named Joe Breen. Most of the publicity was friendly, but some of it then and later was understandably fearful, and ranged from thoughtful concern about his power to personal abuse of him as a blue-nosed censor of American morals, not referring to the fact his job was to prevent official censorship and to represent the industry in all areas of its companies' common, as distinguished from individual, concerns.

Certainly the "self-regulation" aspect of his job sometimes frustrated him, as when the movie moguls, who'd hired him partly to make them toe the decency line, would try their damndest to step over it past him. Tom White told me that once when Tom was driving him to his New York apartment after an especially grueling day, Dad suddenly gusted, "'Cleavage,' 'cleavage,' I'm sick of fighting 'cleavage!' I'd like to wade through a forty-acre field of breasts!" But he laughed when Tom offered, "Say the word, General, and I'll join you."

One of the great many common concerns of the so-called "Motion Picture Producers and Distributors of America" beyond self-regulation of films' contents was the remittance to producers of their shares of boxoffice receipts. This was sometimes difficult, especially from overseas exhibitors. For instance, just prior to World War II, Italian dictator Mussolini, deciding that Italy should have its own exclusive movie industry, ordered his sham legislature to pass a law prohibiting the importation of American movies and impounding millions of dollars owed to American producers. Dad went to Rome to talk "Il Duce" out of that ploy. In the dictator's vaulted, sentried office, a ten-minute audience arranged by the United States ambassador (who acted as interpreter) stretched into a forty-five minute dialogue, at the end of which Mussolini roared something at a hovering aide, who scurried from the room. As the ambassador whispered to Dad, "I can't believe it!" the seemingly towering, barrel-chested, squared-jawed dictator arose from his raised desk, stepped in his elevated boots around it and down to his five-feet, eight-inches of height to shake Dad's hand in parting. Outdoors a few minutes later, the ambassador told Dad in amazement that Il Duce had ordered his aide to order the legislature to "Repeal the motion picture law!" (In telling this story, Dad added, "Wouldn't a President envy such clout with Congress!")

Whatever whirled about father in his daily work—and I couldn't help but be aware that it was intense and grinding—my intimate perception of him was of a kind, sensitive, humorous, principled man who loved me. He had a whimsical sense of fun—for instance carrying oranges we'd bought one night into the Waldorf Towers' entrance one at a time from a taxi, as theater returnees watched and laughed—and he loved the company of chic, pretty women and, when he (rarely) got a chance, to dance and flirt with them and perhaps make love to a very select one or two of them (although this I didn't think about then); and women loved to be with him, as men did.

Among his infrequent relaxations was poker, usually for modest amounts, mostly penny ante, played with friends. The stakes weren't the point, it was the fun. He enjoyed the game's strategy and tactics and especially its psychological aspects. One summer evening when I was vacationing from college at his Hidden Valley ranch, I luckily and very silently got to watch a game between him and some guests—as I recall, Walter Chrysler, Roy Howard, Albert Lasker, and Lowell Thomas. That happening stays in my memory for a reason besides the players. After the company left, Dad and I talked about the game, which had got a bit steep from my teenage perspective, as I mentioned to him. And he said very solemnly to me, "Remember this, Bill Hays: never bet more than you can afford to lose, but just as importantly, never bet more than the other fellow can afford to lose."

He told me one time why he'd never taken a drink. As a boy, he'd loved and lost to alcohol an uncle, and he was afraid the weakness might be buried in him and come back to life. Although he was a teetotaler, he enjoyed parties. "Sure," a longtime friend of his said "he doesn't touch the stuff, but he's always the liveliest, drunkest one at any party—and he dances circles around the rest of us." Dad never made mean fun of drunks, but he told some amusing stories about drinkers. One was about the Welsh coal miner in Sullivan years ago who lost a beer drinking contest—he'd downed nine steins to the winner's eleven—and couldn't understand why, he told bettors, because he'd drunk twelve of them an hour earlier for practice. And there was the time when Dad was making a political speaking tour of Sullivan County, and at each crossroad where the auto caravan was met by an added contingent a jug was passed around. He said that by the hour of his final evening speech on the porch of general store near a coal mine tipple, the county chairman, who was to introduce him, was barely able to stand. That gentleman did manage, however, using the porch railing, to pull himself upright; and staring out at the crowd, he bellowed, "You folks all know Bill, here!" And then, looking down at Dad while waving toward the crowd, he added at the top of his lungs, "And they all know you! So speak to the folks, Bill, goddam 'em, speak to 'em!" That was the most unique introduction of his career, Dad recalled; but it wasn't his only recollection of the event. Near the end of his speech, as he was hitting hard on Republican prosperity, the mine's whistle routinely blasted, signaling work the next day for the miners and incidentally drowning out his voice. Being an old hand at ad-libbing, he shouted as soon as the whistle stopped, "There—that tells my story for me!" And from the rear of the crowd, a voice shouted back, "How's that, Bill, all wind?"

I heard Dad say many times that it wasn't enough in this world to live and let live, you have to live and help live. And he drew a distinction between understanding and excusing, saying you can understand why somebody does something wrong without excusing it.

He "put great store," as Hoosiers phrase it, in compassion. Once he described Abraham Lincoln in a speech as a man "whom sorrow made merciful, and mercy made immortal." I recall his recalling to me, on an occasion I'll never forget, the sometimes forgotten compassion of Herbert Hoover. I had come to New York for a few days' visit during a Wabash College break. Riding with Tom White from the station to the Waldorf, I suddenly was seized by an urgent need to relieve my bladder. I rushed into the Towers apartment, dropped my suitcase, headed for the nearest bathroom, and burst into it—to find the ex-president sitting on the toilet. Feeling awful, I said, "Sorry, Mr. President," and backed out, shutting the door again, and staggered along the hall to the living room, where Dad was waiting. It seemed they'd been talking and Dad had invited Mr. Hoover to stay for dinner—he had an apartment in the Towers, too—and I was so embarrassed that, in the flurry of our greetings, I didn't manage to blurt my ignominy before the dinner guest walked down the hall and into the room. Dad said, "Mr. President, this is my son, Bill. You kindly had his picture taken with you and your dog a few years ago in the White House Rose Garden." As we shook hands, that fine gentleman looked me right in the eye, with a faint twinkle in his, and said, "Yes—we've met, indeed," and he turned the conversation in what was for me a less nerve-wracking direction. I escaped for a few minutes to the bathroom, to compose myself in a couple of respects. Later, when I told Dad what had happened, he said, "Part of Herbert Hoover's great character is his compassion."

Chapter Twenty–four

October 14, 1929

Dear Bill:

What a fine time we had this week end! It makes me very happy to have these visits with you. It was fine having Colin and Ed, too. In a day or two I will know what I can do about next week end. I have to be here in New York Friday night for a dinner for Winston Churchill, the English statesman, who is over here, and on Sunday night I have to go out to Detroit for the 50th anniversary of Edison's invention of the incandescent light. Mr. Henry Ford is having a celebration out there. This will not interfere, however, with my coming out and getting you on Saturday and going out and spending the afternoon and Sunday . . .

I am delighted with the way you are hammering on your studies; keep it up. Please also arrange to get more milk. I don't think you are getting enough sleep and I know that you are not getting enough rich milk.

I love you.

Affectionately, Father

* * *

October 20, 1929

Dear Bill:

I just have your report for the period ending October 18th . . .

The English and Latin, of course are great. We have a little problem ahead on the French and a big problem ahead of you and me on Mathematics and Civics. I wish you would think it over and when we are next together let's discuss earnestly what you and I have to do to lick it.

I love you.

Affectionately, Father

* * *

November 2, 1929

Mrs. Thomas Hays,
Crawfordsville, Indiana

Dear Helen:
    . . . Bill was in at the dentist's on Thursday afternoon and I bought him four suits of medium weight underwear, part wool and part cotton, and he did not think that was so good . . .
    I spoke to him about Christmas Day and he is perfectly happy to be with you that day. He can go down the next day and visit with Charles and John T. and then come back to Crawfordsville and spend sometime with you before you bring him back East . . . Thanks for your cooperation.
    With best wishes always, I am

Sincerely, W.H.H.

* * *

November 12, 1929.

Dear Will:
    . . . Regarding your wanting to take Bill out west to a ranch for a real vacation together next summer, and the possible trouble which might arise from Helen, we should together be able to work that out, since it would not involve a trip across the water, against which there were some distinct embargoes impressed by the divorce judge last June . . . I do not think that after Bill is in Wabash College and Crawfordsville in the winters, when the whole summers naturally go to you, you will find any difficulty in arranging a trip with him abroad . . .

Affectionately, Hinkle

* * *

November 12, 1929.

Dear Bill:
    In connection with my birthday wire from your Dad, one of the things that tickled me most is that last Saturday afternoon he saw you play center for your team throughout the whole game against some other

school, and then he tells me of the fine rides and visits you had over the week-end. Oh, boy!

Business is very bad out here now; there has been an awful panic on Wall Street, in New York, as you probably know . . . In some cases the hard time the whole country is going through now is as bad on the minds on men as the World War was on the bodies of men, and both experiences sometimes affect their hearts and morals. Now with all this uncertainty, I cannot help but think that the happiest thing in my life today is the relation that exists between the five of us together . . . I want to tell you for the ten millionth time how much I love you and how much you mean to all of us here. When you have time, write me. I want the lowdown, because remember no "bull" is ever slung between partners . . .

Affectionately your pal, Hinkle C. Hays
CC: WHH

* * *

(11-17-29)

Dear Miss Fischer:

Well, how's everything, gee I can hardly wait until I see you Christmas, Oh boy! We'll surely get together for a meal or two and some good times then!

I'm located fine and am getting along pretty well in my five subjects, Latin, French, Algebra, English and Civics and soon General Science is to replace the civics as it is only a half year subject . . . I play center on the 4th team and have had no bones broken yet. We play a lot of games with outside teams and have had hard luck in losing most of them. By the way, I hear Wabash is not so good this year; what is the matter?

Well I expect I had better sign off. (That reminds me; have you been hearing *Amos & Andy* any lately.)

Good-bye

I love you, Bill.
!Please Write!
XXX *** OOO

* * *

December 2, 1929

Dear Bill:

It was a fine week-end we had.

. . . I don't think I ever saw you look as well. But I still think, however, you'd do better with the football and the hockey and otherwise if you had more weight. There's just one good way to get weight that's easy—that is to drink milk. Would it be possible to have it delivered to your room? . . .

Congratulations on the splendid improvement in your grades in November. I am delighted with the way you are licking the situation. I know you will keep it up.

I love you.

Affectionately, Father

* * *

WESTERN UNION
1929 DEC 6

W H HAYS=
469 FIFTH AVE=
NEW YORK

NO LETTER BILLIE THIS WEEK GREATLY WORRIED LET ME KNOW=

H.T.H.

* * *

WESTERN UNION
DECEMBER 7, 1929

MRS. THOMAS HAYS
414 WEST WABASH AVENUE,
CRAWFORDSVILLE, INDIANA.

BILL ABSOLUTELY ALL RIGHT WILL FIND OUT TODAY WHAT HAPPENED TO HIS LETTER

W.H.H.

* * *

WESTERN UNION
DECEMBER 11, 1929

BILL HAYS
RIVERDALE COUNTRY SCHOOL
WEST 252D ST. AND FIELDSTON ROAD
NEW YORK CITY

     DEAR BILL MERRY CHRISTMAS ON YOUR BIRTH-
DAY I LOVE YOU

W.H.H.

* * *

Mrs. Helen T. Hays
Crawfordsville, Indiana

Dear Helen:

     I am hoping to get away from New York on Thursday and will be at Beverly Hills Hotel, Beverly Hills, California . . . You will find that Bill wants to ice-skate on Saturday afternoons while you are here. He belongs to a skating club at Madison Square Garden to which Thomas takes him and always stays with him so there is no danger. When Thomas brings him in from school he will take him right to your hotel room and he can lunch with you and then Thomas can take him to do his skating and bring him back to you.

Hastily, W.H.H.

* * *

(1-12-30)

Dear Miss Fischer:

     I'm sorry I have not written you before. I'm here in Manhattan at the Pennsylvania Hotel waiting to go to school and last night I saw Jack Donahue in *Sons o' Guns*, and boy it was good (musical comedy). How are you and every body else at home? I'm O.K. Tell Eugene and all the rest hello. Mother is here in the room.

     Hurry up and write!!!

Well good-bye

I love you, Bill.

XXX OOO XXX OOO XXX OOO

WESTERN UNION
DAY LETTER
FEBRUARY 1, 1930

MISS JULIA KELLY,
24 FIFTH AVENUE,
NEW YORK CITY.

PLEASE READ TO BILL THIS TELEGRAM QUOTE DEAR PARDNER HAVE LEARNED THAT YOU HAD SCRAP WITH A SNOW BALL STOP WHO IS HE? I DON'T KNOW ANY PRIZE FIGHTER NAMED SNOWBALL STOP ANYWAY I AM COUNTING ON YOU KEEPING ME ADVISED AND DOING EVERYTHING NECESSARY TO MAKE CERTAIN THAT THERE ARE NO BAD AFTER EFFECTS STOP KNOW YOU WILL TAKE NO CHANCES WITH YOUR EYE STOP HAPPY THAT YOU ARE LICKING YOUR FRENCH STOP LOVE STOP UNQUOTE REGARDS.

W.H.H.

* * *

(2-19-30)

Dear Father:

Well, I've sure have some good news for you—the day after you called me on the phone we had a math test & I passed. Also we had a French test & I passed that. Whoopee!! <u>Now stop worrying!</u>

I just took Mother to a dog show up stairs here in the Pennsylvania Hotel. (Sealyham terriers). Enclosed is a picture of one. Also I have enclosed two of my drawings.

Well how are you. I'm O.K. Last night, Mother, Sam[1] & I went to see Lon Chaney in the *Phantom of the Opera*. Whew, what a picture.

I guess this is all.

Good-bye, I love you

Bill

* * *

---

1. *A Riverdale friend who lived in Manhattan.*

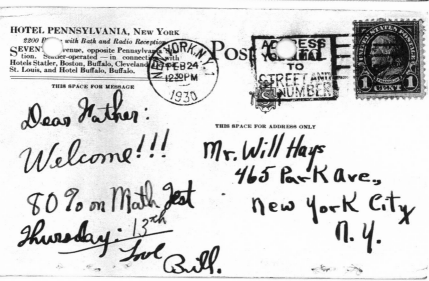

RIVERDALE COUNTRY SCHOOL
RIVERDALE-ON-HUDSON
NEW YORK CITY

Frank S. Hackett
Head Master
February 20th 1930

Mr. Will H Hays
469 Fifth Avenue
New York City

Dear Mr. Hays,

Your suggestion as to his tutoring in Mathematics had been anticipated by us several weeks ago, and I had talked with Mr. Pratt about it. His reply was that Bill strenuously objected on the ground that he knew he could work the thing out himself. Upon receipt of your letter we went into the matter again, and the categorical answer was, "Bill does not want to be tutored." Could you as a father want any spirit finer than that?

Faithfully, Frank S. Hackett

* * *

Chapter Twenty–five

MY father's love, almost reverence, for his parents was as profound as anyone's I've ever known. And his emotional and spiritual attachment to Sullivan, indeed to Indiana as a whole, was similarly deep and abiding. He often said and was quoted as saying that the values and perspectives of his Hoosier upbringing never let him go—or let him down.

When Dad was in New York and I was a Riverdalian, I spent most weekends with him alone or later with him and his second wife, Jessie, but occasionally I brought one or two of my classmates down from school with me.

One such weekend—pre-Jessie—when Dad had to work Saturday afternoon, Tom took Skipper Lofting and Ed Hubbard and me to a hardware store on Lexington Avenue where we bought a roll of electrical cord and some switches and a small panel on which to fasten the switches. Then we took all this equipment back to the Ritz Tower and spent the afternoon wiring the apartment so Dad could operate the lights in all half-dozen rooms from the panel fastened to his bedside table. During the previous week we had learned about electric circuitry in our physics class and we were damn proud of the system we installed for him. When he got to the apartment about six o'clock his reaction was not exactly one of pride; I'd say it was more of restrained appreciation tinged with apprehension. He tried it however and when it didn't explode or set fire to the apartment he accepted our gift graciously. A couple of week ends later the system had disappeared and he said one of the housemaids evidently had reported it to the Tower manager who had urged its dismantling for the sake of the general good and incidentally insurance rates.

Another week end Tom drove Dad and Skipper Lofting and Ed and Bob Hubbard and a boy called Westy and me up to Skipper's dad's Connecticut farm, which I had visited once before. Skipper had invited all of us this time, thinking his father was in England. Dad stayed with Tom at the inn of a nearby village on the pretense of having some business in the vicinity but actually I'm sure to be nearby in case we needed help. Skipper invited him to stay at the farmhouse with us but he said he didn't want to "cramp your style," and had other things of importance to do and would pick us up with Tom the next afternoon for the drive back to school.

When Dad and Tom had let us out and driven away we discovered that Mr. Lofting was in residence after all and indeed not alone; with him was a lovely young lady who, to Skipper's added surprise, had become Mr. Lofting's wife earlier in the day. (I don't remember Skipper ever talking about his mother and indeed very little about his father.) Making the gentlemanly best of what must have been a disconcerting— to say the least—situation for him, Skipper's dad invited us all to join him and his bride at their wedding supper at about nine o'clock that evening. The stunning and probably stunned lady had very little to say throughout the next twenty-four hours, and we had enough sense to make ourselves scarce around the house except to swallow through the bridal supper and sleep quietly in the beds of the one big guestroom. The turn of events didn't at all "cramp our style" because what we had come up there for was to explore the woods and fields and ride the polo ponies in the Loftings' barn which were looked after by a neighboring farmer. We did all those things with gusto and I'm sure noise.

A touching moment occurred at that wedding supper in which I couldn't participate fully because I'd promised Dad a few years previously not to drink: Skipper proposed a really poetic toast to his new stepmother which made her smile and brought moisture briefly to his father's eyes. I touched my glass to my lips but didn't swallow the wine. Not that I didn't wish the newlyweds well. I most certainly did, you can believe that. I had loved Dr. Doolittle, and felt that he was there.

When Dad and Jessie later married I was as happy for me as for Dad, although Jessie and I hadn't had a chance really to get acquainted. She also was a pretty lady and I wrote her saying I loved her. I think that embarrassed her because she never mentioned it. In fact, over the next few years it gradually dawned on me that I wasn't the end of time as far as she was concerned. Among other things maybe I was too unreserved in my regard for people like Ray and Tom and not serious enough about the way I dressed. And after all, she hadn't married me, although circumstantially I went with the bargain, which I guess became a lot of the trouble. In the early days of their marriage he probably talked too much about me in her presence rather than, as later, very little. I can understand how I must have been a pain in the ass to her many times, as well as therefore unintentionally a catalyst of pain to Dad—I'm very sorry to say. But none of these particular horizon clouds cast shadows over my years at Riverdale.

A little at a time, Tom began to teach me to drive, first letting me move the car slowly forward and back in the Riverdale parking lot before he took the wheel for the drive down to the apartment. One Saturday noon he let me take over for several blocks before we crossed the Harlem River from the Bronx into Manhattan. They were the wrong blocks, because a motorcycle officer pulled us over to the curb. While I was sliding with a tight stomach from under the wheel to the other side of the front seat, Tom got out and walked to the rear of the car with the officer; they talked for a couple of minutes and then Tom came back and climbed under the wheel and the officer got on his motorcycle and rode away in his direction and we in ours. I asked Tom how much the fine was apt to be and he said "I already paid it—couple of bucks." That was my first exposure to what neither one of them should have called bribery, simply mutual accommodation. Tom knew his way around New York better than anyone I've ever encountered.

One Saturday afternoon when I was alone in the apartment I was rummaging through a closet looking for a box into which I could put some gravel and a miniature turtle that Tom and I had bought at a pet shop. I didn't find a box—the turtle ended up that post-Mother, pre-Jessie day in a guestroom bureau drawer—but I did come across a bottle of champagne and a negligee, and I was happy for Dad.

When Will Hays was not in New York for the week end—infrequently, except during his month-long quarterly sojourns in Hollywood, where most of the people outside the industry mistakenly thought he spent all of his time—I usually was invited to stay with the Hubbards. Those times, Tom drove Ed and Bob and me downtown after Saturday morning classes and either Tom or the Hubbards' chauffeur took us back to school for its dreary Sunday evening meal and study hours. Occasionally Skipper Lofting came with us or we met him somewhere in Manhattan for a movie or ice skating or shooting a .22 at ducks in a Broadway arcade. I don't know whether or not Mr. Lofting had an apartment in the City. Sometimes Ed's mother and stepfather ate Saturday evening dinner with us at their apartment, but more often they went out for the evening. Almost always their sister, Ginny, had a dinner-theater-dancing date, and we usually didn't see her until Sunday brunch. Late one night while she was still out and before we finally turned in, we "frenched" her bed, meaning we pulled its bottom sheet from its foot upward and folded it over the top edge of the blanket to make a kind of linen envelope which should let her slip only half-way down; and when she came home wearily ready for a good sleep and found our handiwork she went to her bathroom and came back with a pitcher of water and poured it over us in our beds, starting our Sunday off earlier than usual.

Another weekend when we got to Ed's house we found a Koala bear in the apartment; one of Ginny's boyfriends had given it to her. It lived a happy if short life as part of the household. It ate well and got plenty of exercise climbing the drapes and bannister and leaving signs of its passage throughout the duplex. It made Ed and Bob and Virginia happy with its antics. Their pleasant step-father kept his own counsel in the matter, saying only to "keep that damn animal out of the dining room while I'm eating." Their mother simply sighed and went shopping more often than usual. The only people who evidenced unequivocal relief when the bear drowned in a toilet after a week's residence were the butler, the maid and the cook.

Although the doorman of the Hubbards' apartment building wasn't involved with a Koala bear he did have another kind of cross to bear. His problem—I suppose more accurately one of his problems, if he had several like everyone else—was his appeal as a target of water bombs dropped from Ed's and Bob's and Virginia's windows facing Park Avenue. It didn't take him long to discover the shelter of the fabric canopy stretching across the sidewalk from the doorway to the curb; but at the same time he couldn't spot the enemy from under there and since theirs wasn't the only family in the building with kids he had to content himself with looking forward to the armistices that began Sunday evenings.

The only unhappy memory I have of weekends with Ed and Bob and Virginia was of the winter night when their family chauffeur was driving their parents and the boys and me to the theater, and at a stoplight a distinguished-looking man with a battered Homburg and second-hand army coat knocked on a side window of the limousine and asked for a quarter. That was my own most painful moment of the Great Depression then torturing the nation. Before and after that I saw hundreds of men shuffling in Salvation Army bread and soup lines and standing beside boxes of apples given to them by the city to sell for a nickel; but those dramas were more remote, like newsreel pictures of the Oklahoma Dust Bowl, instead of two feet away in the face of a living man with dead eyes.

On a couple of week ends when Dad was in California I stayed with another classmate and his mother, one time at her small west-side apartment and the other at her small farm in Connecticut. I don't recall a father-husband being there. They were good people, obviously less affluent than most Riverdale families, and both the apartment and the farmhouse felt to me more like Sullivan than anyplace I'd been in the East. When my buddy and I arrived at his home the first weekend and he introduced me to his mother, I liked her immediately but I had the feeling I made her uncomfortable; I thought maybe she was shy but I also sensed in her warm welcoming words a kind of defensiveness, certainly not at all apologetic but somehow apprehensive.

It was not the first time I'd felt that people saw me as a shadow of my father's celebrity rather than as myself. Back in Sullivan I'd overheard a few adults—interestingly never kids—make comments ranging from "Probably stuck-up" to "Common as an old shoe, ain't he?" And of course things like the Estes Park ladies' flurry over the *Cosmopolitan* editorial and one or two Culver lieutenants' fake buddy-buddiness toward me when Dad visited there hadn't been lost on me. But this business of making someone, especially as sweet as my classmate's mother, ill at ease just—in Ray's words—"wouldn't get it." I started feeling self-conscious myself and I've always hated the feeling and within the next two hours I helped the nice lady set the table over her protest, ate everything on my plate including Brussels sprouts, which I still can do without, helped her and my friend clear away the dishes, wiped the wooden tabletop with a damp cloth (catching the crumbs off the edges in my palm as Ray had taught me) and, after she washed them, dried the dishes with her son, again over her protests (which however had become more relaxed and faintly bemused). The next time I was their guest—at the farm—everything was old-home week and I had a fine day and a half. In addition to their being very kind, what made it fine was the brisk, silent outdoors in which my friend and I spent most of our time, and the featherbed in his and my chilly upstairs sleeping room.

Dad's half-sister, Martha, stayed at the Ritz Tower for two or three weeks during one of his Hollywood trips before his marriage to Jessie. I think partly he wanted to give Aunt Mattie a good time in New York with a chauffeured limousine and some money to spend, and partly he wanted someone there if I didn't have another place to spend those week ends, and should have had to stay at school. I don't know why in her mid-forties she never had married; she was an affectionate, vivacious red-head about five feet three inches tall and slightly plump, not beautiful but not unattractive either. I think she had worked for a while as a secretary in the family law firm of Hays & Hays in Sullivan, but at that time she had a job in Indianapolis. On the two or three weekends we spent at the Ritz Tower she slept in the apartment's guestroom and

I slept in Dad's room and Tom drove us to some shows and movies and we took walks on Fifth Avenue and ordered most of our meals, except breakfast, from room service. She cooked our Sunday morning breakfasts in the apartment's kitchen. Dad employed a Swedish man named Jerry in those days as a combination masseur-valet-cook, but he probably was on vacation while Dad was in California. Anyhow Aunt Mattie and I had fun together; she related to young people and we laughed a lot. To fight her plumpness she did some floor exercises every morning, including sit-ups, leg-raises and leg-scissors, lying first on one side and then on the other. She did them in the carpeted living room because that's where the multi-record player was and she enjoyed exercising to the Broadway show tunes which Dad also loved—songs like "You're the Cream in My Coffee," "The Best Things in Life Are Free," "Moonlight and Roses," "Button Up Your Overcoat." Incidentally, although one-record-at-a-time Victrolas had been around a long time, automatic changers were a pretty recent innovation. Indianapolis secretaries didn't normally own leotards, so she did her calisthenics in her underwear; at that time ladies' underwear consisted of a brief one-piece chemise or "teddy," rather than bra and panties.

One Sunday morning after I'd got as far dressed as my own underwear I heard the music start and with my ears burning a little I found myself going into the living room and as casually as I could asking Aunt Mattie if I might work out with her. Unconcernedly she said "Sure" and I lay down beside her on the floor; and as she resumed her leg-raises I began mine in time with hers. It was the first time since the onset of my adolescence that I had lain beside a scantily clad female in such an intimate situation. As a child I'd lain in bed with Helen Fischer. And I'd lain on a beach or a pier beside a girl in a swimming suit in the past, but this was entirely different and I was acutely aware of the fact. I had brought it on myself, not contrived it so much as impulsively thrust myself into it. I had no feeling of guilt or even embarrassment; I felt only a warm, intense, pleasant desire to love and be loved. Going through the strenuous motions our hips and knees and arms grazed the other's a few times and my glances brushed the whiteness of her shoulders and breast-swellings and thighs. I half-realized I might be making some sort of overture to her, but it was as achingly loving as it was sexual—if there's a difference. Throughout the twenty minutes Aunt Mattie gave every evidence of being oblivious of my roiling emotions; but I felt an emanation from her gentle, understanding affection tinged strangely with inward sadness.

When our short workout ended, we went to our rooms and showered and dressed, and she fixed us a good brunch and we walked to Central Park and through its south end and by then it was time for Tom to drive me back to Riverdale. That was the last time I saw her but far from the last time I've thought of her lovingly. And sadly. A year or so later she moved to Hollywood, where Dad got her a job; and after another couple of years she died there, alone, of an intestinal problem.

Sometime after Dad's and Mother's divorce and a weekend or two before what turned out to be Dad's and Jessie's marriage, Hinkle Hays showed up at the Ritz Tower to stay overnight; and after lunch on Sunday before I went back to school he took me aside and talked to me about Dad's lonely homelife and very kindly asked me what I'd think if Dad and Jessie got married. I had been aware casually that they'd been dating since his divorce from Mother, and as I've said I was delighted at this prospect and told Hinkle so. He seemed relieved by my response, as though he'd expected some further discussion about the matter, and I sensed Dad probably had wondered how I'd react and had asked his brother to sound me out.

Hinkle told me the wedding was to be on Thanksgiving in Washington at the home of Jessie's brother, retired General Charles D. Herron. That distinguished, now-deceased army officer, a Crawfordsville native like Jessie, had preceded General Short as commanding general of the United States army forces in Hawaii, and some people were to say later that if General Herron had been in charge at the time of Pearl Harbor we'd have been better prepared. I went down to Washington for the ceremony. Hinkle, Lucile, Chuck, and John T. came east from Sullivan for it, and afterward they went home and I came back to school and Dad and Jessie went somewhere for their honeymoon. The following Sunday I read about it in the *New York Times*.

Christmas, spring and summer vacations from Riverdale always began with an overnight train trip from New York to Indianapolis, and always ended with a return one over the same tracks. When I came out, Ray drove up from Sullivan to the state capital to take me the fifty miles to Crawfordsville, where I spent with Mother all of Christmas and spring vacations and three weeks at the beginnings and ends of summers.

The six weeks in the middle of those summers, I spent with Dad and Jessie either on a dude ranch near Cody, Wyoming, or on a Southern California beach. On the Cody ranch visits, they took Ray along. I'm not sure why they did; I guess it was to be helpful to Jessie, or maybe it had something to do with me. Anyhow I was overjoyed because I loved Ray and I loved the West and I wanted the two to get acquainted. Ray also went along on at least one of our California beach summers; Dad had Tom drive the New York town-car through Indiana and pick up Ray and continue across the country to the coast. Another passenger of Tom's on that trip was the Puerto Rican cook Jessie had hired at the Waldorf Towers, to which they had moved by then from the Ritz Tower. Obviously they were planning a pretty social summer that year.

Chapter Twenty–six

(3-5-30)

Dear Bill:

Just now I have your report . . . This is coming along and I don't have to tell you, of course, how important it is that you hit the Mathematics between the eyes . . . You are one hundred percent real man . . . When I see you get a D, I wonder what in the world the dumb ones do . . . I am looking forward with great happiness to seeing you Saturday.

I love you.

Affectionately, Father

* * *

1717 N. Normanidie Ave.
Hollywood, Calif.
March 18, 1930

Dear Bill.

. . . About the boots for Bill Jr., since I've been here I have gone to every store in Hollywood and haven't found just what I think would be suitable . . . I expect to leave here in about two weeks for the ranch, and in Cody I know I can get just what you want in a boot that is really made well and will not hurt his feet . . . Things are slowing up in the studios a bit, but I have found the work most interesting. I intend to come back next Fall and spend the winter at it.

Well, Bill, I hope everything is going fine with you, and also hope to see you at the ranch this summer. Dot joins me in sending her very best to you, and I wish to thank you again for helping me toward a chance in pictures.

I remain

sincerely yours, Leonard.[1]
P.S. We enjoyed the newsreels of you with the Coolidge party.

---

1. *Leonard Morris, whom W.H.H. had met earlier as a big game hunting guide, was also proprietor of Lazy Bar H dude ranch near Cody, Wyoming, and worked for a few winter months in cowboy movies.*

WESTERN UNION
MARCH 25, 1930

MR. LEONARD MORRIS
1717 N. NORMANDIE AVE.
HOLLYWOOD, CALIFORNIA

BILL AND I HOPE TO REACH CODY ABOUT JULY FOURTH AND STAY ABOUT ONE MONTH (STOP) IF WE DO THIS CAN WE GET MY ROOM FOR BILL AND ME AND ONE OF THE LITTLE COTTAGES WITH TWO ROOMS FOR RAY AND JERRY[2] (STOP) . . . AGREE BEST TO WAIT UNTIL YOU GET BACK HOME TO GET BOOTS (STOP) . . . THANKS AND BEST WISHES TO ALL

Will H. Hays

* * *

April 3rd 1930

Dear Mr. Hays

You will remember my note of Feburary 20th in which I told you that it is Bill's idea to work out his own salvation in the Algebra. Mr. Pratt feels now, however, that he would best have tutoring, and we will arrange this promptly upon his return. In French, vocabulary is his weakness. This too may yield to tutoring, but I think Bill is right in wanting to fight the thing through independently . . .

No boy in the school commands greater admiration for earnest sustained effort than Bill Hays. He is just one of our best, and we want you to feel that we are happy in his progress.

Faithfully, Frank S. Hackett

* * *

2. *Swedish masseur and cook, full-time W.H.H. employee for about a year, at Ritz Tower apartment.*

Mrs. Thomas Hays,
Crawfordsville, Indiana

Dear Helen:

Bill got back here in fine shape and looked great. He was very happy and had a fine time with you on his spring vacation, which he needed. I have been a little bit concerned about him having on thin underwear because it has been a little colder for two or three days.

Sincerely, W.H.H.

* * *

(4-29-30)

Dear Father:

Well, we sure had another wonderful week-end, didn't we? Boy, I only wish you knew how much I love you! I sure appreciate your girl "lesson" too . . . I hate not to be with you next week-end while I'm at Buck's farm but we will be together all summer I think I can stand being away from you one week-end. (I really mean this last too. The more I am with you the better I like it). Hello <u>Pal!</u>

I will write later in the week about the country trip and also you can bet your life I'll be careful! Well, I guess this is about all this time. I'll hit the line hard!!!

Good-bye,

<u>I love you</u>

Bill

* * *

May 3rd, 1930.

Dear Bill:

. . . Thomas will have your single shot .22 with him in the case together with a box of catridges when he comes out to take you and Buck to the train Saturday morning. I am sending this along because I have absolute confidence in your promise to me to be careful. I have heard great hunters like Theodore Roosevelt talk about the absolute necessity of eternal vigilance, because however experienced the hunter, he has mental lapses at times.

I know that your conduct as a guest will be worthy of your own high purpose always to do the right thing. I send you forth on this pleasant jaunt with high anticipations for your happy weekend and in absolute confidence. You are very much of a man, my boy, and I am very proud of you as a pardner. Forget your lessons until next Monday and get every possible happiness out of your vacation. Call me Sunday night when you get in and tell me how many woodchucks you have shot.

I love you.

Affectionately, Father

* * *

(5-6-30)

Dear Father:

As I told you, Buck killed two 'chucks and I didn't get a one. Last night when I called you I now realize that I didn't talk very enthusiasticly to you. I was just tired. . .but am feeling perfect now. . . Whoopee! . . . I hope you are all O.K. and boy we will have fun together next week-end . . . I also thought that maybe, if you have nothing else planned, we might try to see *All quiet on the Western Front*. I understand that it is good. I suppose that you have my report card. I'm passing in everything you will note.

Well, I guess that this is about all, good-bye,

I love you

Will H. Hays, Jr.

* * *

(5-11-30)

Dear Father:

Well, it won't be long now till we'll be riding side by side out in the good 'ole West. Whoopee. Even though we had to go out to Sinclair's we had a good time together this week end, and I liked those Kohns very much. Boy, Father, I wish I could do something or say something which would show to you how much I love you. You and I, I think, are about the only Father & son which have the understanding that we do. It sure is great!

Yes, exams are over Wed., June 4, so I can leave soon after that. I suppose that you will write me in Crawfordsville about when I'm to meet you in Chicago etc. Well, I guess this is about all.

Good-bye,

<u>I love you</u>

Bill.

* * *

2 June 1930.

Dear Mr. Hays,

I have just been notified by Mr. Pratt that Billy passed his algebra final examination with a high grade and is thus assured of passing the course. I am very glad, for Billy has worked very hard and certainly deserves some reward.

May I add, too, that I have enjoyed working with Billy this spring very much, for I noticed in him, from the beginning of our association, a commendable quality of seriousness uncommon in present day boys of his age. Once he has acquired the ability to center his interest on the matter in hand his scholastic difficulties should be at an end. He is, in my opinion, one of our finest boys, and I cannot speak too highly of him or of his promise for the future.

Nathan M. Pusey

* * *

Dear Helen:

Bill will tell you about the sudden necessity of my leaving on Wednesday for Europe, to attend a conference between representatives of the German Electrical interests, the Motion Picture Interests in Germany, the German Government and our own Motion Picture interests and our Government.

The one real disappointment in this is that it makes it necessary to delay for maybe a month the trip of Bill and me to Wyoming. He took the news like a real soldier, and I am sure it will be just as satisfactory to you, because it would give him a longer period with you at this time. I want you to help me out as much as you can so as to relieve his disappointment, because he has been counting on it and has been working on a list of things he would take, etc. . . .

With best wished always,

Sincerely yours, W.H.H.

Sunday
Crawfordsville, June 16

Dear Father,

I just wrote to Miss Kelley as you asked me to do every week and told her all about myself in three words: "great," "great" and "great." I am having a dandy time and also having a dandy rest. I drink at least two glasses of milk a meal. Six a day at the minimum rate. At present I am landscaping Mother's back yard here and already a cement walk has been put in, at the end of which will be a bird bath affair. I have been buying clothes, etc., for the West. Boy it won't be long before we will be there! I have seen Doc Jones and <u>every single band, wire and tin can is out of my mouth</u>. Whoopee! (It will go back, though, at the end of the summer.)

Well, so long.

I love you —Bill

* * *

June 22, 1930

Dear Bill:

Well, last Sunday I was on the water and that was pretty far away. This Sunday I am in Paris and it is still further. However, I am not one inch away from you. I am thinking of you this minute and wishing we were riding in the park or on our way to church or something . . . As I told you, I want to congratulate and thank you for the way you rounded out your school year. I am very proud of you. The particular job which you have now is to work hard on that part of the Get-B's that are applicable. You remember the Get-B's—get lessons, get health, be square, be happy. You do not have to get any lessons now and that is slick, but you must keep getting health and you will always be square—that I know—and I want you always to be happy.

Some day I will bring you over here to Paris and show it to you. It is an interesting place. There is plenty of time for that, though. I wish I spoke French. I had lunch yesterday with our Ambassador, which was a pleasant occasion. Friday night I gave a dinner to the German and American delegates to this conference and it was, I think, a useful occasion. General Pershing and his sister are at this hotel and I am going to have a visit with them.

244

I'm sure I'll be back in time to start to Cody the latter part of July.

I love you.

Affectionately your father.

* * *

Sunday, June 23, 1930
Crawfordsville

Dear Father:
Well, another week past and 7 days closer to the big month! Whoopee!! I spent a dandy week in Sullivan with John T. and Chuck and the rest and am feeling fine. Ray is here now, helping me with the back yard. He also is set for the big trip. I'm so happy he's going. I had holsters for your guns and mine made the other day . . . In a little while I will go for a ride with mother to the Shades state park. Well, I guess this is about all now. Keep well!

I love you

Bill

* * *

Hotel Crillon, Paris
Monday morning—June 30, 1930

Dear Bill:
It is a pretty tough job here, partner, about as tough algebra as we ever had to do but we are going to do the best we can, and I am quite hopeful that I will pass.
. . . The only thing on your grades we have to worry about is French and I can understand that. I don't want you to do much studying this summer but between now and August first, when we start to the ranch, you might spend a half-hour every morning on whatever you think you ought to do in order to pass the French examination in the fall.
I love you.

Affectionately your father,
Will H. Hays

* * *

Sunday
Crawfordsville, July 7

Dear Father:
    ... Boy, every day I put on my revolver and sometimes my boots and just sit and dream for hours of the west and our good-time-to-be. We sure are going to have fun together out there ... Hurry home!

<u>I love you,</u> Bill

* * *

Hotel Crillon, Paris
July 6, 1930

Dear Bill:
    As soon as they reach an agreement here I have to go to Berlin to see the German Government. Nothing, however, can keep us here longer than sailing on the *Europa*, which will give me ten days in New York and let us start to the ranch on August first ... I thought on the way home from the American Church this morning how we would take care of the French you have to make up this summer. You get your books, and on the way out to Wyoming we will work on the train and then half an hour every day out there; during the time we simply have to get out of the saddle to rest a few minutes, we will pull out our French books and I will study with you.
    I love you.

Affectionately, Father

* * *

Dear Bill:
    Herewith is a little clipping which will interest you. It is from a French newspaper and shows your Father and the great inventor, Lumiere. I think you can translate this without a great deal of trouble. ... We get very complimentary reports of the work your father is doing.

    Give my regards to your Mother.

Sincerely yours, Julia Kelly

* * *

Dear Helen:

Returning from Europe last night I find your letter and have just talked to Bill. We will stay in Cody practically four weeks, which gets Bill back in time for him to have two weeks in Crawfordsville before he has to leave for school.

There is a good doctor in Cody and we will be in close proximity to him all the time. He will need his heavy shoes for mountain tramping; he has his cowboy boots, which he will want to wear most of the time, I expect. I will watch his covers at night at the ranch. I am glad to have the diet list for him and will have him observe it; he will probably eat everything and like it while he is in that high altitude. I will take the oils and medicine with me so he will be all taken care of. I will be careful about the washing and keep his washable clothes out there as clean as possible... Be sure to include the French books, because I am going to work some at it on the train with him and also out there.

With best wishes,

Hastily, W.H.H.

* * *

(H. V. F. Diary)
Crawfordsville,
August 8, 1930

Ray came to town after B. They left for Wyoming

* * *

Chapter Twenty–seven

I SPENT most of the daylight and several nighttime hours of my first train trip to Cody sitting in a canvas chair on the outdoor rear platform of the observation car with Ray. After we left the kind of farmland I knew, everything about the race westward thrilled me: the speed of the rails clattering under us, pinching closer together as they rushed back toward the distant joining of the tan horizon and the turquoise sky; the gradual upward-heaving of the land until it reached the altitude where it began to wear sagebrush, then the increasing, blunt roughness of it like shoulders under a blanket, then the bald rimrock and the sharper edges jutting above quick, bridged canyons with cotton-woods grasping upward at the train, then the higher country flattening out again for a while and reaching far ahead to low, snow-patched, pine-bearded mountains growing very slowly; the stars and and moon emerg-ing gradually from the darkening sky and shadowing the land with pale silver highlights and gloomy corners; the smell of breezy unstained space mixed with acrid coal smoke from the locomotive hurtling up ahead.

I remember awakening in the morning's light and looking out under the half-raised blind of my lower berth to find we were motionless beside a station platform and a canyon just beyond it that bottomed in a sparkling river. I heard tap water running in the drawing room next to my compartment and I called my question to Dad and he answered "Yes, that's Cody across the canyon. Up and at 'em, Willy-Boy!" He finished shaving and dressing about half as fast as I got my clothes on, but very soon we both were ready to step from the Pullman car which had been left on the Cody siding during the night. After a flurry of good-byes from the Pullman crew we came face-to-face with a man whose name was Leonard Morris—a man and a name to become indelible parts of my life. He was about Ray's size: a couple of inches over six feet tall and powerfully built without an extra ounce of flesh; but his hair was sandy-red, his complexion ruddy and his eyes light blue. Those eyes had a continuous glint of humor except, as I later learned, on the vary rare occasions when he was angry; then they became flinty. Except on those occasions his grin was boyish, too—almost impish. That morning one of his eyes was edged with purple and his cheekbones and mouth showed signs of wear and tear; we learned that the previous night had been one of those angry occasions. A Swedish hay-hand even bigger than Len had thrown a firecracker at Dot Morris's feet, and the fight had lasted for fifteen minutes and ended in what the crowd had allowed had been a draw, with the two fighters groping back up to their feet to give each other a dazed and bloody hug. When I shook hands with Len that first time at the Cody station it was like gripping a rock, and I hoped he should never get mad at me and so far as I know he never did. He died a few years ago in California, crippled by arthritis.

When he had driven us the twenty-five miles to the Lazy Bar H Ranch and we had met his pretty, gracious, five-foot three-inch wife Dot, and been shown to our rooms in the log ranch house and around the rest of the spread, I knew for sure why Dad had chosen this place for our vacation.

The prior fall a small group of Dad's New York friends—Walter Chrysler, Roy Howard and some others—had asked him to go big game hunting with them in Wyoming. He hadn't been enthused about packing into the mountains for ten days or so killing animals but he liked the men planning the trip and had agreed to go at least part way. At their request he had called the state's governor, an acquaintance from political days, and asked the name of a guide for the party; and the governor had said the best man in the business was a young fellow named Leonard Morris, an all-around cowboy, experienced hunter and trapper, former horse rancher with his father, and now, in the Depression, running a dude ranch with his lovely Eastern wife who had been a New York area debutante. As an added note of interest about his recommended guide the governor had said that Leonard's father, who had immigrated to Wyoming from England by way of an American east-coast shipyard, had sent his son to prep school in the East where he had won, among other athletic honors, an inter-scholastic fencing championship; and as Leonard was finishing his final year at the school he had met Dorothy Nauss and they had fallen in love, married and returned to live on the North Fork of the Shoshone River. When the big game hunting party had stopped overnight at Lazy Bar H on its way into the high country—called the "Thoroughfare"—southeast of Yellowstone Park Dad quickly had become so enamoured of the ranch and its setting that he'd decided to stay there while the others went hunting; they were to pick him up on their way back. He and Dot and the wranglers became good friends, and so did he and Leonard when the whole hunting party came back and stayed there for another few days before returning to New York.

That summer and the next one at Lazy Bar H confirmed my baptism in my lifelong spiritual affinity with the West, old and new, its inhabitants, history and traditions. In my heart I became a cowboy. I've had cowboys tell me I ride like one and suit them fine, and no greater compliment has been paid to me. Later stays at Len's father's homeranch on the North Fork of the Shoshone River, after the two of them had consolidated their dude ranches, and at the late Larry Larom's Valley Ranch on the South Fork strengthened my captivation by the life and lore and land between the Kansas plains and the Sierra Nevada Mountains.

The images and scents and sounds of those times and places always will be with me: the spur jingle of boot heels on wooden porches; low log buildings with foot-high grass growing out of sod roofs; the sagebrush smell of the air after a rain; the snorts and grunts and farting and slapping leather of a bucking bronco; the feel of the top corral rail under my buttocks, heels hooked on the second or third rail down; cowboys' whistling and hawing and the remuda's hooves splashing and clacking over the stones of a river fork as the morning began; trying to keep up with Len and his rangy horse on a day-long chase of a wild stallion behind Wapiti under the rimrock of Sheep Mountain; the lady on the Yellowstone Park bus at the Wapiti rest-stop taking my photograph as what she thought was her first real cowboy close-up, and the grin it left in my heart; the way Ray and Len—from two different worlds if those ever were—hit it off from the beginning and kidded each other endlessly, Len affecting a black accent and saying things like "I see you're wearing shoes today" and Ray asking him "You know they have horseless carriages now? Cowboys are out"; the bawling of roped calves; riding my horse Gigi along cottonwood-lined creeks and across sagebrush benches and up scary mountain slopes to jutting points from under which the whole world stretched out like a badly laid carpet; the ugly smell of branded horsehair and hide; my ambivalent feeling about the other dudes: knowing I was one of them and they'd not be there if they didn't love the West too, but at the same time embarrassed and condescending about their cameras and dumb questions and bowed-back sitting in their saddles and their at least initially awkward adjustment to this temporary environment of all of us.

Among my early Shoshone country memories was the day's trip by automobile with Dad and Len and Fred Morris to visit Will James at his ranch, The Rocking R, on the Crow Reservation near Pryor, Montana, and my first venison there, and the two ranch girls with a pack horse riding by on their way down from days in the hills. Another day's auto trip was to see Tom Mix's circus when it played Thermopolis, eighty miles south of Cody, and to lunch in his tent with that fabled man. The awful night in Cody when—I've got to believe aching as he did it—the Movie Czar, with his new wife beside him, whispered to his black employee that the latter had better wait outside the Irma Hotel café until after the dudes had finished their in-town dinner, to which I'd heard several of them invite Ray; and I followed Ray outside and sat with him in the car while he cried and I cried and after a while I went back in, feeling Dad needed me, too; and when dinner was over, we all came out and rode back to the ranch in several cars, with the others in ours making small talk. I never mentioned it to Dad and he didn't to me; I really felt more sorry for him than mad at him, as though it had been an accident that had happened to him and hurt him almost as much as Ray and me. Jessie hadn't the reasons we had for cherishing Ray. But I felt guilty for not speaking up.

Another time of anger and embarrassment for Ray and therefore me, not in Cody but as we were on the way there, was when we were watching a movie in a crummy, single-aisle theater on West Washington Street in Indianapolis while waiting for the train to Chicago, and he was told to leave the place. The fat proprietor, smelling of old sweat, came down the aisle after we'd sat there half an hour and he stared at Ray in the light from the screen and went away. In about two minutes he came back and asked Ray in a hoarse whisper what was his nationality, and when Ray said "American" he left again for another two minutes. This time when he came back he had another moronic character with him, and they told Ray they didn't cater to "you people." Ray said he didn't cater to the movie or the theater or the two of them either and we got up and left. I considered for only a moment telling the slob he'd just kicked out the Movie Czar's favorite son, not to mention favorite chauffeur. I'm sure he shouldn't have given a damn about any goddam Russian big shot, or known what "chauffeur" meant.

Dad's accompanying Swedish masseur, not long in the United States, was still another world apart from both Len and Ray. Fortunately this man had a sense of humor, up to a point. He tolerated without always understanding their joshing until the midnight after an evening of grizzly bear stories Len rode his horse onto the porch of the Swede's isolated cabin. The racket of shod hooves and wild whoops and shouts like "Shoot the damn thing before it breaks in" brought the masseur out through a rear window in an astounding hurry. That of itself was enough to make him mad, but maybe not to account entirely for how very mad; one of the wrangler witnesses later recalled hearing in the confusion a laugh from the cabin's interior, and recognized it as a pretty three-summer kitchen girl's who undoubtedly knew Len's clowning around when she heard it.

Len had a way with dudes; the men admired him and the women got crushes on him. On rides with us he often broke into song; I remember especially "When I Take My Sugar to Tea," because it brought to my mind an intriguing picture of him and Dot tea-dancing at the Plaza when they were courting. One time on a trail at the foot of a sagebrush-covered hill he stopped the riders and told them to sit there while he rode a hundred yards up the hill, turned his mount around and spurred it back down at a leaping gallop—the horse snorting, Len whooping, rocks flying, dust swirling—until he reined the animal to a stiff-legged, sliding stop at the bottom and grinned at the dudes, "Now that's *not* the way to ride a horse down a hill." When a dude once asked him if it were true that mountains grew, he nodded solemnly, "Yes, Ma'am, I remember when that one—" pointing— "was a hole in the ground." He told another questioner that the best way to keep a horse from slobbering was to teach it to spit; and another time when a horse on a single-file trail broke wind loudly and at amazing length Len looked back down the line of riders at the man on the offending animal and said "If you'd fingered that you could've played 'Yankee Doodle.'" On trips to town he drove his vintage Pierce Arrow, which he called "Old Scarface" after a notorious grizzly in Yellowstone Park, as though it were one of the wild horses ranging over the benches under Sheep Mountain, fast and free and recklessly.

One day after Jessie and Dad had a spat, her husband of a few months asked a cowboy to saddle up their horses and asked the Chinese cook to fix a couple of lunches for their saddlebags and told Jessie the two of them were going for an all-day ride, with Len and the wranglers leading the day's other dude riders in a different direction. He smiled at me and winked at Ray as they rode off. I was happy. Jessie seemed to be too.

W.H.H., Sr., and W.H.H., Jr..., riding the range on the Lazy Bar H ranch in Wyoming, 1930.

Chapter Twenty-eight

Crawfordsville,
September 6, 1930

Dear Father:
    I was sure glad to hear from you (Phone) the other night. Boy, I sure am homesick for Lazy Bar! Father, I want sincerely to thank you for the most wonderful time I've ever had!! We sure had a wonderful time together out there... Last night I made up my mind that I was going to begin in work with a running start and hit it hard as bedrock.
    I'm fine & sure hope you are the same. Well, so long, I'll be seeing you!

I love you, Bill

* * *

Dear Helen:
    This is by way of report about Bill. For nearly four weeks we rode together and played together every day and I went to bed at the same time he did every night... The cow punchers all loved him. He really rides very, very well... I sent him a wire last night suggesting that he get a French tutor from Wabash and work an hour a day on French during the two weeks he is there...

Sincerely yours, W.H.H.

* * *

Crawfordsville
September 14

Dear Father:

I've been working every morning from 9 to 10 o'clock on French with Prof. Montgomery. There is not much doing here now, but this next week is rush week for the frats and then all the rest of the winter it will be "studentized." It sure brightens up things when they come. I've been invited over to the Phi Delt house for a meal soon.

I love you, Bill

* * *

Saturday
(9-30-30)

Dear Helen, Miss Fischer or Something (That's the way you told me to start):

Well, I've started school and I'm getting along fine and dandy. Football practice has started and I'm having a good time in it. Father and I rode horseback this afternoon and we are going to a movie tonight. . . I'll write you fuller soon. It was so good seeing you in Crawfordsville. So long,

I love you, Bill

xxx ooo xxx

* * *

October 25, 1930

Mr. D. Earl Gardner,
Assistant Headmaster,
Riverdale Country School,
Riverdale-on-Hudson
New York City.

Dear Mr. Gardner:

. . . It is essential that we carefullly check up just what is necessary for Bill both to graduate from Riverdale in the spring of 1933 and enter Wabash College that fall. It is essential that he graduate; I believe that any boy should <u>finish the job</u>. I am anxious, however, that this be done in the time originally contemplated . . .

With kindest regards, and best wished always, I am

Sincerely yours, Will H. Hays

* * *

Sun., October 26, 1930

Dear Aunt Sallie:

Dad and I have just come home from church and have ordered our dinner from room service. Right after dinner we are going horseback riding in the park. Last night we went to the rodeo which is here in town and I rode in it at the grand entrance when all the cowboys come in. It was great.

I'm well and getting along first rate. My studies are all right. I hope that you are well and are having a good time. I shall see you Christmas and we'll have a good time together. I hope that you are settled down all right now and that you get good things to eat and good heat. My father is in wonderful health.

Well, good-bye

Love to you, Bill

* * *

(10-26-30)

Dear Father:

I'm writing to tell you how much I appreciate the wonderful week-ends you have given me, and I hope you too have had fun . . . I'm going to work and not only that but I'm going to make my ten yards <u>every</u> time henceforth . . . I'll see you off for California next week-end.

Well, so long and I'll be seein' you.

I love you

(never forget that, pal), Bill

Mond. morning

Last night I cried myself to sleep thinking how much I loved you. That's a funny thing to do isn't it.

B.H.

256

October 27th 1930

Dear Mr. Hays:
    . . . Most definitely Bill has mental equipment sufficient to do satisfactory work in college . . . I would suggest he spend the first half of next summer on the ranch about which he is so enthusiastic, and the last half of the summer as he did last vacation, tutor with the Wabash Professor . . .

                                    Cordially yours
                                    D Earl Gardner
                                    Assistant Headmaster

                    *   *   *

(11-4-30)

Dear Father:
    Well, I'm back and ready to hit the line for ten yards this week. I had a fine week-end with the Hubbards after seeing you off (I didn't like that part) and I'm feeling great . . . I have some dandy socks on, those woolen ones you asked me to buy. Tom got them while I was in the show . . . That evening we went to what we though was going to be a musical comedy but turned out to be a drama . . . It was *The Torch Song*. Mrs. Rinestien says to beg your pardon. She said it made her feel guilty for people to see her with two boys at the *Torch Song* (Ha, Ha) . . . All this after noon Ed & I had a paper-wad battle in his play-room.
    I'm glad you liked my letter about our week ends and glad you feel the same way. Knock on 'em out there cowboy! I'll be a-seein' you soon.
    So-long.
                    <u>I love you</u>
                            Bill.

                    *   *   *

WESTERN UNION
NOVEMBER 7, 1930
HOLLYWOOD, CALIF.
NIGHT LETTER

MR. BILL HAYS
RIVERDALE COUNTRY SCHOOL
RIVERDALE-ON-HUDSON
UPPER NEW YORK CITY, N.Y.

HELLO PARTNER WE WISH YOU WERE WITH US. IF WE HAD YOU ALONG WE WOULD WRANGLE A FEW BRONCS AND DO A LITTLE FANCY RIDING. WE HAVE BEEN GOING OVER OLD TIMES AND MISS YOU. BEST WISHES FROM US BOTH

LEONARD MORRIS
WILL H. HAYS

* * *

(11-16-30)

Dear Father:

I spent another happy week-end at the Hubbard's. Their people sure are nice! We went to the Ill.–Army game . . . I got your tellegram & it sure was welcome. Please tell Len that I wish I was a-toppin' the rough string now, all right, or a-fightin' some big, long-horn bahama. You might show him the enclosed drawing of a bucking horse and tell him I wish I was on Gigi now!

I hope that you are all right in every way. I'll sure be happy to see you back this week end. We'll have a happy Thanksgiving!

So-long.

<u>I love you</u>

Bill

(11-24-30)

MEMO for W.H.H. from Julia Kelly:

Mr. Earl Gardner of Riverdale telephoned the message that the school "could not officially sanction any absence beyond a week end, on account of establishing a precedent with the other boys, but if Mr. Hays takes Bill an extra day at Thanksgiving there will be no objection"—and he hopes "they both have a good time." [1]

* * *

HAYS & HAYS
Attorneys-at-Law
Sullivan, Ind.
December 17, 1930

PERSONAL AND CONFIDENTIAL

Mr. M. E. Foley,
Attorney-at-Law
Traction Terminal Building,
Indianapolis, Indiana.

Dear Mike:
. . . All of us in Sullivan hope that Helen will let Bill come down here for a day or two during his Christmas vacation.
. . . Confidentially, Lucile is giving a tea for Jessie on Friday afternoon and having a few couples in for bridge for Bill and Jessie Friday night . . . As her attorney, maybe you can help.

Most cordially,
Hinkle C. Hays
HCH:L

* * *

---

1. *On November 28, 1930, W.H.H. and Jessie Stutzman, nee Herron, originally of Crawfordsville, were married in Washington, D.C.*

Crawfordsville
December 29, 1930

Dear Father:

I hope you are well on your way to California now ... Say, Father, I've lain awake nights lately and I can hardly tell you how terribly sorry I am about the Christmas present that I forgot to give you . . . you were the <u>first</u> on my list <u>as always</u> but I just wish that I could buy you something worth $900,000,000,000,000,000,000,000,000,000 but when I told Uncle Hinkle about it he said it wasn't the length of the step but the direction . . . Gee, I'm glad you had a good Christmas and that you've decided to go to Sullivan more. I sure was glad to get down there to see you and Jessie . . . I'm going to stay up all night every night at school working on Algebra till I get it, and I don't give a d——n if it kills me. Im so gosh darned ashamed of myself I don't know what to do, making you worry about that. You just watch my steam.

Mother just wrote you a note saying that I didn't get her a present. I can prove it by Jessie that I did but that it was lost some way and I am going to get her one but she won't listen. <u>Don't let it worry you</u>. She says that it's the thought, not the gift, and you know, Father, that I did get her one, or at least Jessie does. Well, I'll have to sign off now & work on my Algebra. It's right here beside me.

I love you (<u>never forget it!</u>)

Bill

* * *

(Written in Hollywood)
January 3, 1931

Mr. R. Earl Gardner
Riverdale Country School,
Riverdale-on-Hudson
New York

My dear Mr. Gardner:

. . . Won't you please have a talk with Bill and otherwise give thought to the matter of his applying himself to his work and being required by the school to do that? I would like to have your frank judgement as to just what we should do.

With kindest personal regards and best wishes always, I am

Sincerely yours, Will H. Hays

(1-6-31)

Dear Father:

I have just received the sweetest letter ever written by any human at <u>any</u> time and I shall keep it <u>always</u> . . . My love for you will exist <u>always</u>, in this life and the next. Never forget that, father. You are the best, squarest, most courageous, most honorable, most perfect man that has ever lived. To me you rate with <u>God Almighty.</u>

I hope that you got the lounge-robe I sent you, and the letter, both from Crawfordsville. Well, <u>Good</u>-bye for a little while.

Your Son—I love you

Bill.

* * *

Sun. (1-11-31)

Dear Father:

I'm in at the Penn. Hotel with Mother now and I'm having a dandy time. Yesterday was Ed's birthday. I gave him a hunting knife. I got the money from Tom. That was all right wasn't it? Say, you'll please tell Jessie I'm awfully sorry I haven't written her and that I will right away, won't you . . . You know the present I sent you is a <u>lounge</u> robe so "take it easy" . . . Mother looks fine . . . In the math test of 5 problems I got four right; in English I got a B and in french about 80% for the week. I feel great!

I love you, Bill.

* * *

(2-16-31)

Dear Father:

I just happened to think that we owed Mr. Pusey $15.00 for math tutoring done before Christmas. I expected this had better be paid, don't you? I'm looking forward to the week-end with you like no-body's business!

<u>I love you,</u> Bill

P.S. Would appreciate if you would see if you could get 4 seats together for Mr. Callisen and Mr. Pusey for *Trader Horn*. I would like to pay for two of them but he will pay for the other two. They can go only Wednesday. Two of them are for guests of theirs.

March 5, 1931

Dear Bill:

The enclosed bill from Alex Taylor Co. is for pants. I know you wear pants, but I want to be certain these pants were for you. I don't know—maybe you are buying pants for someone else out there at school. I want you to have pants. I would be ashamed if you were in the same position that Joe Brown was the other night when we went to the wrestling match!

I love you.

Affectionately, W.H.H.

* * *

(3-9-31)

Dear Father:

Here is the way things stand: (1) Im now failing in Algebra; (2) Mr. Callisen says I have more chance to pass in N.Y. Regents' Entrance exams than in College Board Entrance exams; (3) Regents' are excepted at Wabash; (4) Regents' have to be excepted at Riverdale also because Riv. is under N.Y. jurisdiction; (5) Regents', if taken and passed in June, put me in the fifth form at Riverdale regardless as to what my marks have been here the whole year; (6) I take two exams in June, one given by Riv. masters and one by College Entrance Exam Board <u>or</u> Regents'. I think I will pass the Riv. ones, but if I don't those but <u>do</u> the Regents' I get into 5th form any way; (7) Mr. Gardner, our good friend, recommended Regents' for me.

In the meantime I'm going to work hard and try my best to pass, so you can lay to that, dear father. Say, I wish you knew how much that Hays kid loves his old Dad.

Bill.

* * *

(3-17-31)

Dear Miss Helen:

You bet I remember those times. The pictures of Estes Park you sent makes me homesick for the old place and I'll never forget it as long as I live. We sure had fun that summer, didn't we? Remember little old

Brownie, and when we used to take walks down into the village in the afternoon, and how you read *Treasure Island* to me at night? Where did you get these pictures, anyway? Out of a magazine? Well, so long and don't forget to write, please!

xxx   ooo   xxx   ooo

Bill.

* * *

March 24, 1931

Dear Bill:

You are now starting on your spring vacation. You deserve it. I want you to forget all about studies from this minute until you get back. While you are in Crawfordsville you should talk to the Dean of Wabash College or someone about taking the Wabash entrance examination in Latin this summer and thus getting it out of the way at Riverdale too. Also while you are there I wish you would make a little inquiry as to whether or not there is a suitable place nearby to keep Tony this summer. Also I think you should practice baseball some. I am much interested in your being a good first baseman.

<u>YOU ARE A VERY VERY GOOD BOY</u> and I love you very much. Have a good time.

Affectionately, Father

* * *

Mon. morning
(4-6-31)

Dear Father:

Well, I got back here to school from Crawfordsville all right and I feel fine. Gosh, I can hardly wait till you come back from California. I sure hope you're all right. Boy, I was glad Ray brought me to Sullivan for that day you stopped through! Wasn't the Sullivan house great? Jessie sure fixes up a mean house!

I'll bet you're having a good time out there and you just keep having one. Please tell Jessie hello and I'll be seeing you.

<u>I love you</u>

Bill.

Hollywood, California
April 10, 1931

Dear Bill:

Herewith an original letter from Tom Mix . . . If we can go up to Boston in May to see him in the Sells Floto Circus we will. I don't expect it will be possible but it is a dandy invitation for you to visit him there with some buddy and you never can tell . . . A lot of folks out here have asked about you, and I have told them you are well and happy and hitting the ball. By the way—are you hitting the ball? In addition to being a first baseman and catching and throwing the ball, the ball player has to hit the ball . . . Jessie is well and we are getting some pleasure in, as well as getting some work done. It is good for one's work to have some pleasure, and it is good for one's pleasure to do his work well.

I love you.

Affectionately, Will H. Hays

* * *

Hollywood, California
April 15, 1931

Dear Bill:

. . . If we could get a good tutor for part of the summer he could be quite useful and not unpleasant if he is good scout otherwise. You might even arrange to have him drive the car which I am hoping your mother will buy . . . We are going to a ranch out west this summer. That I hope very much to do, and I am assuming you can probably be persuaded to go along. What do you know about that?

I love you.

Affectionately, Dad

* * *

WESTERN UNION
COLLECT=CRAWFORDSVILLE IND
1931 APR 24

WILL H HAYS=
5504 HOLLYWOOD BLVD
HOLLYWOOD CALIF=

WHEN BACK NEWYORK (STOP) WORRIED ABOUT
BILLIE THERE ALONE=

HTH.

WESTERN UNION
<u>DAY LETTER</u> APRIL 25, 1931

MRS. H. THOMAS HAYS
414 WEST WABASH AVENUE
CRAWFORDSVILLE INDIANA

NEW YORK OFFICE IS IN TOUCH WITH BILL EVERY
DAY AND I TALK WITH THEM EVERY DAY STOP HE IS IN
FINE SHAPE IN EVERY WAY AND SPENDING THIS WEEK-
END WITH HUBBARDS STOP I WILL BE BACK MONDAY
STOP

W.H.H.

* * *

May 19, 1931

Dear Mr. Hays:

. . . In the light of Bill's academic immaturity, my suggestion would be that we plan his graduating here in three more years, instead of two . . . giving him the advantage of an entire summer devoted to other kinds of education such as the ranch life, development with horses and other forms of sport, without the pressure of tutoring.

It may well be that in the light of all circumstances, he would best attempt the two-year program, necessitating summer work, but I see so many instances of the futile setting of a goal for a boy, just because he is expected to proceed as others think he should, that I incline more and more to trust an earnest boy to work out his own salvation. Certainly, earnestness is one of Bill's chief characteristics.

With kind greetings, I am

Faithfully, Frank S. Hackett

* * *

28 W. 44th Street,
New York City,
New York.
May 20, 1931
(New office address)

Mrs. H. Thomas Hays,
414 W. Wabash Avenue,
College Hill,
Crawfordsville, Indiana.

Dear Helen:

I am making inquiries at the college about the possibility of a Wabash junior or senior to tutor Bill this summer and be a sort of companion to play tennis, golf and swim with him. (I note what you say in your last letter about Ray and understand your desire not to have him in Crawfordsville.) I'm very anxious he finish Riverdale in two more years.

Bill frequently expresses the hope to me that he can "get out on a ranch again" this summer and I suppose he makes the same suggestion to you. I give no encouragement to this, because I will not plan to do it without your approval . . .

Hastily, W.H.H.

Chapter Twenty-nine

WHEN I got back to Crawfordsville after the first Cody summer I was there for a while in body but not in spirit. Renewing my morning tutoring sessions with Wabash professor Henry Montgomery to prepare for a makeup Riverdale exam, I kept seeing white-flecked mountains and smelling sagebrush and hearing the squeak of saddle leather. Most afternoons I spent swimming at the Crawfordsville Country Club with friends I'd made in town—the Ewoldt brothers, Flora, Jack, Rosemary O'Neall and the rest—and sometimes in the evenings going to movies at the Strand or the Ritz or sitting in front of Mother's Majestic radio playing my drum in time with the music of the "Lucky Strike Hit Parade."

If my return to school after three weeks in Crawfordsville hadn't the pain of my first year's arrival from Sullivan, it still wasn't a joy. I was glad of course to see Ed and Bob and Skipper and Bobby and Walter again but the contrast between Riverdale's fall and Cody's summer was depressing. A bright spot suddenly shone in the nostalgia's gloom however; Ed Hubbard had spent the summer on a northern Arizona ranch and had fallen as hard for the West as I had. He went to Arizona again the next summer as I did to Wyoming and we spent many hours of the succeeding winters talking about those realms of our enchantment.

The years I spent at Riverdale have seemed since to blend into one multifaceted experience rather than a series of nine-months periods. I remember the summers with more definition, maybe because they were spent in what to me were places of more interest and color. Riverdale seemed drab—not the people, many of them were colorful and some were outstanding individuals, and I don't mean the times those winters were all dull. The weekends of course were sparkling and the weekdays at school had their memorable hours and events too, as I've mentioned. Ice-skating on the school's hockey rink and in Van Courtland Park nearby was fun. Watching Ed Hubbard tackle like an axe in varsity games made me proud. Sitting with Ed as non-speaking members of the stage jury of a Broadway murder mystery was a rare experience; the show was produced by a friend of Dad's, and we were told afterward that our pay should be donated to the actors' guild. Irish Bob Hubbard's fistfight with a husky Italian pupil exploding after weeks of creeping animosity over some girl varied one day's routine. So did the night watchman's shooting of a burglar in the locker room and our hearing about it the next morning and staring at the blood on the floor before the janitor cleaned it up. We changed our rooms' furniture around in the spring at some kind of subconscious urge to revenge the winter. We saw Clark Gable's ex-wife come on Saturdays to pick up her son by another husband, but never saw the great movie star himself. I wore a patch over one of my eyes for a week after a cyst had been removed from its lid by the same Dr. Wheeler whose eye operation on the King of Siam the week previously had been publicized nationally; he was a nice man and the father of Charlie, one of the nicest guys at Riverdale. I wonder if the Bloomingdale brothers at school could wander through their family store on Lexington Avenue and pick out anything they wanted, free of charge.

Mother came from Crawfordsville to visit me two or three times while I was in Riverdale, both before and after Dad and Jessie were married. These visits always were timed when Dad, or later he and Jessie, were in California. On his instructions Tom met Mother's train and drove her to the Pennsylvania Hotel. Maybe whoever chose that one did so because it was near the station. It certainly wasn't anything like the Waldorf Towers; it was more like the old Claypool in Indianapolis, a huge convention house. Invariably and despite Dad's offering to pay for a better one, the room she took was the smallest single she could get with a double bed, symptomatic of her compulsive parsimony. I think she usually stayed about three weeks in the cavernous place, "sallying forth" from her cubicle occasionally for short walks in that unattractive area of New York and for a minimum of shopping and for scenic drives once in a while with Tom in Dad's car. On Saturdays when she and Tom came out to school to pick me up, if any of my classy friends there noticed, much less were embarrassed by, her old-fashioned high-button shoes and long dress, they were better than I at concealing it, at least not wincing at it.

As I look back on those weekends with Mother, I guess they weren't happy for her either, because she was a long way from home; but she didn't show discomfort and I also tried not to. We stayed pretty close to the hotel, except for Tom's kindly tours and a couple of Broadway shows to which Julia Kelly got us tickets. We ate in the coffee shop—I loved its guava jelly and cream cheese on toasted nut bread sandwiches—except on Sunday mornings when we read the *New York Times* over room-service oatmeal and milk for me and coffee for her. We slept in the double bed (I don't know whether or not she registered for me, but I don't recall signing into the hotel) and after my reading light switched the room into darkness I'd hear her put her false teeth into the water glass she'd filled earlier and set on her nightstand. It always took me a while to get to sleep—not because of her soft snores, I just didn't feel like sleeping. I remember a surge of sadness once when I thought of Dad and her, long ago, lying side by side in a bed like that in Sullivan. Mother always rode back to Riverdale with Tom and me on Sunday afternoons, and those return trips were even more depressing for me than usual. Maybe they depressed her too. For different reasons.

A page or so ago, I mentioned Clark Gable being a great movie star. I didn't have the pleasure of knowing him, but Dad said he also was a nice man. A later wife of Clark's was the very lovely and popular actress, Carole Lombard, and in the earliest days of World War II, Dad sadly was part of a tragic happening involving them. The United States Treasury Department asked Hoosiers Lombard and Hays to meet in Indiana for a whirlwind, war bond-selling tour of the state. They came from their respective coasts to Indianapolis, and, with Governor Schricker, spent the day flying to and speaking at several cities, ending it at a huge, also successful rally in the capital's Cable Tabernacle. Exhausted, the movie star and the movie "czar" rested and reminisced about the day in a room of the Claypool Hotel before heading for her Los Angeles plane and his New York train. Because she'd done such an outstanding job, he phoned her husband to tell him so, saying to Clark, before giving her the phone, something like, "I know you'll see her in a few hours out there, but I wanted you to hear from her partner of the day how beautifully she served this state and the United States, and that she may very well be the next governor of Indiana!" Of course, that night her plane hit a mountain near Las Vegas. And the nation mourned. Incidentally, I was awakened by a call from the Associated Press before dawn the next morning in Sullivan, from which I was headed into the army from my law practice, asking me where dad was. I replied, with a creepy feeling, that he must be nearing New York—unless he'd changed his mind—and asked why the man wanted to know; and he said that Miss Lombard's plane had hit a Nevada mountain, and the AP thought Dad might have been with her. I spent a hellish few hours until I heard Dad's voice on that same phone from New York.

Before going for the second time to Cody I spent the usual weeks with Mother in Crawfordsville. I had to have some more tutoring in a couple of subjects, and through Wabash College, of which he was a trustee, Dad hired a senior named Ernie Boyd for that. Ernie and I became friends as well as tutor and pupil. He painted in oils as a hobby and got me interested in it, and both of us took some lessons from a local professional named Fritz Schlemmer who had a studio above the interurban terminal. Ray came up from Sullivan for part of that time, taking a room Nellie Akins found for him with a black family in town. Ray and I played a lot of catch on the sidewalk in front of Mother's house and did some target shooting in the countryside; Ernie and I went swimming in the country club spring-fed pool and cruised around town in his car; and the three of us took Mother for afternoon drives. I don't recall thinking it was odd that Ray stayed in Crawfordsville while I was there; I guess I accepted it partly as an analogue of his omnipresence in the Sullivan days and partly as a sign of the protectiveness toward me that Dad showed on the Lake Michigan pier and the Lofting weekend in Connecticut. I didn't learn it might have been prompted partly by Dad's concern about my kidnapping until later.

Chapter Thirty

MOTION PICTURE PRODUCERS & DISTRIBUTORS OF AMERICA, INC.
28 WEST 44TH STREET
NEW YORK CITY

Will H. Hays
President

May 29, 1931

Mr. Earnest Boyd,
410 South Water Street
Crawfordsville, Indiana.

Dear Mr. Boyd:

Bill Hays, aged fifteen, is a Fourth Form student at Riverdale Country School, Riverdale, New York. He should graduate there in 1933, completing a course considerably more extensive and intensive than a high school. It is altogether probable that he will have to do some tutoring this summer in Algebra and probably in French and possibly in Latin, since he is behind a year . . .

I have in mind that you might tutor him during the mornings and then do other things with him at other times which would be useful in building his character, habits, etc . . .

With personal regards, I am

Sincerely yours, Will H. Hays

* * *

271

WESTERN UNION

June 6, 1931

MRS. H. THOMAS HAYS
414 W. WABASH AVENUE,
COLLEGE HILL
CRAWFORDSVILLE, INDIANA

BILL LEAVING NEW YORK TODAY STOP ... HE IS IN
FINE SHAPE AND PASSED SCHOOL EXAMS IN MATHEMAT-
ICS, LATIN AND ENGLISH. GRADE NOT YET IN FOR FRENCH
BUT NO DOUBT ALL RIGHT STOP

W.H.H.

* * *

(6-8-31-)

Dear Father -
Well, here I am in C'ville—all ready to start the tutoring Wed.
or Thurs. (I like to get settled first) ... Ray is coming back here Tuesday
with Tony and Byron as you suggested and will probably stay till the last
of the week for the purpose of taking the rough off Tony, etc.

I LOVE YOU

Bill

* * *

Crawfordsville
June 10

Whoopee!!

Dear Father:
Well, I'll be dog-goned—I've got my arm in a sling. Now wait!
It is absolutely all right—here's the story ... I took the saddle off Tony
because I wanted to ride bareback and left it on the ground, and to make
a long story short I came back later and put the saddle on without

cinching it because I was just going up to the barn—Well, when the horse walked up a little four-ft. hill, I slid off backwards and fell off with the saddle, landed on my arm and got up, the arm not hurting but looking funny. I called Ray and he came over and looked at it and gave it a pull. Later the Dr. said the pull Ray gave set it so all the Dr. had to do was put it in a sling.

Well, I'll be seein' you.

I love you

bill

* * *

(6-10-31)

W.H.H.:

Don't worry. B. is fine & every thing is O.K. and arm being seen after by Dr. Did a boy ever get past 15 <u>with out such</u>!

(He is now a real boy.)

Helen

* * *

WESTERN UNION
JUNE 11, 1931.

BILL HAYS JR.
414 WEST WABASH AVENUE,
CRAWFORDSVILLE, INDIANA

TOUGH BREAK OLD PARTNER BUT YOU SHOULD WORRY ABOUT A FEW BROKEN ARMS STOP NEXT TIME BETTER USE TWO SADDLES AND SOME PAGE'S GLUE TO STICK THEM ON THE HORSE STOP ONLY TWO THINGS NECESSARY AND THAT IS TO BE VERY CERTAIN THAT THE ARM IS MOST PROPERLY TREATED AND TO BE CAREFUL WHILE IT IS GETTING WELL STOP BROKEN ARMS GET WELL VERY QUICKLY AND ARE GOOD AS NEW AND IT WONT BE LONG UNTIL YOU ARE RIDING TONY AGAIN STANDING UP STOP LOVE

DAD

(6-12-31)

Memo. from
C.C. PETTIJOHN to W.H.H.

Boss:
There is not much advice that a "co-father" can give a situation like this. It is an artistic example of "slipping the bad news to father without worrying him". When a boy displays as much "guts" and such a splendid desire not to worry daddy as this fellow shows, there is not much to worry about and there is not much room for advice.

C.C.P.

* * *

(6-15-31)

<u>Dear Father:</u> Report on Arm.
(1.) I walked in Dr. Sigmond's (specialist) office. (2.) Waited 15 minutes. (3.) Nurse came out of hole in wall. (4.) I went in hole in wall accompanied by nurse. (5.) Arm exrayed. (6.) Came out. (7.) Waited 10 minutes. (8.) Dr. came out. (9.) I got up. (10.) Patted me on shoulder. (11.) "Everything is fine—don't worry," he said (shoot, if you must this old gray head—anyway, to get on with the story) "just be careful & it'll heal up all right." (12.) Good-bye. 13.) Good-bye. (14.) The End.
I'll be seein you—whoopee—I love you

Bill

* * *

New York City
June 18, 1931.

Dear Bill:
. . . I hope you ride the calf you told about at the farm where you keep Tony. However, I think you had better be careful because I have known good riders who got thrown off of burros a couple of inches high, and if a cow puncher can't ride a burro I don't know what he could do with a calf. Anyway, go ahead and try the calf. I would do the calf-trying, however, after the arm gets well. In the meantime, if you think you have

to ride something, we will see if we can get a velocipede somewhere. Of course, you could ride your French right hard.

I love you.

Affectionately, Dad

* * *

WABASH COLLEGE
Office of the President
CRAWFORDSVILLE, INDIANA

June 23, 1931

Dear Mr. Hays:

Your son Bill took the Wabash entrance examination in Latin two days ago and I have just had a report from Professor Montgomery, head of the department. Bill made a B in the examination, so he doesn't have to worry about that any more, as far as we and presumably Riverdale are concerned. A couple of days ago I talked with Mr. Ernest Boyd and during the conversation he spoke in most commendable terms of Bill's interest in his work and the progress he was making in French, in which we'll examine him this fall. The mere matter of a broken arm seems to have had no noticeable effect either on Bill or his work.

Sincerely yours, L. B. Hopkins

* * *

June 25, 1931

Dear Helen:

This morning I received here in New York a letter from Bill, written last Sunday, full, as usual, of his desire to go on a ranch. I note also your note on the envelope about your not wanting him to go. Of course, the fact that he is so crazy to go on a ranch presents a real problem for us both . . . I am mighty certain, of course, that he is happy there with the attention you are giving him yourself, with the car and the Country Club, Ernest Boyd and Flora, etc., but if, in spite of all this he still continues to be literally crazy to get on a ranch for a short time, then you will want to consider what course we ought to take. It will not be very

275

long until his interest in ranch life and horses will be succeeded by his interest in dancing and girls, I expect . . .

Think this over very carefully and if you decide that it would make him extremely happy, then why don't you suggest it to him yourself.

Sincerely, W.H.H.

* * *

Crawfordsville, Indiana
June 27, 1931

Dear Mr. Hays:

Bill and I have spent most of today again swimming at the Crawfordsville country club. We met early this morning for our French lesson and went out to the club later. Mrs. Jessie Hays, here visiting as you know, drove us out in her family's car. (Bill's mother said that arrangements had been made for us to go to Indianapolis on July first to get the new Chevrolet. That will facilitate our trips out of town considerably, of course.) . . . Bill's mother bought a club membership . . . We have found time in most cases to play tennis after French class each morning . . .

Sincerely yours, Ernest Boyd

* * *

Crawfordsville
June 29

Dear Father:

Boy—It sure is hot! I've been going swimming everday at the Country Club now that we're members. I went out last night and swam by moonlight. Gee we had fun! Martha (Pierce), Earny, Flora & I all went. Earny is a nice fellow and we sure had fun. I'm goin' to ask mother and see if I can't go out again tonight. I hope I can!

I think the Cody thing will work out O.K. and I think and hope very much that Mother will be happy for me to go out there four weeks in July & August. My arm is all fine and the cast is off. Byron is fine and so's Tony.

I love you.
Billy

Crawfordsville, Ind.,
June 29, 1931

Mr. Will H. Hays
28 West 44th St.
New York, N.Y.

Dear Mr. Hays:

. . . As the novelty of the country club pool wears off, if it does, we will begin playing golf and resume our tennis playing. This all sounds rather stiff, I'm afraid, like our "work" together is mechanical. Rather, at Bill's suggestion—and I think the idea is yours too—we have been playing together as if we had become friends by accident instead of by contract. We try to maintain a certain formality in the class work, but after the daily work hours are up we forget that we are studying French and enjoy ourselves . . .

Sincerely yours, Ernest Boyd.

* * *

H. W. SIGMOND, M.D.
RADIUM AND X-RAY
BEN-HUR BUILDINGS
CRAWFORDSVILLE, IND.

July 1, 1931

Dear Mr. Hays:

Many thanks for the check. It was quite a pleasure for me to be able to help your son. No man could have conducted himself with more nerve and courage than he did. I am looking foward with a great deal of interest to the time when he enters Wabash College because boys like that are the kind of material that we are looking for the future of Wabash.

Yours very truly, Harvey Sigmond

* * *

Crawfordsville, Indiana
July 5, 1931.

Dear Mr. Hays:

To start our celebration of a rather quiet Fourth, yesterday, Bill and I met at 9 o'clock and read French for an hour. Bill's colored friend, who is here from Sullivan for the week-end, took us, with Flora and Martha Pierce, to the country club to see a swimming meet...At the club again last night, we saw some shooting of lawn fireworks. Since Bill hasn't learned to dance, he returned home shortly after ten o'clock, apparently a little bit "griped" because the younger Pierce girl, Flora, stayed to dance with a Breaks boy. Don't you think Bill should be encouraged to dance? From a brief conversation with the colored man I gathered that you as well as his mother would not be adverse to his "mixing" a little more, socially . . .

Sincerely yours, Ernest Boyd

* * *

Crawfordsville, Indiana
July 6, 1931

Dear Father:

HOORAY—WHOOPEE! Mother's given me permission to go out West—Isn't that great? Old Tiny[1] and all . . . Drive in and say, "Why, hello there Dave. How's old Bearpaw?" Dot—Sally—Tiny—W-H-O-O-P-E-E—Boy that's great of Mother, isn't it?

Every thing is going along fine here. Boy I was sore last night at one Flora Pierce—I met a nice girl the other day by the name of Kate Synder. I'm going to run around with her for a while and then you just watch Flora warm right up to me. Hot dog—that's the way to treat 'em. Flora thinks she has me buffaloed by monkeying around with other guys—you know—We'll see about that! . . . Well I'll be running along now. I'll be seein' you.

I LOVE YOU!

Bill

* * *

Dear Helen:

. . . I note what your letter says about Bill going to the ranch and I will make certain that he will be in Crawfordsville not later than one month after he leaves there . . . He will study just as he now is up until the time he goes. Then he begins his studies again immediately upon his

---

1. *Nickname for 6'2" Leonard Morris.*

278

return, before he starts east the last of September . . . Be sure he takes all his old clothes, spurs, riding boots, hat, etc. He knows very well what he needs in that regard. The fact is he is quite a cowboy himself.

Yours, etc., W.H.H.

* * *

Crawfordsville
July 12

Dear Father:

Boy, I can hardly wait to ride into the old Lazy Bar H— Whoopee!!!! Seriously, father, I appreciate this trip and the last one more than anyone can tell—that's all.

Boy I'm havin' fun here lately. Kate Snyder had a girl come to visit her, a cousin named Mary Plummer. I called up Kate the other day to ask her to go some place with me last night and she told me she was going to this party so I asked what Mary was doing. She said "nothing" so I went down to see her (Mary) and we went swimming and then for a long auto ride. What fun! Yesterday Flora and I played some tennis and I met another nice girl—she left today tho. (Worse Luck.) Flora is going to see *Free Soul* with me tomorrow night. We're going out to the farm (Tony & Byron, etc.) in the morning and going swimming in the afternoon. Hot dog.

Whoopie, Leonard! Ride Em Cowboy!!!

I've been playing golf lately. It's a lot of fun. I didn't think it would be. I'll take you on soon! Well, so long. I'll be seein you!

I love you
(Etc. into the night.)

Bill

* * *

Sullivan, Ind.
July 13, 1931

Dear Mr. Hays:

I just have your letter of July 11, regarding the Cody trip. Bill called me as soon as you phoned him about going along and this is what he said: "Ray, I just talked to Father on the telephone and I'm awfully sorry, but he said that you and I—could meet him in Chicago and go out to Cody!" He was almost as happy about it as I was. I am surely very grateful to you for your kindness not only in taking me on these wonderfull trips, but all of your dealings with me. I can but say you are the best Boss in the world.

Best wishes always.

Very truly yours, Ray Russell

* * *

WESTERN UNION
JULY 14, 1931

LEONARD MORRIS
LAZY BAR RANCH
CODY WYOMING

RIDE EM COWBOY STOP BILL RAY AND I WILL BE THERE NEXT TUESDAY MORNING AT ELEVEN O'CLOCK STOP YOU CAN HAVE ROOM FOR BILL AND ME IN THE COTTAGE AND PUT RAY WHERE HE WAS LAST YEAR STOP MRS HAYS WILL COME IN A SHORT TIME AND YOU CAN REPARK US THEN IF NECESSARY STOP BEST WISHES

WILL H. HAYS

* * *

THE STATE OF WYOMING
BOARD OF LIVE STOCK COMMISSIONERS
CHEYENNE

August 13, 1931

Mr. Will H. Hays
Wapiti,
Wyoming.

Dear Sir:

Replying to your letter of august 10th in connection with the brands you ask for this is to advise you that you may have both the brands you ask for: the *Diamond H* and the *Snowshoe*.

The diamond brand is to be placed on the left hip of the horses and the snowshoe brand on the left ribs of cattle . . .

Sincerely yours, D.H. Dalzell, Secretary.

* * *

Northern—*THE NEW NORTH COAST LIMITED*—Burlington
Pacific Route

(8-16-31)

Dear Father—

Just a note to tell you that I had the greatest summer ever & I hope you realize how much I appreciated the trip.

Your Pal till bears grow horns and eat alfalfa.

I love you

Bill.

* * *

(8-23-31)

Dear Father:

Well, one week gone by very happily for me here in Crawfordsville. Boy, I'm havin' a great time—swimming, golfing, and just monkeying around. I've been going somewhere with Flora every morning, golfing or something, and sometimes Martha[2] comes along and then in the afternoon they and Ernie and I play golf. I have dates with Flora set ahead to keep us busy & some day soon, about four-thirty, Flora, Martha, Earny & I are going to drive over to Indianapolis for dinner, supper that is, and then to a show & home . . .

I love you

Bill

* * *

---

2. *Flora's older sister.*

Crawfordsville, Indiana
September 3, 1931

Dear Mr. Hays:

I have just taken Bill home to study his French after we stopped downtown this evening for a chocolate milk-shake . . . After taking a swim this afternoon, I took my "sax" and Bill his drum, drove out toward the country club where no one could hear us, and proceeded to demoralize the pigs and cows. . . Thursday's "event" was a dinner party with the Pierce girls at a chicken-dinner establishment a short distance southwest of the city. . . I think I forgot to say in connection with our golf that we're beginning to go out to play two or three or five balls, instead of holes, each morning. I think a ball lasted for nine holes one day.

Very truly yours, Ernest Boyd

* * *

(9-6-31)

Dear Father;

Earny and I went out to the country club the other night after Mother and I got home from the show at the "Joy." We went "stag" and I had a rotten time. I guess I'm off of dances! I had an awful time trying to get up the nerve to ask any one. Finally, about 10:30 I did after Earny and I made a bet about it. He said if I didn't go in the next dance I'd have to give a cowboy yell in the "Sweetshop" downtown after the dance, and visa-versa if I did. I waited till the song was just about over and took Flora out on the floor. Luckily the piece stoped right away so I won the bet and didn't have to dance long. We got in about 12:30 but the sweetshop was closed so Earny has to yell tonite.

Last night E. & I fixed up a bell—a loud one—on the front of the car & by a string we can ring it from the driver's seat. We went up & down Wabash Avenue ringing it. I expected any minute to be hauled in for disturbing the peace. We're goin' to paint things red tonite. I'll be seein' you.

I love you—Bill

* * *

September 11, 1931

Dear Mr. Hays:

I am writing to Professor Frank S. Hackett at Riverdale certifying Bill's excellent grades on the exams the College has given him in both Latin and French, the latter of which he took yesterday and both of which Riverdale will credit... I congratulate you on Bill's showing and I certainly congratulate Bill.

With kindest personal regards I am

Sincerely yours, L.B. Hopkins

Crawfordsville
September 18

Dear Father:

Knowing that you know the creed of honor between us I hearby make the following statement: I found a cigarette in the house here, lit it and took several puffs. This is the first time this has happened since I promised you several years ago, in fact, about 5 or 6. It will not happen again but I thought I should let you know, knowing the way we do things.

It won't be long now till New York! Whoopee!
I'll be seein' you

I love you

Bill

* * *

October 24, 1931.

Dear Helen:

... I think if I were you I would get the gun for Bill that he wants, just to make him specially happy and appreciative. There is no need to write him of your writing to me about it. Just tell him you will give it to him for Christmas... Note that I have moved to the Waldorf Towers (28-A), Waldorf Astoria Hotel, Park Ave. at 50th St.

Best wishes.

Sincerely yours, W.H.H.

(10-26-31)

Dear Father:

I'm in my dorm room, and this is just a note, because I can hardly move the pen—I'm so sleepy... Doggone, didn't we have fun this week end—and haven't we had fun these last four years together? I sure have, at least. I live for these week ends & summers with you ... So long, puncher—I'll be seein' you Tuesday when I come in from school about my back.

I love you

Your Partner, Bill

* * *

Hollywood, California
November 17, 1931

Dear Bill:

Of course I am just more sorry than I can possibly tell you that I have to stay out here longer that I thought when I left, and so can't be with you for the next two weeks and over Thanksgiving weekend. However, I called up Uncle Hinkle and he, Aunt Lucile and the two boys are coming down to have a great time with you on Thanksgiving. ...I have told Miss Kelly to give you any money you need, and I want you to show the whole crowd a fine time ... I just have to do this Algebra job of my own, believe me ... I know you will not fail to take the osteopathic treatments for your back and drink your orange juice and your milk.

I love you.

Affectionately, Father

* * *

(11-23-31)

Dear Father:

Gee, Bob & Ed Hubbard's mother is fine. She has three towel racks in the bathroom at her house, and over one last week end she had posted a piece of paper saying Bob, another Ed, and over the third, Billy. Isn't that nice. She says to make it my second home.

Well, I reckon you're ridin' her straight up out there (as usual). Boy, I'm goin' to have fun Thanksgiving with the kids—<u>Gee, I wish you were goin' to be there</u>! My back's comin' along fine—straight as an arrow.

I saw Ed Wynn's <u>great</u> show last night, Gosh it's funny! He's great Well, so long & don't forget, if you can, to slip in even a short note every once in a while. I'd rather get a letter from you than from a million girlfriends (of course).

Be good!

I love you

Bill

* * *

Chapter Thirty-one

ONE Sunday Dad and I were changing from our riding clothes in his bedroom at the Waldorf Towers apartment, to which he and Jessie recently had moved from the Ritz Tower. I'd showered after he had and was pulling on my undershorts with my back to him when he said in a concerned voice "Wait a minute, stay bent over that way" and stepped to his desk, picked up a pen, walked over to me and began tracing my spine with it, inking on my skin each of my protruding vertebrae from my neck to my tailbone. When he'd finished he had me straighten and stepped back and looked at the marks. When I asked him what he saw he said after a moment "Your backbone has a couple of curves in it." By the following weekend his doctor had arranged appointments for me with a radiologist and an orthopedist; and to make a long story short, these specialists and their colleagues, after a series of examinations, concluded I had both scoliosis and kyphosis—side-to-side and front-to-back S-curvatures—maybe resulting from the tilting effect of a compression fracture of a lumbar vertebrae caused by Tony's falling on me several years previously in Sullivan.

The doctors told Dad and he told me that there were two treatment options: surgery, leaving me with a straight but stiff spine, so I should have to bend from the waist for life; or a relatively new procedure which had been invented by a doctor named Royal Whitman, and which should involve my lying in a hospital and then the apartment for a number of weeks on my back on a long, narrow "A-frame," with my head and feet about fourteen inches lower than the top of the "A's" upward thrust against the backward bow of my lower spine. The "A-frame" was to be placed on top of a regular hospital bed. Dr. Whitman's theory was that pressure at the small of my back resulting from its being bent frontward over the pressure-point and stretched at the same time by the weight of my head and feet should force both the side-to-side and the front-to-back curves at least considerably straighter than they should be otherwise; and then this straighter condition was to be stabilized by three or four month's encasement of my body from my hips to under-arms in a plaster cast followed by a like period in a corset; and thereafter throughout most of my life, hopefully, I could keep my spine fairly straight and flexible by appropriate exercise, particularly swimming. Dad asked me which of the treatment options I chose, and I said the "A-frame" and he agreed. When Dr. Whitman told us he would take me on as a patient, I left school for the "duration" and was admitted to Manhattan's Hospital for the Ruptured and Crippled.

I stayed in that hospital about three and a half weeks, not turning on either side or raising any part of my body except my hips for a bedpan to be slid under them. I learned a good deal by reading books, ranging from *Lorna Doone* to *Wyatt Earp, Frontier Marshall*, and by talking with nereby patients who could wheel themselves or walk into my room on their therapy jaunts, and with visitors from what even in that short time came to seem like the outside world, and with my own three shifts of eight-hour nurses, and with a tutor whom Riverdale recommended and Dad hired to keep me up on my school work. Dad and Jessie bought a contraption that Tom and a nurse fastened to the top of my bed directly over my head, so I could place an open book on it and read upward through its glass shelf.

When I complained one day the first week about the lack of vigorous life around me, Dad arrived with a canary in a cage; and although I'm sure this didn't thrill the nurses who had to clean its cage, it added a bright dimension to my earliest days there.

Two very bright later days were the ones when Will James brought me his painting of his horse, Smokey, abut which he'd written and Scribners had just published a book, and when Felix Count Von Luckner visited me. While Will was there, he helped me write up an order for a saddle, with recommendations about its roping tree and swells and cantle and ox-bow stirrups. The count was the famous German "Sea Devil" of World War I whose disguised square-rigger had prowled the earth's oceans and sunk thousands of tons of Allied shipping without the loss of one life, taking captured crews and passengers aboard his *See Adler* for debarking in neutral countries, and who had won in the process the admiration and even affection, not only of his captives, but of the diverted world.

Dad had become acquainted with the count through Lowell Thomas, who had written a book about him. I heard his booming sea-captain's voice coming down the corridor ahead of him mingling with nurses' gasps and laughter and patients' calls of greetings, and then his six and a half feet and two hundred and fifty solid pounds filled my doorway. Exclaiming what I'd read was his habitual greeting of "By Joe," with "Bill" added now, he strode to my bed and seized my outstretched hand with one even bigger than Len Morris's. That began two hours of conversation and adventure tales and demonstrations of his celebrated strength by his tearing a Manhattan telephone directory in two, enthralling me and the nurses and patients who crowded into my room and ending with his invitation that I join him and some other boys, whom he was in New York recruiting, on a trip the next summer to Tahiti aboard the full-scale replica of the *Sea Eagle*, then moored at a West Side pier. Things didn't work out so I could make that voyage, but I daydreamed about it for a long time.

Lying in the hospital I did considerable daydreaming about other things too, including girls. Across the hall a very sweet and pretty twenty-some-year-old was recovering from surgery to equalize the lengths of her legs, and when she had progressed to the walking therapy stage she came in to visit me everyday. The fact that she was at least a half-dozen years older than I didn't bar her from my daydreams, any more than Joan Crawford's seniority had kept the actress and me fancifully apart back in Sullivan, years of nights earlier. I imagined that we, too, had fallen in love. Then one morning she broke the news that she would have to be tearing herself away from me because she was to be discharged the next day; and although I couldn't deny this had aspects of good news from her standpoint, it left me with one less incarnate love fantasy object, a vacuum in my psyche I'd have to fill as soon as possible. Luckily (and typically then, I guess) it didn't take long.

Of my three nurses, one was pretty but in love with someone else, another was homely and married, and the third, although no beauty, was not homely and not at all encumbered. My sexual imaginings swept her into their whirlpool. Then I made an amazing discovery: she was as frustrated as I was. I found out this piquant fact one morning when she was giving me my sponge bath. The pleasant warmth of the wet washcloth in her massaging hand produced a sudden hankering in me. And her grazing touch seemed to stir her own ardor, as well. She was a very nice lady, quite shy; but before we knew it, our lips were touching briefly. This confused us both. At least it did her. My confusion was less certain than my excitement; but I managed, with a couple of deep breaths, to regain control of that. The canary burst into song, the blushing lady took the wash basin into my bathroom to empty it, and I plunged into a stream of smalltalk. We avoided personal subjects in our conversation for the rest of the morning; but by the time she got back from lunch in the nurses' cafeteria, we both seemed to have recovered pretty well from self-consciousness, and I managed to thank her for her kiss, and she swallowed a time or two and said the pleasure was all hers.

That broke the ice, you might say, not only between her and me, but among that end of the floor's nurses and me. I didn't mind it when the evening nurse—the pretty one—hinted, soon after her shift had begun, that my new lady friend had kissed and told. Loyal to her own lover, she didn't offer to kiss me, but she said a very young nurse down the hall had bet the others during their dinner in the cafeteria that *she* would. Of course, I knew I wasn't all that desirable. But I sensed those nurses needed relief from their environment's un-life—not only patients' deaths, but as often suspended lives, where pain and hopelessness and disappointment supplanted living. I seemed able to imagine their weariness and I guess they related to my imagining, I don't know. Not that I had any special insight; I just joined the little private party. One thing I do know: it was fine for my morale.

The day nurse's and my antiseptic affair took an intriguing turn about a week before I left the hospital. She was switched to the evening shift. The intriguing thing about it was that it provided some kissing time in the darkness after visiting hours. Although our fervent gropings never fully reached even the limited intimacy that my immobility should have allowed—I give her restaint the credit for that—we came gloriously close. She's another of the people I'll alway remember with affection.

Early in the morning of the day I was to be discharged from the hospital, I was awakened by a covey of nurses around my bed, like grinning quail. It was the morning shift change, and my new night nurse—the homely, married one—said they'd come to kiss me goodbye and that she was first by her own election and that the youngest one who'd made the bet with the others was next and that the rest were on their own. The dazzling thing was they weren't kidding. I asked only to brush my teeth hurriedly, and then one at a time damned if they didn't do what they said they'd come for. I felt like an Eastern potentate; that morning's exalting experience has carried me through many a discouraged moment.

Before lunch, Dad, who had visited me every day, came on his best visit of all: he rode with me in the ambulance to our apartment in the Waldorf Towers, into which he and Jessie had moved during my incarceration. The "A-frame" was loaded on with us, and Tom followed the ambulance in Dad's car. When we reached the Waldorf's driveway between Forty-ninth and Fiftieth Streets, I was stretchered up the Towers' service elevator by the medics, with Dad and Tom alongside and two bellmen lugging the "A-frame" behind us. The bellmen put the frame on a hospital bed which had been set up in the room where I was to continue lying for three or four more weeks before going back to the hospital's therapy room for an hour's stringing up by a head-harness, so the trunk of my body could be wrapped in plaster, after which I was to be amulatory. The medics lifted me onto the frame, and Tom returned to the hospital to get my day nurse and canary, and Dad went back to his office.

I settled into the remaining months of school year, which involved a mosaic of happenings: watching from my horizontal perch on stormy nights as lighting struck the tip of the Empire State Building; drawing Western scenes, inspired by Will James's great sketches; more tutoring until I was able to return to classes wearing my cast under my clothes; talking at length with Dad in the evenings when he and Jessie didn't have to go out; visiting with friendly people who dropped by the apartment to see me, like Ed Hubbard and his mother and Mr. and Mrs. O.O. McIntyre and Tom Mix's daughter, Ruth, or those who called on Dad there for private meetings with him, like movie executives Nick Schenck and Louis Mayer; riding the Riverdale bus to and from school with the "day students," until I could trade my cast for a laced-up corset; waiting for that bus early in the mornings on the corner of Park Avenue and Fiftieth Street, and exchanging greetings with the Sanitation Department workers who were getting their sweeping and hosing done while traffic was light; going along with the gag for a week after my return when some kid would get another to slap me on the back, so he could watch the other's reaction at hitting my camouflaged armor plate; becoming friends with internationally famous chef and Waldorf maitre d', Rene Black, when Dad and Jessie were away on the Coast and Rene came up once in a while to the apartment with the room service waiter who brought my dinner and at other times invited me down to the hotel's Starlight Roof and with great kindness himself acted as my captain; feeling vastly relieved at Gene Tunney's saying one evening at dinner that before the opening bell of every fight he had the same butterflies in the pit of his stomach that I secretly had been ashamed of having in mine while waiting for a football kickoff.

By May, my cast was cut off, and thanks to daily workouts for several weeks after that in the New York Athletic Club pool (to which Tom drove me from school), the corset became unnecessary, except when I had to stand or sit in one place for a considerable period. Before I got rid of the cast, it had become very itchy with the onset of warm weather; but I discovered that, by exhaling as much as possible, I could stick a ruler down from its top and scratch most of my sheathed skin pretty well.

Chapter Thirty–two

November 27, 1931
1:30 p.m.

(Report by H.C.H. to W.H.H. in Hollywood on doctors' conference in New York re Bill's spinal curvature)
. . . X-ray indicates back curvature increasing . . . I would not accept the diagnosis without full consultation with both Capps and Herrick . . . Maximum treatment required not more than two to four months in bed and not more than four to five months in portable cast after patient up . . . Patient absolutely impervious to any reaction of regret or worry other than statement "Only thing I want is that my grades and school work will not be allowed to worry father. Worst thing in world is to see expression his face when he opens envelope containing grades in his office and finds an "f" . . .

* * *

Sunday afternoon
November 29

Dear Father:
Well, another week gone & I've sure had fun. I think the kids & Aunt Lucile & Uncle Hinkle have had a good time too. At least I hope so! We saw *The Cat & the Fiddle* and the Ed Wynn show. In the latter I was sitting star-gazing with my eyes on a point about the level of a person's head, before the show began, and all of a sudden a face butted into my vision and then walked on down the isle. Boy what a thrill. It was Joan Crawford. (Harpo Marx was sitting in front of us last night at the Palace.) . . . Well, I'll be seein' you soon at Chicago when I come overnight to check with Dr. Capps and Dr. Ryerson about my back.

Whoopee! . . . Listen, Father, I want you to know that I absolutely am <u>not</u> worrying about going to bed. Well, I'd say not—see you every night.

I love you, Bill

＊　＊　＊

DR. EDWIN W. RYERSON
PEOPLES GAS BUILDING
122 SOUTH MICHIGAN AVENUE
CHICAGO

December 15, 1931

Dr. Royal Whitman
71 Park Avenue
New York City.

Dear Dr. Whitman:
    I thank you for your letter about Will Hays Jr. Dr. Capps and I have advised Mr. Hays to place the boy in your very able care and to follow your advice. This case is one of great personal interest to Dr. Capps and me, and we are very anxious to have every possible attention given to the boy, on account of our friendship with his father . . .

Very truly yours,

＊　＊　＊

December 17,1931

Dear Helen:
    Today Bill has gone into the hospital and is very happy about it. He was really very anxious to go, insisting he wanted to "get it done and get it over with." He does not want to lose any school, either now or otherwise delay his entrance into Wabash as planned. He said "it seems crazy to go to the hospital when I feel like I wanted to run a mile," but he realizes the vital importance of fixing his back now . . . About the tutor: Mr. Hackett, the Riverdale headmaster, agreed to help find one or more for Bill until he can get back to school . . . And about your winter visit here, Bill is sending you your transportation—the railroad ticket and the

lower in the Pullman—just as he always does, as his Christmas present to you . . .

I am going over this evening and will, of course, go over every morning on my way downtown and spend some time each evening with him. His good friends, like the Hubbards out at school, are going to come every day during the holidays to see him . . . He will have time to write you frequently . . .

Sincerely yours, Bill

* * *

(12-25-31)

Dear Father:

I got your sweet letter here in the "Ruptured" hospital and I appreciate it very much. I only wish that I could give you something that you would cherish as much as I will your gift of the saddle that Will James is going to help us order. I am very happy about it, pardner. Every time I sit in it, my hands resting on its swells, I'll think of you. Thanks.

Your pardner and loving son.

Bill

* * *

January 9, 1932

Dear Helen:

When Dr. Whitman said yesterday that Bill should stay on his back on the frame "three weeks more," I immediately said, "If this is so, then why can't he lie on his back on this frame just as well in the apartment for the next three weeks as in the hospital? To this Whitman said, "He can" . . . The same day and night nurses will look after him and the doctor will come every day to our Waldorf Towers apartment to see him, just as he went to the hospital . . . The night nurse, who watches him all night, turns him over on his back if he gets on his side in his sleep . . .

Sincerely, W.H.H.

293

Tuesday
January 10, 1932

Dear Aunt Mattie:

Well, at last I'm at the Apt. . . . Thank Gosh!

Say, I sure do appreciate your Christmas present. The little iron dog is right where I can see it. Thanks heaps.

Gee, ain't it the craziest weather we're having now? (I hope you won't mind my bad writing because I'm doin' this on my back.) . . .

So long—here's hoping you're OK!

Love, Bill

* * *

February 1, 1932

Dear Helen:

Bill was taken back over to the hospital this morning... they put a pad all around his body about a quarter of an inch thick; then around that they wrapped the wet crinoline which is saturated with plaster . . . then it hardens. It took about twenty minutes. During this time he was held up on his toes by headstraps so that it was not too exhausting, but quite exhausting, indeed, when he had been in bed for nearly seven weeks . . . After he has worn this for about three or four weeks, he gets the lighter cast which he takes off every night . . .

Sincerely yours, Bill

* * *

HAYS, William English V B   2-1-32
(Status Report to Parents)

In many ways the finest writer in the class, I feel nevertheless that Bill is unnecessarily limiting himself by writing as he does exclusively on subjects dealing with the West . . . He can express these thoughts in pencil and oil as well as in words, but I would encourage him to try other fields to write and paint.

I.W. Thompson

* * *

February 9, 1932

Mr. Ed Hubbard,
Riverdale Country School,
Riverdale-on-Hudson
New York.

Dear Ed:

I want you to help me on a matter. Our cowpuncher is going to start to school today or tomorrow. He does not know what I am telling you but I want you to help me put one over on him. He will probably try to play football with his seven thousand pound jacket on, and I don't think that is so good. I want you to help me on keeping him quiet a little . . . Keep an eye on him for me and call him down if he gets too frisky. I have to go to California today. Mrs. Hays is going to Indiana and then joining me. I'll be gone about a month, so I make you head wrangler until I get back. Thank you, Ed.

Sincerely yours, Will H. Hays

* * *

HOTEL PENNSYLVANIA
NEW YORK

(2-16-32)

Dear Father:

Well, there goes one week-end closer to your coming home again. I didn't do much this one. Mother and I are at the Penn. Hotel, and I took her to a good movie at the Roxy (Will Rogers in "Business and Pleasure") and heard that same orchestra you and I did a week ago, directed by the father of the Riverdale kid Rappe. Boy, this is some bright day! Reminds me of those mornings out in Wyoming—Oh Gosh—

Say, Father, Yesterday I went to the apt. after something and you know all the swell pictures I had in my room—fixed up just to suit me and the pasted-up ones of Count Luckner & Bill James' Christmas card, etc., and the bridle and cartridge belts & bridle? Well someone has taken those all away and moved all the furniture around. Dog-gone—I just had it fixed up and now look at it. Also, whoever did it has put up, in place of the western pictures, a crazy fool Chinese one! I asked the Towers house keeper but she knows nothing about it and said ask your butler, but Dawson wouldn't do that on his own. That's funny, isn't it. I'm going to put em all back next week-end.

Well, I've gotten all settled down & doin' the medications great. I'll be seein' you—

I love you, Dad

Bill.

* * *

Hollywood, California
March 2, 1932

Dear Bill:

. . . The three thousand dollars Aunt Sallie left you in her will I think you may want to set aside toward your college education. She was a great school teacher as well as a fine person and that might please her. Or you might use it on law school expenses. Or maybe together we can take care of all those expenses and save this three thousand for you to get married on.

I love you, Father

* * *

<u>Mon. afternoon.</u>
(3-4-32)

Dear Father:

. . . Doctors, eye-men, liver of oil by Cod, drops, salve, etc., all O.K. Don't worry. Since you have been away I have missed just 15 drops out of about, well, at least 315 or 320. Ed just came along & dumped my books—wait a minute, I'll pick 'em up—O.K., they're fixed. We heard Buttrick (that great minister we like so much) preach a <u>swell</u> sermon Sunday. he talked about temptations and will power . . . A man sees something very tempting, or hears it, this travels along the nerves' road to his mind's headquarters where it is labeled and presented to the will. Here takes place a terrible struggle—a one-sided one. A dull, uninteresting sense of duty against pleasure, relief or satisfaction. The will usually loses, and the messengers go out with the news. Now, the place to make a victory, and usually the only place, is to shut the outer door (ear

452

******

112 Natoma Ave
Santa Barbara, Calif.
March 17, 1932

Dear Jack and Mary:

Well, I had to hoist a few to day to St Patrick,
and I thought of you folks, I bet you done the same and maybe
things turned out just as wild as they did when you all
got together and scribbled me the letter I received the
other day. It was sure thoughtful of you cusses to write us
and we sure appreciated it.

Say, Jack, did you receive an order from Will
H. Hays for two saddles. If you didn't I expect you will soon.
I seen Will Hays the other day and he said he'd ordered 'em.

The way that come about was that young Bill Hays
asked me what kind of a saddle he should get. I told him the
same kind he rode at my ranch and that suited him fine. Do
you remember the plain saddle I had you make me?-- The one
with the Ladesma tree. Remember how I had you sort of fill
and round out the swell and widen the front of the tree ?
I think that tree was ordered special, and if you dont remember it you'd better write Fred at the ranch and have him
send it to you. The rigging was single and between a Spanish
and three quarter, round skirted, and the only saddle you
made me with sheepskin lining.

Well, they both want that tree. I dont know if
they'll want plain or stamped covering or round or square
skirts but they can tell you and I told 'em that whatever they
wanted in saddles and such, Jack Connolly was the man to do it.

Will Hays amounts to as much in Hollywood and in
the moving picture game as Mussolini does in Italy.

Things are going pretty fine here with us, Alice's
mother is with us again for a spell and we're all busy, specially me. I managed to sell LONE COWBOY to Paramount for the
movies and got $ 10.000 for it. Not so bad for an old decrepit.
I think I can sell two more too.

This is a long letter so I better stop. Tell all
who know us hello and that I'll be along July 4th, with bells on.

Best of luck to you two.

Your friend

Bill JAMES

or eye) so the temptation can not get a hold and get started inward . . . If we are listening for the doorbell, we run to the door at the first clang, if we are not, we may not even hear it! Some idea, huh? Well, so long—I'll be seein you

I love you, Bill

* * *

March 8, 1932

Dear Hinkle:

The Riverdale nurse says Bill is getting his bone and other medicine with absolute regularity. He got so tired of eggnog every night that they are giving it to him every other night, alternating with Ovaltine . . . The nurse commented particularly on his good spirits . . . Also Thomas, the Chauffeur, says Bill is absolutely all right. In fact, Thomas is quite "cocky" on the subject and takes a lot of credit to himself for Bill's improvement.

Sincerely yours, J.K.

* * *

WALTER ELLIOTT TAYLOR, D.D.S.
2 EAST 54TH STREET, NEW YORK
March 9, 1932

Mr. Will Hays
28 West Forty-fourth Street
New York City

Dear Mr. Hays:

. . . I found Bill's teeth in a deplorable condition as regards decay, despite his taking very good care of his mouth . . .

Yours sincerely, W.E. Taylor

* * *

Pencil sketch by W.H.H., Jr., 1932

(3-10-32)

Dear Father—

Well, things are coming right along here now. We thought for a couple of days that we were going to have Spring here, but it got cold day before yesterday and gummed up the works. I'm gettin' spring fever—homesick for Wyoming. Medications, etc, are fine, so don't worry. Am enclosing a composition I wrote. Use it for scrap paper if you don't have time to read it. Say, I've started a savings account, keeping the money in that metal cigarette box you gave me, and already I have two dollars. I got some more today by selling an old scarf, & tie, and a pair of suspenders . . . Sure be glad when you're back!

I love you, Bill

* * *

Sun Eve,
(3-13-32)

Dear Father:

. . . Tho' the weather might warm up by the time you get here, don't come cavortin' back here in your shirt sleeves just because you've been in Calif. for a month! Mother and I are at the Penn. Hotel but I was up at the apartment today, and found everything in great shape, all waitin' for you. I also was up at the club[1] today. Horses are great! Well, I've got to study now—so-long till only a little while!

I love you, Bill

P.S. Hope you like the drawing

* * *

New York City
March 22, 1932.

Mr. Hinkle C. Hays,
Sullivan, Indiana.

Dear Hinkle:

. . . There is speculation that Bill's curvature resulted from a compression fracture of lumbar vertebrae due to Tony, Jr. falling on him

1. *Probably Sleepy Hollow Country Club, near Yonkers, N.Y.*

some years ago in Sullivan, which I didn't know about until all this came up. He has an adolescent bone condition and the doctors are very certain that this softening condition of the bones happens to be coincident with and not the cause of, the twisted condition of his frame. Both have to be treated . . . He has no doctors here except Dr. Royal Whitman, the orthopedic physician, with occasional observance by my local Dr. William Herrick, who prescribed the medicine and who is working in conjunction with Dr. Capps of Chicago.

Love to all,

Affectionately, Bill

* * *

March 24, 1932.

Dear Helen:

Bill got away in good shape yesterday. I know he will have a pleasant Spring vacation with you in Crawfordsville . . . He is not planning, of course, to go to Sullivan during this vacation, as you suggested he not, since he missed Christmas in Crawfordsville.

. . . As far as this summer is concerned, the doctors advise that the prime requisite for his health is to get him where there is corrective water and sunshine . . . The most practical way to meet this suggestion would be for me to plan my work so that instead of being in California two or three weeks as usual, I am there for three months . . . I would get a house on the beach at Santa Monica, only twenty-five minutes from my office . . . I would be doing the right thing from the standpoint not only of Bill's health, but of successful execution of my job.

Sincerely yours, W.H.H.

* * *

WESTERN UNION
MARCH 25, 1932

HON. M.E. FOLEY,
TRACTION TERMINAL BUILDING,
INDIANAPOLIS INDIANA

THINK IT IS ALL RIGHT FOR BILL TO HAVE A DRIVERS LICENSE BECAUSE HE HAS PROMISED ME HE WILL

NOT USE IT UNLESS RAY OR ERNEST IS IN THE FRONT SEAT WITH HIM AND THEN VERY CAREFULLY AND ONLY IN SAFE PLACES WHILE HE IS LEARNING TO DRIVE STOP REGARDS

WILL H. HAYS

* * *

March 25, 1932.

Dear Bill:

You passed for the term in English, German and Physics, which is good having in mind your absence, but you flunked Geometry ... You might be studying Geometry while Dr. Whitman is putting on the new plaster cast the day you get back to New York! . . . Mr. Gardner recommends that you tutor Geometry during Spring Term at school and take the Wabash examination when you get back to Indiana, like you did in Latin and French last year. He thinks you will pass that Math examination, along with all your courses here, and be all set for next year, including graduation at the end of that . . .

I love you.

Affectionately, Father

* * *

Crawfordsville
March 28

Dear Father:

... Your help in getting Bill James's books made into movies sure means a lot to him and he certainly appreciates it, believe me! I'm havin' a great time driving and I'm being very careful, so again I say: DON'T WORRY! . . . Well, so-long, and take care of yourself.

I love you, Bill

* * *

April 2, 1932

Dear Helen:

When Bill got back here to New York early yesterday he went right to the hospital and had the jacket taken off at 11 o'clock. At one o'clock they took x-rays and at two o'clock Dr. Whitman put on the new plaster jacket. It is a very tough experience, but he went through it all right . . . He will leave the hospital tonight and go back to school on Monday. Incidentally, he'll be living here at the Towers so I can watch his diet better, and he'll be riding the Riverdale Day-School bus, leaving at 7:22 A.M. and returning by 6:00 P.M. every week day . . . I appreciate your letting him have John T. and the other Wabash boys from Sullivan in to eat with him at your house while he was there.

Sincerely yours, Bill

* * *

April 13, 1932.

Dear Helen:

. . . When they took that x-ray ten days ago without any cast Bill's curve sank back, proving that the recovery is not being held. This makes especially important the sunshine recommended by Dr. Whitman . . . We have failed to provide for him enough food which builds bones in early youth and that has to be provided now. You and I simply have to take our medicine and get him what he ought to have this summer . . . I will be very grateful if you will write me at once and tell me that if the doctor insists that the one best place for Bill for three months this summer is the sun, the beach and water of southern California, that you want me to go ahead and arrange to take him there . . . I know you will realize that from next year on he will be in Crawfordsville a great majority of the time . . .

I realize the importance of your suggestion that he does not get the idea that he is sick, or that he has to nurse himself, etc. Believe me, he does not have that idea . . . He does not pamper himself a bit.

Mattie went to the hospital in Hollywood last Thursday afternoon with an intestinal obstruction, she had a sinking spell and was unconscious until Tuesday afternoon when she died at five o'clock. It has been a very real grief to me . . .

Sincerely, W.H.H.

M. E. FOLEY
LAWYER
INDIANAPOLIS, IND

April 15, 1932.

My dear Will:

If it is necessary in your judgement for Billy to spend his summer vacation in California near the seashore, Mrs. Hays will not object to this plan, but she will go West for the summer and spend her vacation in California where she will be in position to see the young man whenever she desires to do so.

Yours very truly, M.E. Foley

* * *

May 26, 1932

Dear Helen:

On yesterday they took off Bill's plaster cast to try on the framework of the new removable brace, which has a light, steel frame . . . He'll wear it all the time for some weeks except when lying down or swimming . . . The little operation to remove the cyst from his eyelid went very well. It was done by a Dr. Wheeler, who recently operated on the King of Siam, the latter coming all the way here for that purpose because Wheeler is such a top eye man. Bill had to wear a patch for only a few days.

Sincerely yours, W.H.H.

* * *

June 2, 1932.

Dear Helen:

. . . For Bill to put his brace on every morning upon arising you'll have to have a hook put in the middle of the door "header," as we have done in the apartment here, so as to give him room to swing as he pulleys himself up by his head-strap apparatus. I think the thing to do is for me to have Ray there when he arrives day after tomorrow so as to organize it . . . Also Bill will have to have somebody help him each morning put it on . . . Although he doesn't have to sleep on his frame, which I expressed there yesterday, he has to have a folded blanket under the small of his back at night and lie on the frame frequently during the day.

Sincerely yours, W.H.H.

* * *

WESTERN UNION
JUNE 3, 1932

MRS. H. THOMAS HAYS
414 W WABASH AVENUE
COLLEGE HILL
CRAWFORDSVILLE, INDIANA

BELIEVE IT WILL BE BETTER FOR BILL TO COME OUT ON THE TRAIN WITH LON OWENS WHO IS COMING THEN SO LON CAN HELP WITH BRACE STOP BILL PASSED ALL OF HIS FINALS INCLUDING MATH AND IS IN GOOD SHAPE SO NONE NEED BE TAKEN AT WABASH

W.H.H.

* * *

71 PARK AVENUE
June 4, 1932

Mr. Will Hays
TO DR. ROYAL WHITMAN, DR.

For professional services rendered to Will H. Hays, Jr., $3500.00

* * *

DR ROYAL WHITMAN
DR. ARMITAGE WHITMAN
71 PARK AVENUE

June 7th, 1932

Dear Mr. Hays,
Dr. Whitman has asked me to thank you for your extremely prompt payment of his bill. As you know, people as a whole are lax about

paying their doctors' bills and the depression has provided an especially good alibi. Therefore your action is all the more appreciated. We shall miss having Bill come to the office.

Very truly yours, Alice C. Wainwright
Secretary

* * *

Sunday night
Crawfordsville
June 13, 1932

Dear Father:

Well, it won't be long now until we meet in Chicago and head for California! I'm having a great time, and I feel ashamed to say it because I know you're working so hard now. Listen—this is the dope!—this summer you've got to <u>rest more</u>, spend time each day on the beach, and all of each night in bed, away from a phone! No kidding, I'm telling you, not asking you! That's that.

Earny and his girl, and Rosiland Remely, who John T says is the best kid in Montg'm'ry County, and I all had fun at Turkey Run Park the other afternoon, hiking and eating supper at the hotel there and then back here in time for a movie.

Tom came thru in your car with Dawson heading west, and I guess now they're in Oklahoma some where. Tom is about to bust open, honestly; he's having the time of his life—he was in France in the war but has never been across the Hudson River before!

I love you, Bill.

* * *

Chapter Thirty-three

To continue my swimming and get all the outdoor exercise and sunlight I could, Dad decided I should spend that summer vacation on a Southern California beach; so he rented Ben Lyon's and Bebe Daniels' three-story mansion on the sand at Santa Monica. Going back to the Cody ranch was out, anyhow, because it was too soon for horseback riding. In fact I never again was able to be comfortable on a horse, although I returned to somewhat more conservative riding in future years at other spreads, like Len Morris's and his father's consolidated place on the North Fork and Laroms' Valley Ranch on the South Fork of the Shoshone. As it turned out, I spent the next summer also at the beach, just before entering Wabash College, in the Las Tunas beach house of comedian Buster Keaton and his wife, actress Natalie Talmadge, which Dad had rented. It had a soda fountain in its playroom, just indoors from the sand.

Being in that house reminded Dad of having had dinner one evening with Buster and Natalie Keaton—whether there or not, I don't recall—when the soup plate of one of the guests had parted in its middle, cascading its hot contents into the genleman's lap. Dad said that as Natalie had jumped up to help the guest's frantic mopping, she'd glared at her husband and mouthed a silent "Buster!" Dad heard later that without the knowledge of the guest (who wasn't Buster's favorite person) the host had conspired with the chef before dinner to break the plate and lightly glue the halves together and let its steaming contents do the rest. It may have been a week before the hostess spoke to her husband, if the rest of the story was true.

Some of the people in addition to Dad and Jessie who made those beach summers memorable for me in one way or another were household staffers Tom and Ray and the Puerto Rican cook Dawson and a muscular young valet-masseur whose name I don't remember (not the Ritz Tower-Cody Swede), my teenage buddies Mary Plummer and Kate Snyder and Dad's, and successively my, friends Bud and Helen Kron, the Hollywood Athletic Club's swimming coach Clyde Swensen and wrestling coach Carl Johnson, Johnny Weissmuller, Buster Crabbe,

Photoplay editor Jimmy Quirk (who died late the first summer) and his former movie-star wife Mae Allison, the Los Angeles Sheriff's Department deputy assigned to guard our house nightly the second summer because of kidnapping threats—with which officer Ray played horseshoes in the side yard's floodlit sand and whom he dubbed "Night Man"—director of the 1926 *Ben Hur* film Charles Brabin and his kindly, erstwhile glamour-queen wife Theda Bara, superstar Norma Shearer who owned a nearby beachhouse with her Metro movie-executive husband Irving Thalberg, and publishing tycoon William Randolph Hearst and his beautiful and generous moviestar mistress Marion Davies, whose parties at their Santa Monica beach mansion as well as their San Simeon castle up the coast were legendary.

One evening, as we were walking beside the surf in front of the Hearst-Davies house, Dad told me that, although he knew both of them, he had the warmer feeling for Marian. He said that at some time previously, Hearst had been in financial danger of losing at least one of his chain's newspapers, and had called together for dinner in that house a few of his top executives and some other people whose judgment he respected, like Dad, to discuss his problem. Marian, the hostess and only woman present, listened to the lengthy discussion of the need for "bail-out" money in a hurry and of where possibly to get it; and as coffee was being served, she excused herself for a few minutes and came back carrying a shoe-box-size metal case which she set on the table in front of Hearst. Putting a hand to her temple, she said something like, "Gentlemen, I hope you'll forgive my leaving you now to your cigars, but I seem to have a headache. However, I think some relief for your much bigger headache may be here—"tapping the case and looking down at Hearst—"and I'm returning it to you, my darling, with love." And she left for the upstairs. Under the circumstances, Hearst was pretty much obliged to open the box then and there; and in it were at least most of the jewelry and deeds to buildings he'd obviously given to her. Dad said that she may not have been a great actress, but that she was grateful. (One of his favorite saying was, "There ought to be an eleventh commandment: 'Thou shall not be ungrateful.'")

My daily week-day routine at least the first of those summers hardly varied. I got up and ate Dawson's breakfast in time to drive myself to the Hollywood Athletic Club by nine-thirty; I worked out first with gentle, shaggy, cauliflower-eared Carl Johnson, not wrestling with him I'm lucky to say, but going through a sixty-minutes series of exercises under his supervision; after that I headed for the pool where Clyde Swensen put me through another hour of swimming the crawl and breaststroke and backstroke and kicking a small board length after gradually increasing length, sometimes alongside, or I should say far behind, Johnny Weissmuller and Buster Crabbe, but with their friendly encouragement; next I ate a locker-room lunch with those and other men, including actors whose studios had ordered them to lose weight or gain it or keep it firm (I was embarrassed for Johnny one noon, but he didn't seem to be, when his hot-tempered girlfriend, or maybe wife by then Lupe Velez, screamed at him from the top of the stairs to get his ass up there); and then I dressed and headed back to the beach for the afternoon's ocean swimming and beginner's surfing and generally relaxing in the sun until dinnertime, often with Mary Plummer and Kate Snyder.

Those two girls were transplanted Hoosiers whom I'd met when they were visiting Kate's aunt in Crawfordsville. In California, Mary was vacationing with Kate, who had become a student at U.C.L.A., and the three of us fell into a warm, laughing, energetic companionship. Bud Kron called us a "menage-a-trois without the menage." They were really the first post-gradeschool female friends I'd known, as distinguished from my version of "sex objects" born of my monastic Riverdale experience. I don't mean they both weren't pretty and sexy or that I didn't think about sex in relation to them; I guess we were just too comfortable together to get romantic, or maybe the fact there were always three of us inhibited the pairing off we assumed then was essential to making love or anything approaching it. When we went to movies, I sat between them and surreptitiously held one hand of each; I might have known they'd quickly become aware, as sharing young women, of that little dodge. Kate and I one day on the third floor of the Lyons' house did find ourselves briefly and I think unintentionally separated from Mary down on the beach, and I remember being acutely conscious of lovely Kate's hip pressing against mine as we rummaged through a drawer for something, and feeling she should have responded if I'd put my arms around her; but for some dim reason I didn't (shades of the Estes Park lovely!), and the moment passed, and I regretted its passing until we got back to the beach and I saw Mary standing there with her sweet grin.

During the second beach summer, before which they had only heard about each other, Ray and Tom became friends, as Ray and Len had in Wyoming; and as in the case of Ray's and Len's, Ray's and Tom's dialogue of banter and different life-experiences gave them and me and Dad and Mary and Kate and, among our other frequent guests, Bud Kron much amusement. It didn't amuse Jessie; she didn't encourage social-

310

izing with the help. In answer to Ray's questions, Tom told him what living in the nation of Brooklyn was like, and Ray gave the New Yorker some insights into what Tom called "life in the sticks." The citizen of Sullivan was fascinated by Tom's accent, and the New Yorker by Ray's contrast to the urban racial stereotype. I gained most from their new friendship, because I was the old friend of both.

I got along fine with Dawson the cook and Muscles the valet-masseur, but they didn't get along with each other for some reason too obscure for me to understand in those days. I think now it was a love-hate relationship. They had spats and made up and had more spats, much to Ray's and Tom's glee and Jessie's annoyance. I stayed carefully on the outer edge of that particular domestic scene.

The only Olympic Games I've been privileged to see were held in Los Angeles the first of those summers. For me their most dramatic moments were Eddie Tolan's winning of one of the dashes, and Buster Crabbe's victory in the 400-meter freestyle swim. Ralph Metcalfe's win in another dash was thrilling, too, for us hundred thousand spectators in the Los Angeles Coliseum.

With all my incidental hanging around the fringes of Hollywood, I've had an urge to be a movie actor only once, and that was during my summer at Santa Monica when I met Dad's good friends James and Mae Allison Quirk. She had quit making films then to devote herself to her family. I never had seen her on the screen, but I'd heard how beautiful she was, and I found—to use the old but apt phrase—she was as sweet as she was beautiful. I immediately fell in love with her, either without her and her nice husband's knowing it or more likely with their tolerant but veiled amusement. (Of course I did the same thing with Dad's friend Irene Dunne later.) Inexplicably I wanted to be in the movies; maybe I imagined that Mrs. Quirk and I could do a romantic film together. I asked her one day how a person went about breaking into pictures, and she answered that unanswerable question as though it weren't inane by saying gently there were as many ways as there were actors and actresses. That slowed me down some, but not entirely. I hardly can believe it now—I was almost college age—but I tried once more: I asked her if she would put in a good word for me with some producer or director friend of hers. At this she became faintly evasive, probably wishing someone else should come into the Lyon's room where we were talking, but did say that since her retirement from the screen she hadn't kept in touch with many of those types. I let her escape, gave up my movie career, and returned to other interests to ease my disappointment, such as going to Ocean Park with Kate and Mary.

In those days Ocean Park was a busy amusement pier jutting into the sea off the little Santa Monica suburb of Venice. It was replete with roller coaster, ferris wheel, bumper cars, shooting galleries and, especially at night, throngs of strolling, laughing, gawking people of all ages and pursuits, from elder statesmen to pre-teen pickpockets, with an assortment of movie stars thrown in. One evening I was there with Dad and Jessie and a convivial group of their dinner guests; and Helen Kron, who took astrology very seriously, pulled me into a fortune-teller's booth and paid to have my future prophesied. I don't know why she was interested in my future instead of hers. I remember the dark lady in the black wig with the trailing orange hair-wisps saying that I was going to be married three times; maybe Helen was considering a child-groom if Bud, who had a healthy interest in all girls, were to overdo fatally.

Our 1932 summer trip to California was by the Santa Fe's great Chicago-to-Los Angeles train, the *Chief*. Within an hour of departure, Dad discovered that Walt Disney was on board and went to visit him, taking Jessie and me along. Entering Mr. Disney's drawing room at his muffled "Come in!" in response to our knock, we found him sitting on the floor in his shirtsleeves with a screwdriver in his hand, taking apart the mechanism of a swivel chair. After getting to his feet for introductions all around, he sat down again on the floor, saying he wanted to know how the contraption worked, and resumed his efforts to find out, carrying on a pleasant conversation with us as he worked. I was fascinated by his intense curiosity, his almost childlike absorption with this small wonder he had encountered. I'm certain it wasn't for some sort of effect; it was simply his way, and helped explain for me the particular quality of his genius's contribution to the world's beauty.

Chapter Thirty–four

LEWIS GREGORY COLE, M.D.
86 EAST 61ST STREET
NEW YORK

September 26, 1932.

Master Wm. Hays, Jr.   Mr. Wm. Hays, Sr.
Riverdale Country School   Waldorf Astoria
Riverdale-on-Hudson   New York
New York.

Roentgen Findings:
    . . . From a study of these recent films after the summer in California it is evident that there has been a progressive improvement in the scoliosis . . .

Respectfully submitted,
Lewis Gregory Cole, M.D.

*   *   *

November 29, 1932

Dear Bill:
    Yes, we certainly did have a fine time over another Thanksgiving, as you said in your letter. I never have better times any place, doing anything, than I have with you. We are going to have a lot more grand times, believe me. It is cold weather now, and those flannel pajamas will come in good. Be sure and write your mother if you failed to get the letter off Sunday. Probably you did write but Sunday was a pretty busy day and maybe you missed it. See you again this week end.
    I love you.

Your partner, Father

*   *   *

THE FRANKLIN SQUARE AGENCY
49 EAST 33RD ST.
New York,
December 10, 1932

Dear Mr. Hackett

    I would like to take a few minutes from the press of a busy day to express my sincere appreciation of your forethought in placing our charitable program's magazine subscription business in the hands of so capable a person as Billy Hays . . .

                    Very truly yours
                    FRANKLIN SQUARE AGENCY
                    Maxwell Forsyth
                    Assistant Manager

              *   *   *

December 23, 1932

Mr. Bill Hays
414 W. Wabash Avenue,
Crawfordsville, Indiana.

Dear Bill:

    I had hoped up until this afternoon that I would get to come home to Indiana for Christmas. This is not going to be possible. I am all right and feel fine but am very busy . . . The Christmas present I was going to bring, I can't bring. When you get back here, however, I will have it for you. In the meantime enclosed is a little extra to have a good time on. If you don't take Rosemary to a movie on this you ought to have your so-and-so and so-and-so and so-and-so—

    I am especially anxious that you have a happy Christmas in Crawfordsville. You are well and that means everything. You are a good boy and that means still more. I <u>know</u> you will be careful of your health, sleep a lot, eat a lot, do your exercises and the other things necessary for your health and progress. <u>I know that you will be a good boy because you are a good man</u>. So I am very happy that you are happy.

    I love you.

                    Affectionately, Tonkafather

Friday
(1-20-33)

Dear Jessie:

Well, I hear you're spending a while in C'ville while Dad is in California—Boy, I envy you. I hope you'll excuse this school paper, but it's all I've got. Nothing much going on around here now—except work. The bane of my life (Chemistry) hasn't been going so hard lately.

I went down to the New York Athletic Club for a swim Wednesday—sorry I didn't see you before you left. I get a great kick out of those work-outs two or three times a week. Tom and I have fun talking on the way down and back. Oh, oh—there goes the bell for supper. So-long, and I hope I'll hear from you soon. (Say, by the way—will you do me a favor by telling Mrs. O'Neall's beautiful daughter to <u>hurry up and answer my letter</u>? Thanks.) I'll be seeing you.

Lots of Love, Bill

* * *

Hollywood, California
February 14, 1933

Dear Bill:

Here is a copy of Whittier's *Barbara Fritchie*. Commit this as soon as you have a chance, and we will practice. Your grandfather worked on this; I worked on this; I think your Uncle Hinkle worked on it; I expect John T. worked on it. It is an old standby—there is no better speech to make . . . I'll be back next week.

I love you.

Affectionately, Father

* * *

Wed. eve., Feb. 23

Dear Father:

Gee, I was sort of disappointed today—it would be that on the only day you could get away from the office in order to come to the Athletic Club the water would be cold, and I wouldn't be feeling in good form, etc! Darn it, I sure hope you can get away from the office about 5 mins. on Sat. aft. That pulling to one side in the crawl, I had completely overcome and was going along fine until today. I guess I wasn't just loosened up properly, or something. My wind is coming along fine, though. It was swell to see you! B+ yesterday in a Chem. Test. (Hot dog.) I'll see you again this week-end. Whopee!

I love you

(Vergessen sie es nicht!)

Bill

P.S. I hear Buster Crabbe is coming in a picture to the Paramount soon.

* * *

March 1, 1933

Dear Bill:

Congratulations on being out of the "red ink" in your grades! You know, when you fail in business, they put it in red. Seriously, I know that you know how I feel when you "make the grade." There is one thing I think we want to work on those profs a little about: If we can get C's with "fair efforts," we could knock down some B's with "Commendable effort" . . . I think we will work so hard from now on that they can't help but notice it. See you Saturday.

I love you.

Affectionately, Father

* * *

Fri. night,
March 24

Dear Young Tonkafather:

I've had two good sleeps and 4 good, hard exercise sessions since I've been here in C'ville for spring vacation. Maybe, someday, I'll have a <u>whataman</u> chest like yours! . . .

I have been seriously thinking it over, and have decided definitely to say "yes" to the Phi Delt pledge that John[1] has said will come about this week. He thinks I ought to stay Saturday night for the dance, too . . . I'd rather be in your outfit than any in the world. Also, there's John & the old Unc' and I hope Chuck next. There are a few nuts but

---

1. *Hays, cousin, brother of Charles (Chuck), son of Hinkle*

a lot of great fellows in it. John says the nuts will be thinning out to nothing through graduation. So now forget that!

Gosh, I'd given one heck of a big sum if you were having this vacation in my place. Oh, Oh—time to eat heap big food. I'll be seeing you.

I love you

Bill

* * *

WESTERN UNION
MARCH 25, 1933

BILL HAYS,
414 W. WABASH AVENUE
CRAWFORDSVILLE INDIANA

HAVE TALKED TO DUKE HACKETT AND WE BOTH THINK YOU SHOULD STAY FOR FRATERNITY PARTY SATURDAY NIGHT . . . IF YOU WANT ME TO SEND YOUR TUXEDO AND REST OF OUTFIT WIRE RIGHT AWAY.
W.H.H.

* * *

WESTERN UNION
MARCH 29, 1933

WILL H. HAYS, JR.
CARE JOHN T. HAYS,
PHI DELTA THETA HOUSE,
CRAWFORDSVILLE, INDIANA.

DEAR BILL FROM BROTHER JOHN T HAYS I LEARN THAT YOU WILL BE PLEDGED TONIGHT TO PHI DELTA THETA STOP THIS GIVES ME GREAT PLEASURE AND I CONGRATULATE YOU STOP . . . REMEMBER THAT A DUTY WILL REST UPON YOU AS A MEMBER TO BRING HONOR TO THE FRATERNITY AS IT BRINGS GREAT CREDIT AND USEFULNESS AND JOY TO YOU . . .

AFFECTIONATELY
YOUR FATHER.

April 6, 1933.

Dear Bill:

Dawson will not be at the Towers while I am in California but the apartment will be, so if at any time you want to go into it you can. Jessie is not going with me because of the rush of work. She is going to Crawfordsville again tomorrow to be with her mother . . .

I love you.

Affectionately, Father

* * *

Monday eve, April 12

Dear Father:

. . . I'm back at school now, and Ed, Pedro, Devy and I had a great time. I certainly appreciate your letting us use the apartment while you're out there. It was great of you! Saturday night Tom drove us to see *Gabriel over The White House.* I enjoyed it immensely. We ate downstairs here most of the time, in the Norse Grill. (When I say ate I don't mean we just sat around a table and talked. Boy, we fed our faces!) Today at the Club as I was practicing racing dives someone behind me said, "Keep your can down a little more, and stoop lower." I turned around and there was John Weissmuller! I thanked him, and tried what he said. Then he showed me how to do it by diving a couple of times for me himself. We talked for a awhile. He's a swell fellow. Maybe he'll be back tomorrow. What a big son-of-a-gun he is!

I saw Jessie off the other day. Everything was all right, I guess. Say <u>hello</u> to the Krons. Rosemary is one peach of a sweet girl. She can swim too, what I mean. She is better than I am in proportion to the mens and womens records. Do me a favor, will you? Give Dorothy the blond telephone girl in your office a piece of Beman's gum and say I sent it? Thanks. (It's a joke we had.)

Say—here's something I'd like to talk to you about, Father. I know how busy you are and all, but I said I'd say this, and I'm interested in it too, so here it is if you can spare about two minutes! Gene Fischer, Helen's brother at C'ville, says he can get to California with about two weeks notice, and I thought maybe some <u>electrician</u> or <u>carpenter</u> or <u>doorman</u> in a studio would need a helper, or maybe they're short of <u>prop-boys</u> or <u>stage hands,</u> or something. You see, Father, he figures if he can just get "inside those walls" on any kind of job at all that he can, if he's good enough, work up to an electrician or cameraman in a few years time.

I sort of think he could . . . Well, there it is—as hard for me to write it as for you to listen, and if you're too busy, etc., why just let it go . . . I guess I've rambled on and said about enough now, so I'll sign off. Gosh, I wish you were here. I'll see you soon tho'. Say <u>hello</u> to <u>all</u>, and <u>don't work too hard</u>. So long.

I love you

Bill.

* * *

WESTERN UNION
APRIL 13, 1933.

HON. WILL H HAYS
CHATEAU ELYSEE
5930 FRANKLIN AVENUE
HOLLYWOOD CALIFORNIA

. . . HAVE FOLLOWING MESSAGE FROM CRAWFORDS-VILLE ADDRESSED TO YOU QUOTE HAVE BILLY WRITE FULLY IMMEDIATELY NOTHING ANY KIND SINCE LEFT UNQUOTE STOP HAVE CHECKED WITH BILL AT SCHOOL AND WIRED PARTY[2] FOR HIM STOP HE HAD MAILED LETTER TO PARTY.

J K

* * *

Hollywood, California
April 20, 1933

Mr. Bill Hays,
The Waldorf-Astoria,
New York City.

Dear Bill:

. . . I had a talk yesterday with Jack Warner about Eugene Fischer. I read to him your letter as he is the one man I have felt I could talk to about it because he has a boy. They are closing down their studio for a while but he said he will give it thought and I will follow it up with

---

2. *H.T.H.*

him. I am pleased to do it and we both got a kick out of reading your letter. It made a big hit with him.

I talked to Bill James on the telephone today and he is coming in at ten o'clock tomorrow to see me. He is not drinking anything now and talks fine over the telephone.

I love you.

Affectionately, Father

* * *

April 21, 1933

Dear Mr Hays

Thank you ever so much for so promptly enabling us to have your check, through Miss Kelly, for $1000.00 as a six months loan to Riverdale at 5% ... You will be glad I know to have the enclosed progress letters about Billy. If I were you I should feel deeply encouraged with such an impression by my boy on teachers who have known him so long.

Faithfully, Frank S. Hackett

Progress Reports upon Bill Hays (April 1, 1933)

By a herculean effort, by an indomitable will, and by a sweet nature under adversity, this boy has accomplished almost the impossible. Need I say more?

D.E. Gardner

Dormitory
Billy has changed very much during this school year. He is quite given to practical jokes at times verging on pertness. He takes an interest in keeping his room orderly.

Martha O Shiffert
House Mother—1st Floor

German IV
Bill has done fairly satisfactory work this year and has so far passed all his tests ...
Five years ago, Bill seemed a little boy, very quiet and retiring, and now he is an outstanding personality in the Sixth

Form and his word carries influence whenever he speaks. He has grown in self reliance and poise and carries with him a quiet independence that comes only from a boy's having found himself.

I doubt if there is a more generally popular boy in the school than Bill and popularity with this school body practically is never won except on the basis of character and solid worth. Bill has figured prominently in the charity undertakings backed by the school and it is not surprising that he should give his time to such matter for he is one of the most unselfish and sympathetic boys we have ever had. His quick smile, his dry humor, his capacity for selfless friendships have endeared him to all who have known him here and he will be greatly missed when he leaves us.

Marc L. Baldwin[3]

History IV

Despite the fact that Bill is not a quick student, he has maintained a passing grade by serious, honest effort. I am puzzled to find the reason for the errors in his March examination paper, for I am sure he knew such items as the importance of the bank issue in the campaign of 1832 and the connection between the Dred Scott decision and the Republican platform of 1860. But I feel confident that his persistence will see him through successfully in June.

F.C. Murray

Chemistry

Bill is to be complimented on his work during the winter term. 79% on the March examination leaves a good margin of safety. Continued good work will insure his success.

F.W. Cobb

English VI

The integrity of this boy is equalled by too few in school and surpassed by none. His composition, written and oral, shows

---

3. *Note: I was surprised (and embarrassed) by Mr. Baldwin's effusiveness, given his characteristic gruffness. W.H.H., Jr.*

intelligent, independent, constructive thinking, which has made his progress in English steady and gratifying. In reaction to literature "Bill" is mature; in interpretation adequate always, sometimes far more than just satisfactory; in original work, effective. His place in Riverdale will not soon be filled.

Clough

* * *

W.W. HERRICK, M.D.
16 EAST 90TH STREET
NEW YORK CITY

May 12, 1933

My dear Mr. Hays;
. . . I have been over the radiographics. The most satisfactory result shown by a study of these serial negatives is that the anterior curve of the spine has been established, I judge permanently. The lateral curves are still present, perhaps not as marked as at first but they are none the less significant. In the way of exercise, swimming is ideal. Something should be accomplished by special exercises under the personal direction of an expert trainer. I would suggest consulting Mr. Joe Fitton . . .

Your sincerely, W.W. Herrick

* * *

May 15, 1933

Dear Bill:
I have just talked to Mr. Joe Fitton . . . He wants to see us on Thursday afternoon . . . and tell you what exercises to take to build up any muscles he finds are not up to standard. I will send this letter out by Thomas on Tuesday when he comes to take you to the Athletic Club to swim.
I love you.

Affectionately, Father

* * *

May 19, 1933

Dear Helen:

I appreciate what you say about Bill and understand thoroughly how much of a sacrifice it is to have him away from you this summer. As suggested, however, he will be in Crawfordsville for four years at Wabash College, beginning next fall, and that will be splendid for both of you. I still hope to go to California late in June . . . I will pick Bill up in Chicago just as I did before. If there are any earthquakes out there, however slight, I will immediately have a wire sent you . . .

I do not know why there should be any talk going around about Billy being ill, because he certainly looks like a million dollars, except that he has to get this orthopedic curve corrected; that simply has to be done, but it ought not be considered an "ailment" . . . When they see him in the swimming pool at Crawfordsville, nobody will think he is ill!

Sincerely, W.H.H.

* * *

June 2, 1933.

Dear Bill:

The contents of this letter is my graduation present to you.

With it goes my sincerest love and affection and my very highest respect, as well as my congratulations on <u>finishing the job</u>. Most intimately, of course, I have watched you accomplish this five years' work, and I know whereof I speak. The progress has been uniform and most gratifying. You conclude in the best shape, physically and mentally, in which you have ever been. Spiritually you stand erect now, as always. All of this makes me very happy and I am particularly gratified by the four-square manner in which you have approached and conquered all the incidental difficulties. I know you will continue giving the same attention to this right conduct . . .

I was, of course, moved very deeply when you finally decided and told me what it was you wanted—and, as you said, the only thing wanted—as a graduation present, i.e., a promise from me that I would take a vacation this summer and "for one month earnestly and conscientiously work at the business of having a vacation, resting and having fun." That promise I now give you and this letter is the pledge so to do.

I wish I could adequately express to you what your period at Riverdale and your association with me incident to this period have meant to me. This is impossible. I know what it has meant to you, too.

In this connection I think of the spirit expressed in the card you drew for me of the two cowboys walking out together toward the rising sun. As full partners we carry on.

Affectionately your father, Will H. Hays

Crawfordsville
June 13, 1933

Dear Tonkahemanfather:
Hi! Boy, you should see the muscles coming up all around, chest and stomach and legs and everything. Hot dog. Boy, I've been working on it, & has it been hot around this place! Wow, 94 in the house. I pulled a stomach muscle the first day, and had to lay off for 2 days, but for about a week now I've been back on schedule. Everyday I leave here at 12:30, arriving in Indianapolis 1:45, and swimming from 2:00 till 3:00 or 3:15 at the Indianapolis Athletic Club. I really get a work out, too, believe me! (I do my exercises from 9:00 till 10:30 in the morning.) I've seen Rosemary lots. Wed. night she & I are going to Indianapolis, swim & then to a movie or something ... Gosh, I wish you were here, or some place away from the office, but it won't be long now! California, here we come.
So long
I love you
Bill

* * *

June 15, 1933

Dear Bill:
It now seems certain that my plans will be so changed that next week we can start to California by way of a trans-Canada train and then a ship down to Los Angeles ... Don't forget to get your teeth fixed while you're there in Crawfordsville.
Love.
Affectionately, Father

UNIVERSAL PICTURES CORPORATION
730 FIFTH AVENUE
NEW YORK

R.H. Cochran
Vice President
Wednesday. (6-20-33)

Dear Mr. Hays:

Go ahead and enjoy your boy. If you don't, you ought to take a licking. There is nothing in the picture business or in any business or in the world half so important as this. If you ever get the idea that a motion picture crisis is more important than keeping your promise to Bill, then make up your mind that you are taking yourself too seriously and life too tragically.

Now, I like you so well that I am going to hurt your feelings, deliberately but with fine intent. Prepare for a hurt!—I do NOT like the letter you wrote to Bill. You told him it was not intended as an admonition, but it really was. It was an attempt to lead his mind along the right line, when I happen to have heard enough about Bill to know that he does not need it and that he is smarter than you give him credit for. Fools rush in where angels fear to tread, so I am going to give you another note to write to Bill, even if you have to hand it to him in person and let him read it while you are not around. Here it is:

> *"Dear Bill:—I have read over the letter I sent you on June 2, and I am chagrined to find that it does not express half of what I really wanted to get over to you. Let me try again. What I really wanted to say was that I have never had such a kick out of anything in all my life as I got out of the fact that you really wanted me to take a vacation and take it <u>with you</u>. A great many boys consider their dads saps and poor company, but if I have succeeded in making you actually like to be with me, then I am a pretty fortunate sort of a fellow.*
>
> *"Upon reading over my other letter, it sounds a little bit preachy. Forget that part of it. If you ever catch me preaching at you, I hope you will preach right back at me, because you are just as likely to be right as I am. In other words, if you are glad to have me as your dad, I am eternally glad to have you as my son."*

If you don't like to write that to Bill, you have the inalienable privilege of tearing it up and wafting it to the winds. I have avoided even a suspicion of preaching at either my son or daughter, because I do not feel fit to preach to anyone. I told both of them that whether they passed their exams or flunked them, they would still be the same to me. I explained very carefully to both of them that they were far above the effects of high marks or low marks, so that in the one case they would not get a swelled head and in the other an unnecessary mental depression or feeling of inferiority.

I do not even apologize for suggesting that you write another note to Bill. If you don't realize the sentiment which animates me, nothing I could say would ever explain it. But I think you do. Now go on and have fun and to hell with everything else for the time being.

Cordially, Bob

* * *

Leonard and Dot Morris with Will Hays and Will, Jr., on the Lazy Bar H Ranch, Cody, Wyoming.

Chapter Thirty–five

AFTER my early-June graduation from Riverdale in 1933 and a couple-of-weeks' visit with Mother in Crawfordsville I headed for my second beach summer in California. This time however, instead of just the three of us on the Chief across the United States, Dad and Jessie and I rode a trans-Canada train to the Pacific coast in company with Dad's secretary Earl Bright, Bud and Helen Kron and two other of their friends, Gene and Win Hillsmith. Our party was to visit Banff and Lake Louise and Victoria and then take a ship from Vancouver south to San Pedro—Los Angeles' harbor—with a day's stop at San Francisco.

When the train was in the middle of the western plains of Canada one morning, the conductor came to Dad's and Jessie's drawing room next to Earl's and my compartment and said that none of us was to get off the train at Moose Jaw, its next stop, and that we were to keep the car's blinds lowered until we pulled away again after taking on coal, water and mail. While the train ws standing beside the little station with the wind humming about it, I looked under the edge of my compartment window's blind and saw a dozen red-coated, campaign-hatted Mounties lined up on their horses parallel to the car, with rifles across their saddles. After the train pulled out, Dad and Earl and the other two men of our party had another conversation with the conductor; and then Dad let me in on what had been going on. The United States' Federal Bureau of Investigation had notified the Royal Canadian Mounted Police of an informant's tip that some American gangsters were going to take me off the train at Moose Jaw and hold me for ransom. If there was such a plan, obviously those twelve armed Mounties put a crimp in it. I had mixed feelings about the whole thing; I was thrilled but also a bit shaken.

An echo of this experience came to me a couple of years later at Wabash College when an F.B.I. agent called on me in Crawfordsville, cautioned me to be alert to the threat of kidnapping and handed me a state-police concealed-weapon license his Bureau's office in Indianapolis had obtained for me, as a result of which I bought and carried for several months in a hip-pocket holster a snub-nosed revolver—which fell out one night onto the floor of the Indiana Theater Ballroom in Indianapolis during a fraternity state dance, and marked me as a man of mystery to everyone except my Wabash chapter brothers and their dates, who already knew about the gun.

The voyage down the coasts of Washington, Oregon, and California was my first time at sea except for a childhood crossing of the Santa Barabara Channel from San Pedro to Avalon on Santa Catalina Island. The cruise ship wasn't as large as many transoceanic liners, and several times we were in sight of land, but it was an educational as well as exciting experience for me. For one thing, we saw a pod of whales blowing plumes of spray into the air as I'd read they did, and for another I encountered a pretty young school teacher on vacation. She was different from the one on the Yellowstone bus who had taken a snapshot of me and my horse. This one's camera wasn't in evidence, but her curly black hair and pretty figure and obviously happy disposition were. Her travelling companion was another nice but less lighthearted teacher.

After exchanging glances with the pretty girl at dinner the first night and more lingerlingly at breakfast the next morning, and smiles along with our glances at lunch, I blurted a greeting as Bud Kron and I approached her and her friend on our pre-dinner promenade. They were standing at the ship's rail. She smiled and said hello, and I found myself stopping and intoducing myself and Bud and happily acknowledging her introduction of herself and her friend; and then, as Bud was saying something to her friend about the nice sea voyage, I proudly heard myself ask her if she planned to attend the dance that evening, saying we had to eat at the captain's table, but that afterward I had no commitments if she hadn't.

I was amazed at myself, because I was a real novice at dancing, having previously at the Crawfordsville Country Club tried to better myself under the faintly discouraged tutelage of Rosemary O'Neall. She said "Yes" brightly, and realizing as I said it that I was going beyond the point of no return I added recklessly something like "Save a dance for me." After we walked out of the girls' hearing, Bud, his fortyish eye for female beauty gleaming, gave me the conspiratorial elbow and grinned that he was impressed by the progress I'd made with the young teacher. I said I wondered if I'd made more progress than I could handle, in view of my limited dancing experience; and he said that if his wife, Helen, didn't shut him off he'd be happy to dance with the lady, and between dances I could talk with her. I told him I appreciated his gesture of true friendship, but thought I'd give the dancing a try, since I'd brought it up with her, and if it didn't go too well I could take her on a walk around the deck. He accepted this gracefully, but I assumed correctly that with me as his excuse he wouldn't let the evening go by without at least one set with her. Bud and I took another lap around the ship, and I stopped at his and Helen's cabin for a moment to borrow a book on my way to my own cabin ahead of dinner; and as I was closing his door behind me, I met the two teachers in the companionway and we reaffirmed our deal to meet later.

As soon as I entered the dining saloon the pretty girl's and my eyes met and we waved, and during the meal we exchanged smiles over every course, and then it was dance time. Dad and Jessie and the other two couples of our party took a few turns around the floor while I sat at the table with Earl Bright getting my legs ready to walk across the room and ask the lady to dance. Bud obviously had briefed Earl on the evening's drama, and the latter asked if he could help by walking across with me and inviting the other teacher to dance with him. I hardly could turn that down, so we went to their table and I introduced Earl, and the four of us took to the floor.

The girl in my arms was very nice and very patient with my dancing and smelled very good and looked very pretty, and all of a sudden I felt very warm toward her. I held her a little closer and she responded at once by holding me a good deal closer; in fact, I felt the whole length of her body against mine down to her knees, and it was so pleasant that I relaxed my vigilance not to step on her feet and immediatlely did so. Her wince pained me, too, but her quick laugh eased at least my pain, and I offered to save her further damage by taking her for a walk. Her laugh bubbled up again and she nodded and we went out into the sea-chilly night.

A few minutes later we'd climbed a ship's ladder to the boat deck and were standing by the rail looking down at the dark sea hissing backward under us, and not saying much, but shivering quite a bit. I fumbled my arm around her waist with some inane comment about keeping her warm, and she leaned against me and I could make out her eyes' solemn gaze into mine. Turning to her and putting my other arm around her and kissing her seemed an utterly natural thing to do, and I did it. I kissed her a number a times, and each time she taught me more about kissing. Both of us began breathing a little faster, and at least my heart began beating a little harder, and when we paused to swallow and catch our breaths she whispered a question which I didn't hear except for the word "wind," but I pretended I did, because the wind indeed was blowing and my muttered "yes" seemed logical. She quickly pressed her mouth on mine once more and said "Hmmm." When our lips parted,

I suggested we move out of the wind, and her glance was quizzical for only an instant before she nodded and we found a couple of deck chairs in the lee of the ship's warm funnel and stretched out side by side on them and took up our kissing where we'd left off. Within a few minutes both of us were murmuring, the deck chairs creaking, my ears ringing, my spine melting, and I felt as though I'd never be alone again, and I was deeply if somewhat awkwardly content. She may have sensed the rather abrupt ebbing of my passion, but it didn't keep her from whispering— maybe for the second time—that she was cold and that we should go to her cabin to get her coat. She stood up, and I did too rather shakily, and she led me down to her empty quarters, saying she knew that her friend wasn't coming back for another hour, and kicked off her shoes, slipped out of the jacket of her dress, sat down on one of the bunks, half laid back, patted the spread next to herself and whispered a wide-eyed "Please!"

I knew for sure I was in over my head. Thoughts of headlines discrediting the Movie Czar banged around in my mind with embarrassment at not knowing how this lovely lady's game was played, but remembering how Reverend Gray's was, and with fear of her cabinmate's unexpected return and with other nameless, annoyingly characteristic anxieties. I had to get out of there; I didn't want to hurt her feelings, but I was in the wrong place. Glancing at my watch, telling her I'd promised to be somewhere else in fifteen minutes and that I was happy to have met her, I fumbled for the doorknob and lurched out of the cabin. I still recall with remorse the confused look on her face; and its recollection the next morning prevented my appreciating Bud Kron's otherwise amusing sequel to the story.

At breakfast Bud told Earl and me that after he and his wife— who was miffed about his obvious interest at dinner in the young teacher—had gone to bed, a gentle rap had sounded on their door, and he had got out of bed to answer it, but had recognized through the door's louvered bottom the girl's pretty shoes and ankles. Quickly, he had headed back to bed. Helen, however, hadn't let him get by that easily; she'd ordered him, for heaven's sake, to answer the knock, or she would! That had got him up and to the door again in a hurry. He said he'd opened it a couple of inches, told the startled girl that she was at the wrong cabin, closed the door in her face, and assured Helen as he returned to bed that it had been nobody he'd ever seen before.

I saw the girl about noon as we were debarking and smiled at her apologetically. She looked straight through me. I didn't blame her.

Chapter Thirty–six

Dictated en route
June 26, 1933

Dear Bill:

     You'll get this when we've reached California.

     I told my good friend, Bob Cochrane, about your suggestion to me about our vacation as your commencement present and let him see the letter I wrote you. He said I didn't go strong enough, and I believe him. What I want to say now is this:

     I have read over the letter I sent you on June second, and I am chagrined to find that it does not express half of what I really wanted to get over to you. Let me try it again. What I really wanted to say was that I have never had such a kick out of anything in all of my life as I got out of the fact that you really wanted me to take a vacation and take it <u>with you</u>. A great many boys consider their dads saps and poor company, but if I have succeeded in making you actually like to be with me, then I am a pretty fortunate sort of a fellow.

     Upon reading over my other letter, it sounds a little bit preachy. Forget that part of it. If you ever catch me preaching at you, I hope you will preach right back at me, because you are just as likely to be right as I am. In other words, if you are glad to have me as your dad, I am eternally glad to have you as my son.

                      Affectionately your father,
                      Will H. Hays

* * *

Hollywood, California
July 18, 1933

Dear Helen:

     Bill is in fine shape and I am only writing this letter because I want to report to you, as I would want you to do to me . . . This morning when he woke up he had a fever and a good deal of pain centered in his right side . . . I telephoned Harry Chandler, who owns the Los Angeles Times and is an absolutely fine and reliable citizen and knows everybody here . . . He called up Dr. John L. Kirkpatrick and had that fine doctor call me. Kirkpatrick came right out to the beach house...He thought Bill might have appendicitis and should go to the hospital and have tests made. Bill, Thomas, the doctor and I rode down together . . . You can be very certain there will be no operation unless it is <u>absolutely necessary</u> . . . The hospital is called the Queen of Angels.

    Best wishes.

Sincerely, W.H.H.

* * *

Hollywood, California
July 19, 1933

Dear Helen:

    Yesterday evening, it was evident something would have to be done . . . Bill was perfectly marvelous about it, actually wanting them to go ahead and do it. The pain helped induce that state of mind, of course . . . I went with him to the operating room, and as he went in he hollered at me "So long, I'll be seeing you," just as much concerned as if he had driven up to a gas station and ordered some gas in an automobile. The operation was very successful. The doctor told me it probably would have broken today and that would have been very serious . . . As soon as I found out how he was I wired you. I have been at the hospital practically all day today and will go back again after supper . . . The doctor says he is in perfect condition and his patience makes him an ideal subject. The fact is, there is absolutely nothing to worry about and we are very, very lucky.

    Best wishes.

Sincerely, Bill

* * *

WESTERN UNION
1933 JUL 19

WILL HAYS=
5504 HOLLYWOOD BLVD=

I WILL NOT ENTERTAIN ANY THOUGHT OTHER THAN THAT BILL WILL COME THROUGH QUICKLY AND WITH FLYING COLORS KEEP ME POSTED WHEN AND IF CONVENIENT WARMEST REGARDS=

R H COCHRANE.

* * *

WESTERN UNION
NEW YORK
1933 JUL 19

WILL HAYS=
5504 HOLLYWOOD BLVD=

DEAR GENERAL JUST HEARD OF JUNIORS OPERATION YOU HAVE MY DEEPEST SYMPATHY I KNOW EVERYTHING WILL BE ALL RIGHT WITH ALL YOUR OTHER PROBLEMS IT IS TOO BAD YOU HAVE TO HAVE THIS PERSONAL ONE KINDEST REGARDS=

SIDNEY KENT.

* * *

WESTERN UNION
NEW YORK NY
1933 JUL 19

WILL H HAYS=
5504 HOLLYWOOD BLVD=

MISS KELLY PHONED ME AND AM GLAD TO KNOW THAT BILLIE IS COMING ALONG OKAY AND DELIGHTED THAT HE HAS THAT INCIDENT BEHIND HIM STOP IT IS ONE WORRY SCRATCHED STOP HOPE EVERYTHING OKAY OTHERWISE WITH YOUR TRIBE REGARDS=

ROY HOWARD

POSTAL TELEGRAPH
NEW YORK NY
1933 JUL 20 AM 10 40

WILL H HAYS=
HOLLYWOOD CALIF=

SINCERELY REGRET HEARING OF JUNIORS ILLNESS HOPE HE IS GETTING ALONG NICELY AND WILL VERY SOON BE ENTIRELY RECOVERED WILL APPRECIATE YOUR ADVISING ME OF HIS CONDITION KINDEST REGARDS FROM MRS WARNER AND MYSELF=

HARRY M. WARNER

* * *

WESTERN UNION
NEW YORK NY
1933 JUL 20

WILL H HAYS=
5504 HOLLYWOOD BLVD=

HAVE JUST LEARNED OF YOUR SONS OPERATION I KNOW WHAT THIS MEANS TO YOU AND I AM HAPPY THAT HE IS DOING WELL BEST WISHES FOR HIS SPEEDY AND COMPLETE RECOVERY=

DAVID SARNOFF

* * *

WESTERN UNION
NEW YORK NY
1933 JUL 20

MR AND MRS WILL H HAYS=
5504 HOLLYWOOD BLVD LOSA=

LOVE FROM US AND BEST WISHES FOR THE EARLY RECOVERY FOR YOUR FINE SON=

DOT AND DEAC AYLESWORTH

WESTERN UNION
NEW YORK NY 20
1933 JUL 20

MR AND MRS WILL HAYS=
5504 HOLLYWOOD BLVD RM 408 LOSA=

WE ARE JUST CONSTANTLY KNOWING THAT THE SAME POWER WHICH GAVE HIM TO YOU ALSO PRESERVES HIM FOR YOU WHO LOVE HIM SO MUCH MUCH LOVE TO YOU AND JESSIE=

THE O O MCINTYRES.

* * *

WESTERN UNION
NEW YORK NY 20
1933 JUL 20

MR AND MRS WILL HAYS=
5504 HOLLYWOOD BLVD ROOM 408

SO DISTRESSED TO HEAR ABOUT YOUNG BILL STOP IS HE OKAY AND WERE THERE ANY COMPLICATIONS TO THE OPERATION STOP WHAT HOSPITAL IS HE IN GIVE HIM MY LOVE I MISS YOU ALL TERRIBLY ALL DEVOTION=

MAY ALLISON QUIRK

* * *

WESTERN UNION
LELAND MICH
1933 JUL 20

EARL BRIGHT, CARE WILL H HAYS=
5504 HOLLYWOOD BLVD=

PLEASE SEE THAT BEGINNING TODAY I AM WIRED COLLECT DAILY UNTIL BILLS DANGER PERIOD PASSES

STOP ASKED YOUR BOSS THIS BUT DO NOT WANT TO ADD
TO LOAD STOP AM GREATLY DISTURBED ABOUT BILL

H C HAYS

* * *

(Hollywood)
(7-3-33)

Memo to J.K. from W.H.H.

. . . As heretofore reported, Bill has been constantly improving
every day . . . The plan is that he will go out to the beach tomorrow and
be a few more days in or near bed there before starting much exercise .
. . The Doctor says in two weeks he will be doing everything he ever did
in his life . . . About all his athletic friends have had their appendices out
except Buster Crabbe, the champion swimmer, who is going to have it
done right away, so Bill thinks he is "in the swim" in more ways than one
. . .

* * *

En route
August 3, 1933

Dear Bill:

I am rattling eastward somewhere between Winslow and Gallup,
still in my pajamas in bed although it is afternoon. I am staying in bed
out of respect to you—you are in bed at the beach so I stay in bed. I had
breakfast and lunch right here, worked a little and read some, and have
looked long at the red desert. So I am all right—and I hope you are the
same.

I meant to tell you before I left what your wrestler friend Carl
Johnson said the other day when I was in the Athletic Club talking with
him about your future exercises. "I want to tell you something," he said
and was quite timid about it but he finally said, "There was one thing,
Mr. Hays, Bill did before his operation that I worried about and thought
I ought to mention. He was inclined to drink too much cold stuff when
he had been exercising and was hot. It isn't good for an athlete." I said,
"That is right, Carl; I'll tell him about it." So I have told you and I know
you will watch about it . . .

I appreciated the assurance you called to me from the top of the
stairs as I left the beach house that you would be very careful and not try

to do too much too quickly. Get your strength and flesh back that you have lost and a little more. You can take up the strenuous muscle-shaping a little a later . . . I will get back the first minute I can.

I love you.

Affectionately, Father

* * *

En route to New York
August 3, 1933

Dear Ray:

I want you to look after Bill there at the beach in the same way you did when he was a little boy and you would take him hunting. That is, at night I want you to watch to help him with anything he needs until he is completely recovered. In the daytime, I want you to help see he does nothing which would hurt him in any way in his recovery, his health or general welfare . . . Of course, the detective assigned there by the Sheriff to guard against kidnappers will be around, but that's not the same . . .

Best wishes.

Sincerely yours, W.H.H.

* * *

August 6, 1933

Dear Helen:

I got to New York this morning and have just talked to Bill on the telephone . . . He is carefully following the doctor's orders . . . He is playing the game one hundred per cent. Ray is watching him and he is sitting out on the beach everyday, which is the one very best thing for him . . . He showed me his telegram to you about the radio in your car before I left, to see if I thought it was all right about each of you paying half of it, which I do. If you don't feel you want to pay half, you can say you will and I will send it to you . . . He is looking forward with the very greatest pleasure to Wabash College, and I think he is going to make a fine student and give you a lot of happiness watching him there . . .

Best wishes.

Sincerely, Bill

Ray Russell

* * *

Back at the beach from his New York trip that summer, Dad had to drive into his Hollywood office everyday, of course, and he and Jessie were occasional dinner guests of friends, but he and I seemed to have a little more time together than during the previous summer. We talked some about his work—not much, his daylight hours were too sated with that—and about my impending, and his past, Wabash College days, and we exchanged ideas about life and living from a father's and a son's standpoints.

Some of his friends, most of whom became Jessie's, were visitors on week ends. One of those was the great star of the silent-screen era, the legendary Theda Bara, whom I never had seen in films, but came to know and like. She had been the original "sex goddess," the personification of glamour and of press agentry's hyperbole, with her exotic costumes and the pet leopard that in her heyday had ridden beside her in the back seat of her chauffeured convertible. A very practical reason for the chauffeur, aside from his symbolic value, had been her really disabling nearsightedness which still gave her huge eyes their famous allure, but should have made her driving a public hazard. She was a lovely middle-aged woman in the 1930s. Her fine husband, Charles Brabin, was a towering, hawked-nosed, hearty Englishman—a sort of slightly toned-down English version of Count Luckner—with a store of fascinating anecdotes about Hollywood. A few years later on a 4th of July at Dad's Hidden Valley ranch, Theda gave Dad a bugle with this handwritten note attached: "Dear Will: This is the bugle that blew the surrender of the German Fleet at Scapa Flow. It was presented to me at Victory Way in New York City. I am giving it to you because you are the finest American Citizen I know—and in deepest Friendship! I should like it to remain in your Family—after you, Young Will, and then his eldest son. I was the first girl in the History of the U.S.A. to whom a regiment of 3800 men presented arms. I should like this little story to be told to each in turn—it will give me a sense of joyous permanency." It's in my home in Crawfordsville today, and my son knows it's his at my death.

During our beach summers in the early 1930s Dad had been working at his Hollywood job about ten of its eventual twenty-five years, and it was clear to me that he was working at it too hard, it was devouring too much of his small frame's and powerful mind's phenomenal energy; but there wasn't a damn thing I could do about that, except laugh with him when he wanted to laugh and try to do right and let him know I loved him. I don't pretend I gave the matter intensive thought or conscious effort most of the time. I was busy with my own life, as intertwined as that always had been with his at a geographical distance and in temporal fits and starts, but if we weren't always or even often as close literally as I'm sure we both should have liked, he never really was out of my mind, or I out of his, I never was indifferent to his activities and welfare, or he to mine. One thing I saw those summers at much closer range than before was the torment that one or two of the movie company heads caused him, and I was grateful he had some allies like Bob Cochrane, Sidney Kent, Louis Mayer, and Irving Thalberg whose cooperation most of the time helped offset the rascality of some jerks.

I was saddened one evening during the Keaton beach-house summer when Dad and Jessie and I were being served dinner by Ray and suddenly Jessie got mad at me. I don't remember knowing why at the time, and I'm still not sure; maybe I said something subconsciously threatening to her, possibly to her tenancy of Dad, or maybe looking at me she suddenly became consciously aware she didn't like me, or maybe I simply was picking my nose literally or figuratively. Anyhow she suddenly lit on me. Ray's face abruptly became a mask; Dad's took on a half-pained, half-angry expression and, staring at her, he ordered her to let me alone. Almost as soon as he'd said it his expression seemed to change to surprise and then to apprehension as, her face as red as her hair, she threw down her napkin, arose, gritted to Ray to follow her upstairs and help her pack, and said she was "leaving this house!" The storm was so sudden, so dam-breaking, that Dad was shocked speechless; he sat numbly and watched her march to the stairway, managing only a slight nod at Ray's questioning eyebrows. Ray put down his serving tray and walked after her, and I sat looking at Dad, feeling bad and good at the same time—bad to have caused him suffering, good for his defense of me—until he turned to me with one of the saddest looks I've ever seen and asked me softly please to go up to Jessie's room and tell her I was sorry. I felt that anything he asked wasn't too much to lessen the misery in his eyes. I got up and patted his head, went upstairs and apologized to Jessie's back, and was interested to sense her relief. None of us ever referred to the incident again.

I don't mean to say the strain that seemed to have been tightening gradually between Jessie and me was her fault. I'm not judging, I'm stating the fact. Those things usually aren't anybody's fault, or the fruit of anybody's cultivation, anyhow. But it was too bad. Both of us simply learned to live with it.

The rest of the second beach summer—the swimming, exercising, sunning, surfing, movie-going, enjoying of companionships, even the appendectomy—went fine; and on the train trip back across the vast American plains to Crawfordsville, my thoughts were partly back in California and partly in Indiana and partly in Wyoming, as they have been so often since, each place.

Beyond those summers lay the then-unknown, which I know now should encompass—among other doings and places—college, law school, law practice, the army in World War II, two novels, a movie script, sixteen televised scripts, mayoralty of an Indiana town, Indiana chairmanship of a President's campaign, executive service in a large foundation, two marriages (three magnificent children by the second one of those)—all such things in habitations from a coal-mining town to Beverly Hills, and most importantly and fortunately in company with a multitude of beautiful human beings.

The years to come should hold great love, great excitement and, as always, great luck.

None, however, could hold greater delight than those years which went before them in closeness, one way or another, with Will H. Hays—lawyer, politician, statesman, "Movie Czar," and most of all, my dad.

*   *   *

... AND SO, AS SOMEONE SURELY HAS SAID,

"EVERY ENDING IS A BEGINNING...."

Will Hays in his early state political days, with wife Helen and son Billie at Sullivan, Indiana, about 1918.

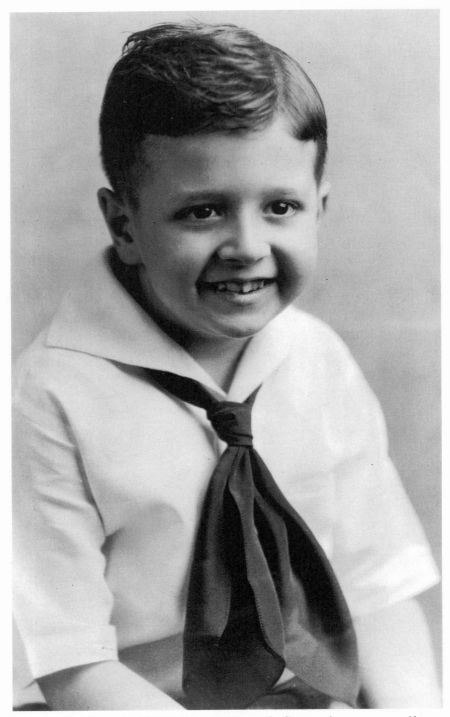

Will H. Hays, Jr. ("Billie") a Sullivan, Indiana, elementary pupil.

Will Hays' swearing in as Harding's U.S. Postmaster General, 1921.
Wife Helen and step-sister Martha are behind him.

First movie industry board meeting with its new "Czar";
1st row, (l. to r.) L. Selznick, Hammons, Williams, Hays, Zukor, Loew,
Laemmle; 2nd row, Sheehan, M. Selznick, Cole, Smith, Fox, Goldwyn,
Atkinson, Cochrane; 1922.

Will Hays and George Pershing, one former "General" congratulates another,
the great military General of World War I; 1927

"Cowboy" Billie Hays, Estes Park, Colorado, 1925

Billie Hays and his pal, "Don," in Sullivan, Indiana.

Billie Hays during his first summer at Culver Military Academy, 1926.

Two "Czars" and three cowboy movie stars, 1926. (l. to r.) Hoot Gibson, Kenesaw Mountain Landis (first commissioner of baseball), Art Acord, Will Hays of the movies, and Jack Hoxie.

A Riverdale School week-end at "Dr. Doolittle's" country house. (l. to r.) W.H.H., Jr., Ed and Bob Hubbard, W.H.H., Sr., Westy Westerfield, and Skipper Lofting.

Will Hays and "America's Sweetheart," Mary Pickford—the Movie Czar and the Movie Queen.

(l. to r.) Douglas Fairbanks, Will Hays, Mrs. Coolidge, President Calvin Coolidge and Mary Pickford on a studio visit in 1930.

Mrs. Warren Fairbanks, Will Hays, Loretta Young (very young!), Mr Fairbanks the second, (son of Pres. Teddy Roosevelt's Vice President, and publisher of The Indianapolis News*), and the second Mrs. Hays (Jessie) during a 1931 studio visit in Hollywood.*

Will Hays, Walt Disney and Friend!

(l. to r.) Will Rogers, humorous writer Irvin S. Cobb, Emma Kerns (Mrs. O. O. McIntyre's Aunt), N.Y. columnist O.O. McIntyre, and Will Hays at Rogers' California Ranch, 1935.

Charles Hays, W.H.H., Jr., President Herbert Hoover and John Hays in the White House Rose Garden.

Will Hays and Will Hays, Jr., 1937.

Movie stars Robert Montgomery and Rosalind Russell with Will Hays and Indiana's George A. Ball on set of MGM's Live, Love and Learn, *1937.*

On a Paramount Pictures movie set, 1938.

Included, among others, are Ernst Lubitsch, Mary Livingstone, Will Hays, Cecil B. de Mille, Betty Grable, Buddy Rogers and Rudolph Zukor.

*On the set. Entertaining Montana Senator Burton K. Wheeler and guests,
are Sam Goldwyn, Merle Oberon, Will Hays and Gary Cooper.*

Senator Wheeler, Gary Cooper and Will Hays.

Indiana World War II bond sale drive by Hoosiers Governor Henry F. Schricker, Carole Lombard, Will Hays and friend, 1942. That evening Miss Lombard tragically died in a plane crash returning to Hollywood and to her husband, Clark Gable.

Will Hays and Cecil B. de Mille at the 1942 Waldorf-Astoria (N.Y.) luncheon honoring de Mille's thirty years in the motion picture industry.

Just a couple of old timers; Will Hays and Sam Warner, 1941.

Gloria Swanson in 1927.
One of the screen's all time beauties.

Mary Astor's career was one of diverse artistry;
she was as talented as she was lovely.

Bebe Daniels and her actor husband, Ben Lyon, owned the Santa Monica beach house which the Hays family leased for a happy summer.

Dolores Del Rio, a Mexican beauty—fascinating!

William Powell, famous as "The Thin Man," among other memorable parts.

"To Will Hays, with a good old fashioned hug—Bill Fields."
W. C. Fields was one of the great comedians of all time.

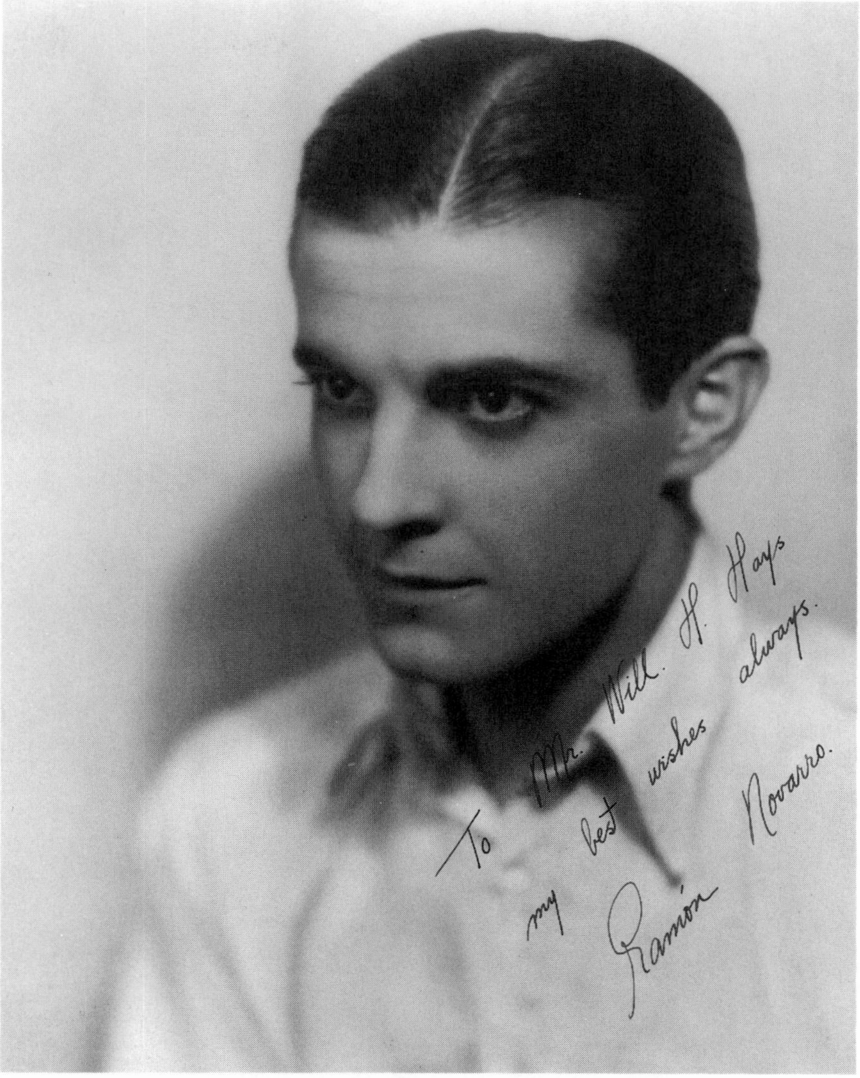
To Mr. Will. H. Hays
my best wishes always.
Ramón Novarro.

Ramon Navarro, a great romantic star of the maturing movies.

Clara Bow, known as America's "It girl."

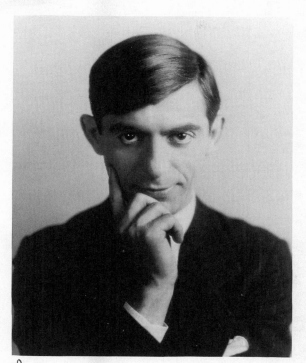

Eddie Cantor: from Broadway to Hollywood he kept America laughing.

Shirley Temple was Will Hays', and America's, favorite child star. She has starred ever since in her country's service as Shirley Black.